DREAMS MADE SMALL

ASAO Studies in Pacific Anthropology

General Editor: Rupert Stasch, Department of Archaeology and Anthropology, University of Cambridge

The Association for Social Anthropology in Oceania (ASAO) is an international organization dedicated to studies of Pacific cultures, societies and histories. This series publishes monographs and thematic collections on topics of global and comparative significance, grounded in anthropological fieldwork in Pacific locations.

Volume 1
The Anthropology of Empathy: Experiencing the Lives of Others in Pacific Societies
Edited by Douglas W. Hollan and C. Jason Throop

Volume 2
Christian Politics in Oceania
Edited by Matt Tomlinson and Debra McDougall

Volume 3
*The Death of the Big Men and the Rise of the Big Shots:
Custom and Conflict in East New Berlin*
Keir Martin

Volume 4
*Creating a Nation with Cloth: Women, Wealth,
and Tradition in the Tongan Diaspora*
Ping-Ann Addo

Volume 5
The Polynesian Iconoclasm: Religious Revolution and the Seasonality of Power
Jeffrey Sissons

Volume 6
Engaging with Strangers: Love and Violence in the Rural Solomon Islands
Debra McDougall

Volume 7
*Mortuary Dialogues: Death Ritual and the Reproduction of Moral Community
in Pacific Modernities*
Edited by David Lipset and Eric K. Silverman

Volume 8
*Mimesis and Pacific Transcultural Encounters: Making Likenesses in Time, Trade,
and Ritual Reconfigurations*
Edited by Jeannette Mageo and Elfriede Hermann

Volume 9
Dreams Made Small: The Education of Papuan Highlanders in Indonesia
Jenny Munro

Dreams Made Small
The Education of Papuan Highlanders
in Indonesia

Jenny Munro

First published in 2018 by
Berghahn Books
www.berghahnbooks.com

© 2018, 2026 Jenny Munro
First paperback edition published in 2026

All rights reserved. Except for the quotation of short passages
for the purposes of criticism and review, no part of this book
may be reproduced in any form or by any means, electronic or
mechanical, including photocopying, recording, or any information
storage and retrieval system now known or to be invented,
without written permission of the publisher.

Library of Congress Cataloging-in-Publication Data

Names: Munro, Jenny, author.
Title: Dreams Made Small: The Education of Papuan Highlanders in Indonesia / Jenny Munro.
Description: [New York]: Berghahn Books, 2018. | Series: ASAO Studies in Pacific Anthropology ; volume 9 | Includes bibliographical references and index.
Identifiers: LCCN 2017059996 (print) | LCCN 2017061130 (ebook) | ISBN 9781785337598 (Ebook) | ISBN 9781785336843 (hardback: alk. paper)
Subjects: LCSH: Dani (New Guinean people)—Indonesia—Wamena. | Dani (New Guinean people)—Education (Higher)—Indonesia—Sulawesi Utara. | Minority college students—Indonesia—Sulawesi Utara. | Ethnology—Indonesia—Papua. | Papua (Indonesia)—Ethnic relations. | Papua (Indonesia)—Social conditions.
Classification: LCC DU744.35.D32 (ebook) | LCC DU744.35.D32 M86 2018 (print) | DDC 305.8009951/6—dc23
LC record available at https://lccn.loc.gov/2017059996

British Library Cataloguing in Publication Data

A catalogue record for this book is available from the British Library

EU GPSR Authorized Representative

LOGOS EUROPE, 9 rue Nicolas Poussin, 17000, LA ROCHELLE, France

Email: Contact@logoseurope.eu

ISBN 978-1-78533-684-3 hardback
ISBN 978-1-83695-686-0 paperback
ISBN 978-1-83695-716-4 epub
ISBN 978-1-78533-759-8 web pdf

https://doi.org/10.3167/9781785336843

Contents

List of Figures and Maps	vi
Acknowledgements	viii
Introduction. New Promises, Old Problems	1
Chapter 1. Ethno-racial and Political Dreams of Education in Wamena	33
Chapter 2. 'Newcomers' and 'Masters of the Land' in North Sulawesi	56
Chapter 3. Stigma, Fear and Shame: Dani Encounters with Racial and Political Formations in North Sulawesi	78
Chapter 4. 'Discipline Is Important': Aspirations and Encounters on Campus	100
Chapter 5. Belonging, Expertise and Conflict in Highlanders' Social World Abroad	123
Chapter 6. 'Study First': Sexuality, Pregnancy and Survival in the 'City of Free Sex'	141
Chapter 7. Doing Good Things in a Dani Modernity	158
Conclusion. Koteka Questions	175
Bibliography	185
Index	198

Figures and Maps

Figures

Figure 0.1. Dani and other highlanders at President Yudhoyono's speech — 2

Figure 0.2. Crowd of onlookers during the presidential visit, Wamena, 28 July 2006 — 3

Figure 1.1. Misi market area, Wamena — 36

Figure 1.2. A young girl ready for school in Wouma — 37

Figure 1.3. Dani gathered at the Office of Statistics — 45

Figure 2.1. Bakar batu, Unima campus — 71

Figure 2.2. Final examination celebration, Unima campus — 71

Figure 3.1. Dorm room poster — 90

Figure 3.2. A Dani student is baptized by a Pentecostal minister in Tondano — 94

Figure 4.1. Dorm room decorations may depict political views, represented by the Morning Star flag drawing, and Christian commitments — 104

Figure 4.2. Examination panel, Unima — 109

Figure 4.3. Student with his professor after his thesis examination, Unima — 110

Figure 5.1. Students at a soccer match featuring Persiwa, the team of Wamena, in Manado — 125

Figure 5.2. GIDI followers leading an event to mark the founding of the church — 131

Figure 6.1. Three generations at a Unima graduation ceremony — 152

Figure 7.1. A graduation moment, Unima, 2006 — 160

Figure 7.2. Unima graduation   161
Figure 8.1. Indonesian tourists at the Baliem Valley Festival battle
            re-enactment   176

Maps

Map 0.1. Eastern Indonesia showing Papua/West Papua and
         North Sulawesi   7
Map 0.2. Central highlands of Papua, including Wamena and
         Baliem Valley   15
Map 2.1. North Sulawesi province   57

Acknowledgements

This book is the product of my own education abroad, and it has been made possible by many generous, insightful and supportive people in diverse places and times. In Indonesia, I owe tremendous thanks to my Dani friends and informants, especially those who allowed me into their lives in the Yepmum dorm in North Sulawesi. In Wamena, I am grateful to everyone who accepted me into their homes and shared their thoughts and sweet potatoes with me. In Manado, I had the good fortune to make friends with Maureen Roble from New Jersey, who found her long-lost cousins in Davao, in the southern Philippines. Maureen was a great companion on an exploration of the best and worst of North Sulawesi charm and prejudice. She also gracefully handled the privilege of having a typhoid and dengue-infected friend convalescing on her couch for a number of weeks in 2005.

Dr Lucky Sondakh and Pangky Pangemanan in Manado arranged my sponsorship by Sam Ratulangi University in 2005 and were highly professional and helpful. My fieldwork was supported by funding from the Anthropology Department at the Australian National University (ANU), then part of the Research School of Pacific and Asian Studies, and by the ANU's International Education office. I also received funding from an Australian government International Postgraduate Research Scholarship.

My ANU mentors Kathryn Robinson and Chris Ballard provided thoughtful, compassionate direction and helpful advice. This work also owes much to the inspiration, support and enthusiasm of my friend and mentor Leslie Butt, who, like it or not, is at least partly responsible for me being on this path. Any path that leads to Wamena is a good path, I think.

I would like to thank the manuscript reviewers who provided astute feedback. Rupert Stasch, the series editor at Berghahn Books, encouraged me to write this book and then provided brilliant comments on a complete first draft manuscript in the span of what seemed like a weekend. I would not have finished the book without his kind and grounded guidance, but all the shortcomings are my own.

Research fellowships funded by Lynn McIntyre of the University of Calgary, Canada, the Canadian Institutes for Health Research, and the State Society and Governance in Melanesia Program at ANU provided time to develop publications based on this research. Some of these materials are reworked into this book, with thanks to ANU Press, Taylor & Francis and *Indonesia* journal. I also thank the School of Social Science at the University of Queensland for additional support to finish this manuscript during my first semester as Lecturer in Anthropology.

Over the years, despite our mobile lives, a few close friends have shared the trials and joys of living and working in Indonesia, including Traci Sudana, Michael Cookson, Sarah Richards, Yohana Baransano, Feryana Wakerkwa, Todd Biderman, and Martin Slama. I owe my biggest debt of gratitude to my family in Canada, especially my parents, Peg Shelley and Keith Munro. During my doctoral fieldwork in Indonesia, my caring relatives worried on my behalf about 'bird' flu, earthquakes, typhoid, imprisonment and a host of other unlikely dangers so that I could enjoy myself. Only once did they call the Canadian Embassy in Jakarta to have me tracked down.

Introduction
New Promises, Old Problems

On 28 July 2006, the Indigenous Dani people of Wamena, the main town in West Papua's central highlands, received their first-ever presidential visit, some four decades after West Papua was handed to Indonesia by the United Nations.[1] Despite the heavy police and military guard that surrounded Susilo Bambang Yudhoyono, a modest turnout of Indigenous highlanders gathered on a sunny hillside in Honelama, on the city outskirts, to see the President. In order to hear his speech, some highlanders had walked for up to two hours from other parts of Wamena because the roads to the site were blocked, except for vehicles carrying government employees and Indonesians.[2] Upon arrival at the site, Dani and other Indigenous attendees were directed by police officers to climb across a ditch and through a large break in a chain-link fence to a grassy area that faced the side of the main stage, where Indonesians and their guests sat in chairs facing the stage. Fenced in on all sides, people told me that the hills behind us were full of soldiers. In case of any unrest, there would be no way out of the enclosure. Perhaps not surprisingly, the crowd around me was subdued and quiet, and seemed to come to life at only two moments – first, during the opening prayers and, second, when the President announced that there had been much talk about 'progress' (*kemajuan*, which may also be translated as modernity or advancement) with few tangible results. This time, he said, things were going to be different. There was shouting and applause from the crowd. Perhaps it was the acknowledgement of their feelings that modernity has not yet come to the highlands despite decades of rhetoric, or hope for a better future based on the President's promise to 'accelerate development' (*mempercepat pembangunan*). Of course, the attendees might have read such statements any day in the newspaper, but there was cultural significance attached to coming face to face with the national leader, even behind a fence and from an awkward angle.

Reports were that the reason the President had travelled to the highlands at all was because he wanted to visit a remote area that had suffered a devastating famine a few months earlier. The famine, like other human crises, briefly sparked national conversations about the apparently shocking extent of poverty and hardship in remote Papua. Indonesians on the populous main island

2   Dreams Made Small

Figure 0.1. Dani and other highlanders at President Yudhoyono's speech. Photo by author

of Java could see that Papuans are poor in ways that seem vastly different from the slums of Jakarta, the national capital of Indonesia. Local conversations surrounding the presidential visit and views in the media (particularly the national radio station, which was the most popular source of news at the time) focused anew on 'underdevelopment' in the central highlands. Why were people so poor, 'backward', 'illiterate' and hungry? Was it geographical isolation and lack of telecommunications? Were the Indigenous people not growing gardens anymore? Which problems could be blamed on Indigenous officials in the highlands? Whose fault was it if teachers did not teach school and students did not study? Though some of the streetside conversations blamed the Indonesian government for treating Papuans with violence and repression, many Indigenous people were also questioning themselves. 'We are low-quality human resources (*sumber daya manusia,* often abbreviated as SDM)', some said. 'We are still backward', said others.

I take these comments as an indication that highlanders find themselves problematized by dominant national and popular Indonesian perspectives (see Lattas 1998: 314). Tania Li (2007) has developed the concept of 'rendering technical' to describe the process by which complex dimensions of human problems are reduced and simplified in order to produce generally applicable, uncontested approaches that fit the agendas of state governments and international organizations (cited in Munro and Butt 2012: 335). Jenny Munro and Leslie Butt (2012: 335) write that 'as part of improvement schemes, those development objectives are characterised in technical terms, carrying with them forms of judgement, vocabularies of implementation, and ideas about human abilities, all simplified in the service of getting the job done.' For decades, Indonesians, foreigners and coastal Papuans have stigmatized highlanders (especially men) as primitive, unsophisticated, backward and violent. Martin Slama and Jenny Munro (2015: 3; see also Stasch 2015: 77–79) draw attention to the 'remarkably persistent association of Papuans with primitivism, especially with the "stone-age" as the ultimate realm of the primitive other'. This study asks: when people (their constitution, lifestyles and capabilities) are deeply problematized or, to use another concept that will be elaborated throughout the book, 'diminished', in this way, what dreams emerge and why? How are these dreams continually reshaped? The study addresses these questions by looking closely at one way that Dani see themselves moving forward, namely, education.

It is no coincidence that after his promises on the hill, President Yudhoyono sped through the main street in a heavily guarded motorcade, with

Figure 0.2. Crowd of onlookers during the presidential visit, Wamena, 28 July 2006. Photo by author

his window halfway down, to the cheers of neatly organized and uniformed school students as if showing the way forward to a better, albeit securitized future, or that he went to a local school, which attracted the following media report (*Cenderawasih Post,* 28 July 2006):

> President SBY pays great attention to children's education. This was demonstrated yesterday when, on his way to Kurima, he found the opportunity to drop in on Junior High School Number Three in Wamena ... The president gave a lesson on the importance of loving one's country and requested that the students study well. 'All of Indonesia's children are the same, because of this Papua's children are also Indonesia's children and so they all need to study diligently ... I am proud of Papua's many high achieving children ... so you must study diligently so you can become intelligent people and useful people.' The president asked one of the students what he dreamed of becoming in the future, and the student said he wished to become a doctor. The president stated that all of Indonesia's children have the same chance to achieve success, including children of Papua ... The president also taught children about school manners, which require students to always respect their teachers and their parents ... he also asked for the children to sing songs, such as 'Fly My Flag', 'Indonesia Raya', and 'From Sabang to Merauke'.

The President seems to acknowledge that Papuans do not feel much like Indonesians, but he argues that they should, and the way that they can become equal and Indonesian is through education. Education is, more than any other development project, about children's dreams and, by extension, the dreams of parents, clans and nations. Education is a long-term project of cultivation and improvement by which, through diligence and submission, children overcome the ignorance and laziness they are presumed to possess. Education promises to close the gap. Education is a process of remediation for 'stone-agers' to catch up with cultural, racial and intellectual 'moderns'. Moreover, the political power of Indonesians is, according to Dani, at least in part due to knowledge and cleverness that has allowed them to take over Dani lands and domains of authority. Dani experiences of education, charted through this study, produce feelings of inadequacy, vulnerability and smallness, alongside cultural pride and political critique. Dreams of education are reconfigured by various kinds of violence, but other dreams are clarified or consolidated. This introductory chapter lays out the key ethnographic and conceptual terrain of the book, focusing first on local cultural, racial, political and historical configurations that have shaped projects of education for Dani highlanders, then explaining concepts of racialization, diminishment and technocratic racism that I use to make sense of dreams that emerge from stigmatization.

For the last half a century, Dani and other Indigenous inhabitants of West Papua have struggled with the oppressive and violent conditions of Indonesian rule. On 1 May 1963, the United Nations Temporary Executive Authority transferred authority over West Papua to the Indonesian government, on the basis of the 1962 New York Agreement signed by the Netherlands, Indonesia and the United Nations, subject to a self-determination plebiscite to be held before 1969. After a sham referendum in 1969, the United Nations ratified Indonesian control in spite of Indigenous opposition, leading observers to describe Indonesian rule as 'colonial' from the start (Budiardjo and Liong 1988; Drooglever 2009; Osborne 1985; Sharp 1977). Indigenous resistance and aspirations have persisted (Giay 2000, 2001; Lawson 2016; Raweyai 2002), and have typically been repressed by the state through violence, killings, arrests, harassment and intimidation (Braithwaite et al. 2010; Franciscans International and Asian Human Rights Commission 2011). Beyond the historical act of incorporation and violation of Papuans' right to self-determination, scholars also point to the violence perpetrated by Indonesian state forces instructed to enforce settlement, migration, patriotism, development and order (see, for example, Elmslie 2003; Giay 2000; King, Elmslie and Webb-Gannon 2011; Kirsch 2007: 54). Military forces continue to murder, rape, torture, detain, disturb and intimidate the Indigenous population with impunity, particularly in the highlands (Farhadian 2007; Haluk 2013; Human Rights Watch 2007, 2014; Komnas Perempuan 2010). In 2012, when I was in Wamena, Honelama (the village where Yudhoyono gave his speech in 2006) was burned to the ground. A Dani man was killed and about a dozen others were stabbed by Indonesian soldiers. Earlier in the day, Indonesian soldiers on a motorbike sped down a road in the area, striking an Indigenous child. His relatives, attending a funeral, believed the child to have been killed, and attacked the soldiers. One soldier was beaten to death on the roadside. Hearing of this, two trucks of soldiers from the nearby army battalion attacked Honelama (see International Coalition for Papua 2013). State violence in West Papua relies on a racialized logic of Indonesian superiority. This book demonstrates that the racialized everyday violence of Indonesian rule is as important as state violence for understanding Papuans' experiences and aspirations.

The possibility of a return to power is proving highly attractive to those Indigenous men and women who are able to complete secondary school and secure the funds to embark on postsecondary studies. The Indonesian national census of 2010 suggested about four per cent of youth in Papua (including Indigenous Papuans and Indonesians) make it to postsecondary studies (Badan Pusat Statistik [BPS] 2010). More recent surveys suggest that 15 per cent of youth aged 19–23 are at university in Papua (Badan Pusat Statistik Provinsi Papua (BPSPP) 2013). About 2.4 per cent of women and 3.7 per cent of men in Papua are university graduates (BPSPP 2013: 50). These achievements must be set against limited to no education among many people in Papua and high rates of illiteracy. In Jayawijaya, the regency around Wamena, 31 per cent of males and 56 per cent of females aged ten years and older have never been to school (BPSPP 2013: 47–48). The illiteracy rate among men and women aged twenty-five and older in Wamena is about 10 per cent, but 63 per cent for areas of Jayawijaya outside the city (BPSPP 2013: 63–64). It is not only the older generation who cannot read or write, as 12 per cent of males and 37 per cent of females aged 15–24 are also reportedly illiterate (BPSPP 2013: 56–57).

As discussed later and in the next chapter, education aspirations are coming out of powerful constructions of Indigenous inferiority, Indonesian colonialism, Dani traditions around knowledge and power, and Christian emphases on knowledge and writing. The result is Dani desires for cosmopolitan cultural connections in a place that appears increasingly connected, but, as Jacob Nerenberg (cited in Slama and Munro 2015: 11) points out, where so much of daily life unfolds in missed connections, delays and trucks stuck in the mud. Very few Dani have the resources to study overseas, but some, mainly because of critically timed injections of cash that sustain educational participation, are able to go to other parts of Indonesia for a few years before they hopefully return home to look for employment. This book follows a cohort of students in their late teens and early twenties from the highlands to North Sulawesi and back home again to Papua. It is based on sixteen months of ethnographic fieldwork in Wamena and North Sulawesi (another province of eastern Indonesia) that began in October 2005. In North Sulawesi I first lived with students in a Dani dormitory on the campus of the National University of Manado for about seven months, then spent two months living with a family in Wouma, on the outskirts of Wamena, and then returned to live in a different dorm that included Dani as well as Indonesian students in Manado, the capital city of North Sulawesi, until the end of December 2006. In addition to participating in everyday activities and informal conversations (in Bahasa Indonesia, the national language), I went to campus, sometimes attended classes, observed student seminars and examinations, and accompanied students around town and to visit their friends and relatives. Attending church services with students was an important research method. I learned about their interactions with each other amidst Indonesians, as well as their relationships with Indonesians. Students welcomed me in their group meetings, discussions and social organizations. To understand their academic pursuits, I also read their organizational documents and theses. I held some group discussions to focus on topics such as experiences on campus and experiences of early schooling in Wamena. Students appreciated the formality of these small-group activities. I employed a questionnaire in the later stages of my fieldwork to elicit anonymous descriptions of experiences of bribery and discrimination on campus to complement the first-hand information from key informants. In Wamena

I lived in a garden hut near the We river and participated in everyday life, as well as funerals and marriage celebrations. I returned to Wamena in 2009 to follow up with some students and graduates who had returned home, and I have been back to Wamena and other cities in West Papua almost every year since 2011.

Highlanders have been travelling to North Sulawesi to attend institutes of higher education since the late 1980s. This is around the time when the first students began to complete Indonesian secondary school in the highlands. Papuans see studying outside Papua as more prestigious, and universities are seen as better quality than universities in Papua. Experience abroad is a compelling draw for young people from small remote towns such as those found in much of Papua. Papuans also go to other areas of Indonesia for university studies, but this province, on the island of Sulawesi, attracts more Papuan highlanders to its higher education institutes than any other province. Students say they are attracted to North Sulawesi because it provides an affordable educational experience in a Christian, modern, safe atmosphere. They say they want to get away from negative influences in Papua. Today, students are also following the paths set by their kin and sponsors, and are attracted to the security of living where there are other highland Papuans. There are approximately three thousand Papuan students in North Sulawesi.[3]

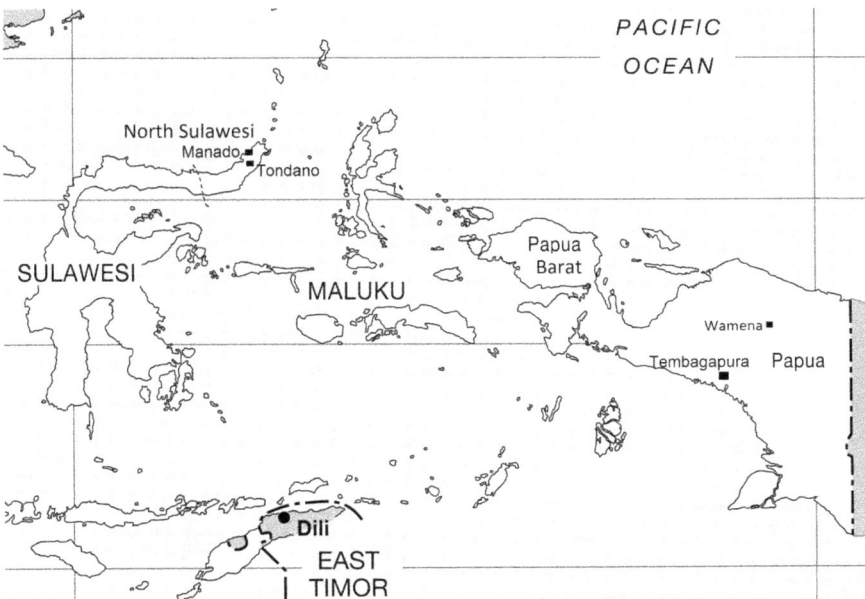

Map 0.1. Eastern Indonesia showing Papua/West Papua and North Sulawesi. © Australian National University, College of Asia and the Pacific, CartoGIS

Dani students hope that going to university outside Papua will facilitate mixing with cosmopolitan Indonesians and an educational engagement with modern ways of being. The acquisition of knowledge will enable them to contribute to development, have new authority and status, and do 'good things for others' (Zimmer-Tamakoshi 1997: 110) when they return home to the highlands. This is not only because of the potent national and local association of education with power, but because Dani leaders and elders in general expect young people to bridge the gap between Dani and Indonesian systems, and to help return Indigenous people to power. Young educated Dani go away with aspirations for belonging as well as transformation, for recognition as well as power. They end up feeling heavily confined by the continuity of racial formations in North Sulawesi and return home after a few years with a new understanding of their inability to belong with, and be accepted by, Indonesians. They may come back newly dedicated to highlands culture, have different perspectives on living in Wamena, or redouble their efforts to build connections with other Dani. Education processes, meanings and practices are thus not neutral. Schooling seems a mundane activity, but this study shows that education is an important site of racialization, regulation, diminishment and resilience. Following Amanda Lewis, racialization is a process that 'draws on old notions of race as a biological characteristic' and 'new notions of culture as a marker of difference' (Lewis 2003: 877). Genetic presumptions are enacted and reinforced (Bridges 2011). Racial logics link identity markers with negative practices and values (Al-Faham and Ernst 2016), and enable local social, political and economic hierarchies.

Since I began my initial fieldwork, ten years of President Yudhoyono's period of 'stability and stagnation' (Aspinall, Mietzner and Tomsa 2015) has come to end. A new President, Joko Widodo, has emerged with a flurry of promises for Papuans. So far he has failed to control conservative, capitalist and pro-military agendas (Munro 2014a, 2015a), and the human rights situation has deteriorated throughout Indonesia (Human Rights Watch 2017). There is growing evidence of the power that racialized views of Papuans have in shaping acts of state violence by police and military, particularly towards groups of unarmed, agitated Indigenous men (Human Rights Watch 2014). Sadly, violence towards Papuans in the rest of Indonesia continues, including in Manado, the city with the motto 'we are all family', where I began my research in 2005 (see Berita Kawanua 2014; Kompasiana 2014).[4] Anti-highlander and anti-Dani sentiment is on the rise in Papua, and it is coming from coastal Papuans as much as Indonesians. Racialization, and the political mobilization of 'racial' difference, is on the rise. Papuans increasingly talk of 'saving Papuans' from extinction, and the young generation is seen as particularly threatened by state violence, poverty, alcohol and HIV/AIDS (Berita Satu 2016; Munro 2019). Violence breaks out along the cultural lines that people increasingly see as important and firm. Perhaps above all, as the Special Autonomy Law passed in 2001 provides (in theory) more opportunities for Papuans in governance and politics (see Chauvel 2011), including the first highlander Governor, Lukas Enembe, highlanders are increasingly blamed for failures in these domains. They are said to be demonstrating 'tribal' or 'clan' mentalities and practicing 'wantok-ism'. Marcus Mietzner (2007: 13) refers to Enembe's election campaign's 'appeal to politically archaic tribal communities'. But this book reveals, first, that these 'failures' are a continuation of Indonesian and foreign racialization of highlanders, and, second, that if they exist, these failures are as much created in the Indonesian education system and via Dani experiences of it than anything that supposedly lurks in Dani or highland cultural traditions. Dani experiences with Indonesians and their systems and institutions, which are also shaped by global forces, teach 'wantokism' and facilitate 'clan' allegiances. 'Underdevelopment' in the highlands has now been laid at the feet of the Indigenous inhabitants, especially the few (mostly men) who have acquired education, a government or entrepreneurial position, and perhaps a modicum of wealth. This book is important for understanding those men, even though the vast majority of Dani graduates are not, and do not become, elites.

Indeed, in many ways this study is much more about men than about women. Male students outnumber female students considerably, and reports are that the numbers of female students from the highlands in North Sulawesi are now lower than when this study took place. Racial stigma is gendered towards Dani men much more than women. It is the 'penis-gourd', for example that symbolizes 'primitive' highlands culture in the Indonesian imaginary. It is mainly men's bodies that are stigmatized as violent, drunken, hypersexed, resistant and physically strong. Women are stereotyped as having loose morals, but duped or dominated by men into 'shameful' situations like premarital pregnancy, explored later in the book. Indonesians do not see Dani women as serious students, but not for the same reasons that they question Dani men. Men's intellect, commitment and diligence are questioned by Indonesians, where Dani women are presumed to be distracted by hypersexed men into premarital relationships and childrearing. That Dani women have the gall to be pregnant and studying, to have children and still be out and about finishing their degrees, stuns the local (evangelical Christian) population in North Sulawesi. Women are assumed not to be political or activists, though they are. Men are more numerous in education and employment, and are positioned by and seeking to recover traditional male domains of authority in leadership, territory and people. Desires for and the right to pursue education are not seen as the sole prerogative of men, but women have to work to maintain this right by reminding men and challenging gender unfairness when it arises.

This study is situated in relation to several sets of questions and themes, which I discuss in the rest of this introduction. As mentioned above, I am interested in how women and men live with stigma, how it is produced, racialized, gendered and resisted, and what is created from these experiences. Fine studies of Papuan nationalism focus on government policies, historical events or human rights (Chauvel 2005, 2011), but do less to capture the day-to-day experiences and understandings that contribute to Papuan desires for a sovereign Papuan state, described locally as *merdeka* (independence or freedom). To understand this decades-old conflict better, we must consider how racial and other conditions shape highlanders' views of the present, the future, themselves and others. Next, I aim to shed light on schooling in contexts of violence, regulation, suspicion and racialization. In this case, education fails to cultivate nationalistic political sentiments or a feeling of connection and belonging within the nation. The third theme that this study speaks to is political conditions in West Papua, and particularly Indigenous understandings and experiences of colonialism from everyday vantage points and at the level of daily and sometimes intimate forms of engagement with Indonesians. Finally, this study is also an ethnography of urban, educated Dani youth who are today's political leaders, government officials, rebels, activists, parents and survivors. For them, what, indeed, does freedom look like?

Who is Who: Racial, Temporal and Cultural Configurations

In this section I pause to introduce many of the relevant categories of ethnic geography and ethno-racial taxonomy that appear throughout the study. I also delineate important inequalities and social dynamics in West Papua that form the context in which young people come to desire and pursue education.

'Race', 'Tribes' and 'People'

In Indonesia, the concept of race (*ras*) was banned from public and media discussion during the administrations of Sukarno (1949–65) and Suharto (1965–98) as a controversial subject likely to incite conflict. Race does not officially exist, and the term is rarely used in local discourse. Yet ideas like *suku* (ethnic group or tribe) or *suku-bangsa* (ethnic nation) do the work of racialization, tying traits, tendencies and capabilities to skin colour and cultural heritage. There is a word for white people – *bule* – and there is certainly quite a bit of popular focus on skin colour and facial features. In my North Sulawesi field site, the majority cultural group is Minahasan, and people speak of the traits of *suku* Minahasa or Minahasa tribe/ethnic group. At another level, there are also 'people' (*orang-orang*) – Indonesian people and Papuan people, for example. *Orang* links a person and his or her population to a place, an identity, an ethno-cultural background. In North Sulawesi, locals who live in the capital city sometimes refer to themselves as 'Manado people' (*orang Manado*). Similarly, students from the central highlands of Papua sometimes call themselves 'Wamena people' (*orang Wamena*). Two very important categories of people in this study are 'Indonesians' (*orang Indonesia*) and 'Papuans' (*orang Papua*). I have been asked a few times: are Papuans not also Indonesians? In terms of citizenship, the answer is yes. But in terms of how people talk about one another, Papuans talk of 'Indonesian people' (*orang Indonesia*), while Indonesians and Papuans talk of 'Papuan people' (*orang Papua*). I have never heard anyone refer to Papuans as 'orang Indonesia'.

These conceptualizations have historical roots that relate to what Europeans thought they were observing in the region and how they depicted the local populations in their writings. 'Racial' observations and representations were, and continue to be, tangled in ideas of primitivity and the politics of territorial expansion and defence.

'Papuans' and 'Indonesians'

Chris Ballard notes that the concept of *orang Papua* (Papuans) and their supposed distinctiveness from Malay people emerged as a subject of interest for explorers and naturalists as far back as the sixteenth century (Ballard 2008). While initial presumptions and definitions of 'Papuan' varied in terms of name and content, by the nineteenth century, a pervasive, if inconsistent, colonial racial logic had developed (Ballard 2008; Giay and Ballard 2003; Ploeg 1995). This racial thought was initially influenced by a science of race in which key external diacritics came to stand for morality, intelligence and abilities (Giay and Ballard 2003). These observations positioned Indigenous populations 'within a gradient or hierarchy of value' (Giay and Ballard 2003: 2). Perhaps the most significant legacy of these early writings is the emphasis on the racial difference of Papuans and Malays (Ballard 2008: 187). George Earl, a British anthropologist who wrote several volumes on Papuans but never visited New Guinea (cited in Ballard 2008: 173–74), stated: 'The physical characteristics of the Malayu-Polynesians are so distinct from those of the Papuans, that a single glance is sufficient to detect the difference between the races.' Moreover: 'The Malayu-Polynesians had left their influence even in New Guinea in a "line of improvement" that extended along the northern coast and eastwards into the Pacific' (Ballard 2008: 174). Later, the Dutch and other European explorers in the highlands in the 1920s–1930s were interested in assessing the capacities of 'the natives' for labour, just as they wished to learn of the region's exploitable natural resources. They based their assessments in part on so-called racial characteristics (Ploeg 1995) that were thought to reveal Papuans' innate qualities, and thus their suitability for labour, and whether they were hostile or submissive. The earliest research in the highlands, undertaken as part of European explorations, focused on assessing the racial characteristics and capacities of highlanders (Ploeg 1995: 231).

West Papua in the 1930s was seen as the final frontier of the Dutch East Indies colony, the last place where officials could experience isolation and 'strange natives', and bring peace, order and law (Rhys 1947). Dutch and Indonesian constructions of Papuans intensified in the post-World War II period. Though the rest of the colony formally gained independence in 1949, the Dutch argued that they could not give up West Papua, then called Netherlands New Guinea, to Indonesia. From 1949 to 1962, the Netherlands was in a dispute with Indonesia over the territory of present-day Papua (see Penders 2002; Saltford 2003). The Dutch side argued: 'Any form of Indonesian influence ... will lead to infiltrations and agitation in a region which needs a complete and undisturbed tranquillity in view of the stage of development of the population' (Lijphart 1966: 161–62). Danilyn Rutherford (1998: 268) also suggests that the Dutch desire to retain West Papua was influenced by plans to provide a homeland where colonial racial hierarchies could be safely maintained.

During the Dutch administration, the government enabled racialized inequalities between Indonesians (of Malay heritage) and Papuans (of Melanesian heritage), giving tangible meanings to representational discourses. Education was an early site of racialization. For example, teachers from the Kei Islands located west of Papua were employed in the Timika area. Coming from highly stratified societies that even included Papuans as slaves, these teachers reportedly treated the local population with contempt (Suwada 1984 [1971]). Richard Chauvel (2007: 33) also suggests that Indonesian settlers were a small but influential part of society in West Papua under the Dutch colonial administration.

Ideas about the categories of Papuan and Indonesian evolved further as Indonesia took possession during the early 1960s. Under former dictator Suharto's New Order government (1965–98), the government enforced development programs throughout Indonesia (Heryanto and Lutz 1988; van Langenberg 1990). The military provided 'order' so that development could proceed unhindered, ostensibly in the name of progress for all Indonesia's citizens. This ideology had particular implications for so-called tribal populations, referred to as 'isolated tribes' or 'estranged populations' (*masyarakat terasing*). They were denigrated as 'different and deficient' (Li 1999: 3). According to Gerard Persoon (1998: 281, 289):

> The government looks upon these groups as deviating from the cultural mainstream, and policies are aimed at bringing these people back into the mainstream of Indonesian life ... The official view is that for a variety of reasons and at various stages in history these groups have lost touch with the main processes of social, religious,

political and economic change, and it is the obligation of the state to help them return to the mainstream.

Most of Indonesia's *masyarakat terasing* are in fact, according to the government, located in Papua (Lenhart 1997). Christopher Duncan (2004: 90) proposes that the concept has had a significant impact on mainstream Indonesians. But where other 'isolated populations' are arguably able to overcome their primitive conditions and capabilities and become part of the Indonesian *bangsa* (race-nation-people), because of racialization Papuans have never been afforded this possibility. In West Papua, racialized identities like *rambut lurus* (straight hairs, a reference to Indonesians) and *rambut keriting* (frizzy hairs, a reference to Papuans) are prominent. The Indonesian government initiated migration programs to bring Indonesians from other parts of the country to Papua to ostensibly contribute to development and cultural improvement (Gietzelt 1989). Thus, Papuans refer to Indonesians as 'newcomers' or 'migrants' (*pendatang*). Dale Gietzelt (1989) refers to this migration as an attempt at 'Indonesianization' of West Papua, and many Papuans continue to point to in-migration (both government sponsored and unofficial) as an attempt to displace their control over land and cultural identity (see McGibbon 2004; Richards 2015).

It is one of the key demographic features of Papua today that Indonesians are the majority in the major cities, notably Jayapura and Merauke, in Papua province, and Manokwari and Sorong in West Papua province (Ananta et al. 2016: 470–72), while the majority of Papuans reside in rural areas. Not all Indonesians are recent migrants, and in some communities there is a distinction drawn between Indonesian who are 'old people' (*orang lama*) and 'new people' (*orang baru*). Indonesians are economically dominant, especially in terms of commercial enterprises, professional, technical and service jobs, and in many aspects of government administration, despite an emphasis in recent years on Papuan employment in the public service and in promoting Papuan private sector activities. The majority of Papuans are rural-based farmers, gardeners or fishers of some sort. Those who are employed in the formal economy are concentrated in the public service.

The category of 'Papuan' is generative of positive sentiments, not just negative assessments from Indonesians and others. Sarah Richards (2015) describes a growing sense of 'Papuan' identity that unites people of considerable cultural, geographical and linguistic diversity. She writes: 'Papuanness is a sentiment of pan-tribal identification that is generated through histories of perceived cultural and racial oppression and relies on stereotypes to position Papuans as a collective that is distinct from Islamic Indonesians' (2015: 146). In contrast to migrants, Papuans might also be referred to (and claim titles such as) as 'sons/daughters of the place' (*putra/putri daerah*), Indigenous people (*orang asli*), traditional or customary community (*masyarakat adat*), or landowners (*tuan tanah*, literally, masters of the land).

The definition of who is 'Indigenous Papuan' (*orang asli Papua*) has become the subject of more debate in recent years. The Special Autonomy Law of 2001 prescribed affirmative action provisions for Papuans and Papuan empowerment as a guiding principle. It defined Papuans as people of Melanesian racial heritage who are descendants of the Indigenous tribes of Papua, or those recognized by traditional communities.[5] The latter category might potentially include long-time migrants or their descendants. However, because the identity now enables preferential access to government positions such as Regent and Governor, and preferential access to programs like the 'Healthy Papua Card' (*Kartu Papua Sehat*), some Papuans have argued that the criteria needs to be more restricted, tied to racial features, and should exclude the descendants of Indonesian fathers and Papuan mothers (see International Crisis Group 2006: 8; Slama 2015: 263–64).

With identity categories having real implications for interactions with Indonesians in Papua, it is not surprising that Dani students are aware that, in North Sulawesi, they are the 'migrants'. Dani students abroad sometimes refer to local Indonesians as 'masters of the land' (or the house, *tuan rumah*). This designation acknowledges the power of being Indigenous to a place and the broad consensus among students that they can learn something from the locals, their institutions and their city. It also reflects the fact that students are ultimately not treated as equals regardless of what they learn or achieve. Dani students also call people in North Sulawesi 'locals' (*orang sini*), 'the community' (*masyarakat*) and variations on 'Manado people' (*orang Manado*). Students also become aware of local understandings of ethnic and cultural difference, including racial ideas about 'whiteness' (*putih*) that have particular salience. In North Sulawesi, locals express that the presence of Portuguese and then Dutch activities, including intermarriage, has contributed to the presence of white skin colour. Being 'black' (*hitam*) attracts criticism ranging from denigration to teasing, for Papuans as well as some locals. However, being Papuan is a certain kind of 'black' that comes with its own set of stigmas. In North Sulawesi, locals mostly do not differentiate between Papuans from different cultural groups, calling them all 'Papuan' or 'Irianese' (*orang Irian*) after the former name of Papua until 2001, Irian Jaya. Locals who have closer relationships with Dani students, such as church ministers with small congregations or some of the university professors, may refer to students as 'Wamena people', and some of them do develop particular notions of what that means.

Locating 'Wamena People' in the Baliem and Other Valleys

My focus in this book is mainly on Dani students from the Baliem Valley and the Wolo Valley, which connects to the Baliem Valley in the northwest. Because

Introduction 15

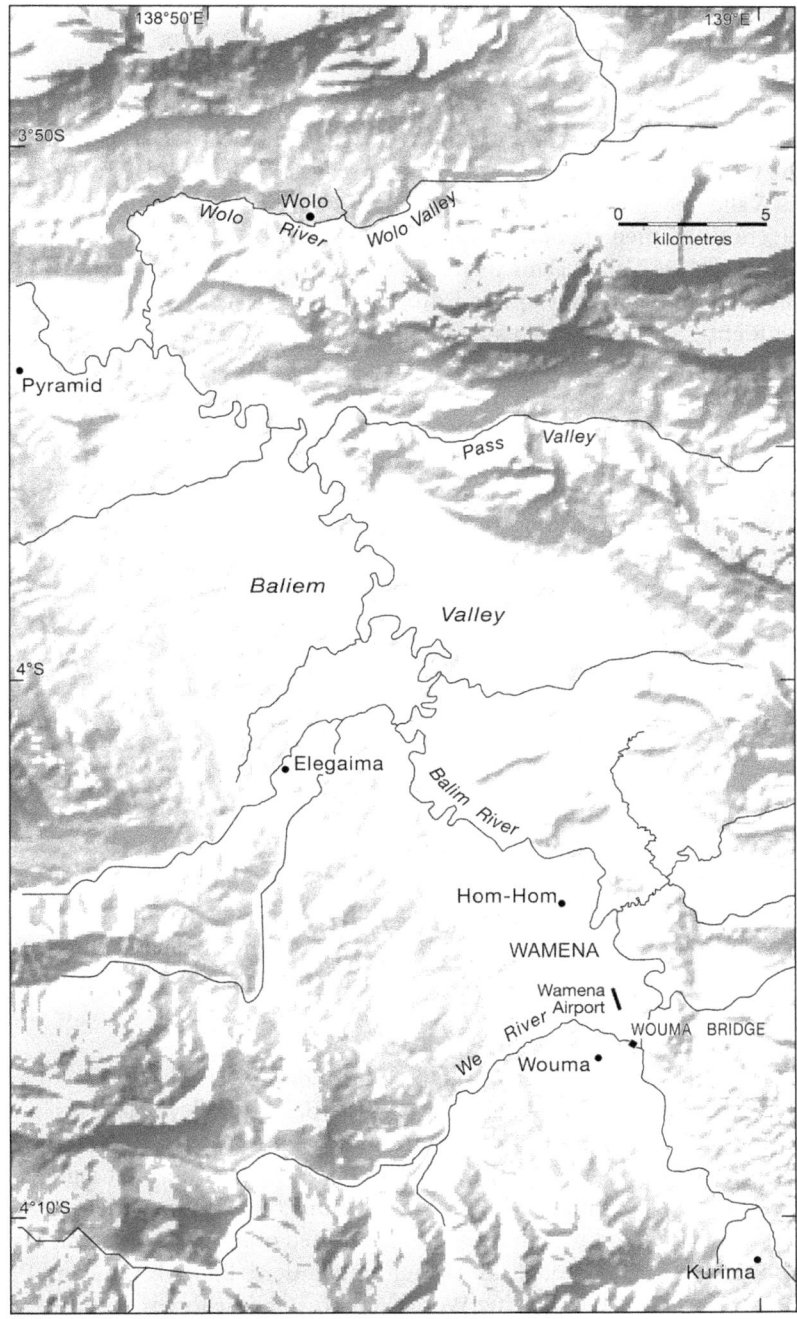

Map 0.2. Central Highlands of Papua, including Wamena and Baliem Valley.
© Australian National University, College of Asia and the Pacific, CartoGIS

of its size, about 80 km long and 20 km wide, the Baliem Valley was first described as the 'Grand Valley' (Heider 1979; Ploeg 1995, 2004). Anton Ploeg (2004: 291) uses 'Grand Valley' to mean 'the lower reaches of the Baliem River where it flows southeast through a wide Valley with a relatively flat floor before it leaves the Highlands via the Baliem Gorge' and denotes this as the habitat of the Grand Valley Dani. To refer to themselves, Baliem Valley Dani use the term 'Valley people' (*orang lembah*), among other possibilities such as 'Dani', 'Indigenous Wamena people' (*orang asli Wamena*), or *Hubula, Nayak* or *Balim meke*, which are Valley Dani words.[6] The students from Wolo identify themselves as Walak, and they speak a different Indigenous dialect from the Valley students. The perspectives and experiences of other central highlanders, namely Lani and Yali, also appear in this study. 'Lani' refers to people originally inhabiting areas west of the Dani; thus, they are called 'Western people' (*orang barat*) or 'Western Wamena people' (*orang Wamena barat*). At the same time, these 'tribal' (*suku*) designations and identities are also broken down into clan groups and with reference to particular areas of the central highlands. 'Yali' people originate from areas to the southeast of the Baliem Valley and speak a different language from the Dani and Lani, although all of the young adults in this study and most youth in the highlands also speak Bahasa Indonesia.[7] Together they may be described as central highlanders, or just highlanders (*orang gunung*), though there are also highlanders to the west in the Paniai Lakes region. Most of the students in my study have spent at least some time in the city of Wamena, and thus they also sometimes refer to themselves as 'Wamena people', including while living in North Sulawesi.

It is a testament to the significance of administrative boundaries and bureaucratic channels for the group of 'Wamena people' in this study that they also refer to themselves using the names of their home districts (*kabupaten*, usually translated as 'regency'). This is less so for students from Jayawijaya regency, the oldest regency in the central highlands, but during my research students often described themselves as Puncak (from Puncak Jaya), Yahukimo or Tolikara, after highlands regencies. As will become clear later on, these identities are reinforced in North Sulawesi as district governments provide crucial financial support and fund student dormitories.

As this study demonstrates, highlanders continue to deal with stigmatization. From the early days of 'discovery', the Baliem Valley was described as peopled by 'stone-age' tribes and cultures that were soon to be 'lost' to modern influence (i.e. Matthiessen 1962). The Archbold Expedition first sighted the Baliem Valley on 21 June 1938, but throughout the early twentieth century, Dutch, American and British expeditions reached other parts of the highlands and encountered Dani people and other highlanders (Ballard, Vink and Ploeg 2001; Heider 1970: 303). During World War II, Japanese forces occupied parts of coastal Papua, imprisoned administrators in camps and put Papuans to work as labourers under the watch of Indonesian supervisors (Pouwer 1999). In 1954, the Christian and Missionary Alliance (CMA) landed some of its personnel on the Baliem River (Naylor 1974: 11). The first Dutch administrative post was established in the Baliem Valley in 1956. This marked the first permanent presence of foreigners in the Valley. Christian missionaries established the first schools (Lake 1989; Naylor 1974), and today, education still retains connotations of moral goodness and modern progress even though it is now also associated with Indonesian colonization and violence.

Some of the earliest descriptions of the Indigenous inhabitants of the Baliem Valley were produced by missionaries (Bromley 1962, 1972; Larson 1987) and Dutch administrators (Broekhuijse 1967; Pospisil 1962; for a discussion of this work, see Jaarsma 1991). The Dani became iconic in the ethnographic record as tribal warriors in Robert Gardner's (1963) film on warfare, *Dead Birds* (see also Gardner and Heider 1968). More broadly, Dani, Lani and Yali are still sometimes referred to (and refer to themselves) as '*koteka* people' (*masyarakat koteka*) after the penis gourd (*koteka* in Indonesian, *holim* in Dani) traditionally worn by men. In the Indonesian era, these people are still considered to be among the most 'primitive' of Papua's 'tribes'. Conditions of discrimination and violence are intense in the highlands (Butt 2001; Mote and Rutherford 2001). Nation-state institutions and ideologies attempt to force the Dani to become more Indonesian (Naylor 1974; Soepangat 1986). At the same time, the 'primitive' is part of what draws both domestic and international tourists to the Valley. A number of tour operators provide guided treks around the valley and nearby areas, stopping in villages, while the annual Baliem Valley festival showcases tribal dance, singing, dramatic performances, mock battles and pig races. At a Baliem Valley festival I attended in 2013, the overwhelming majority of onlookers were Indonesians and highlanders. These dynamics affirm the importance of Rupert Stasch's (2015: 62) project of examining how Papuans 'take up the category of the primitive as a self-understanding, acting toward and through this category in their relations with outsiders'. My study shows that educated Dani resist racialization as primitives by Indonesians, in part because discrimination and exclusion encourages processes of questioning and defending cultural values.

In this study I ethnographically explore current social formations, as well as everyday life among (mainly) educated Dani. But their contemporary experiences and values are very much shaped by the ongoing cultural significance of, among other things, land and gardening, control of territory and securing the future of Dani populations, social reproduction and relations of reciprocity, including leadership that is generous, hardworking and accountable. Dani scholar (and until his sudden death in 2011, head of the Papuan Peoples' Assembly, or *Majelis Rakyat Papua*) Agus Alua (2006: 154–56) describes the Dani 'big man' as having good hands, a good heart, a good voice and good behaviour. This means he demonstrates his ability to work hard on collective activities, his generosity and his ability to speak the truth and compel followers. These understandings of leadership are incorporated into Dani students' aspirations for education and leadership. Dani have used sophisticated agricultural techniques to turn a variety of marshy, rocky or steep landscapes into fertile gardens (Heider 1970; Sugandi 2013). They grow sweet potatoes as a staple food and raise pigs for ritual, exchange and economic purposes (Alua 2006; Heider 1979; Ploeg 1965, 1966, 2004). Even Dani university graduates will sometimes refer to themselves as 'gardeners', whether to show how far they have come, to explain their relative lack of material wealth or to assert their capacity for hard physical work. Pigs continue to be significant in competitive exchanges and social events such as weddings or funerals, as well as in bridewealth and compensation payments (Butt 1998; Farhadian 2003). Raising and selling pigs is one of the main ways that young people acquire enough money to depart for university abroad, while the work of their mothers and sisters growing and selling garden produce frequently provides them with money while they are at university. Eating *bakar batu* (literally 'stone cooking', referring to the technique of using heated rocks to steam pork, sweet potatoes and greens under banana leaves) together is an essential part of all celebrations, even among students in North Sulawesi. Dani societies have traditionally been relatively egalitarian in terms of male social hierarchies, with men improving their social standing and leadership status through achievements in warfare and their ability to attain and redistribute wealth (Alua 2006; Heider 1979; O'Brien 1969; Peters 1975). Young people view education and employment through this cultural lens that emphasizes tangible results (*hasil*) that should also benefit others (see also Glazebrook 2008). In the past, clan leaders tried to control marriages and fertility, including through supernatural and spiritual means, to ensure healthy future generations and build economic and political alliances (Butt 1998, 2005a). Today, 'saving Papuans' is a common goal among young Dani.

Yulia Sugandi (2013) argues that Dani elders in particular are focused on recovering collective dignity that has been lost during the Indonesia era. According to Sugandi (2013: 34) they feel 'made naked' or 'stripped' and 'dishonoured' by the impositions of the Indonesian state, including being treated as inferior and manipulated by outsiders, being kept in a subordinate position (Naylor 1974: 237), and being excluded from land and development decisions (Farhadian 2005: 42). Sugandi (2013: 42) focuses on the loss of control over sacred and taboo knowledge that is essential for good relations with the ancestors and continued fertility. Thus, Dani experiences and values today cannot be understood without acknowledging the effects of an equal number of Indonesians who now live alongside them in Wamena.

The term 'migrant' (*pendatang*) does not reflect the fact that some Indonesians are long-term settlers. Most of the migration of Indonesians to Wamena is not part of official transmigration programmes that funnelled Indonesians into rural areas to develop rice paddies and other similar activities. Migrants in Wamena are rarely engaged in farming or rural activities, but work in the private sector, in professional jobs, and in government and military roles. Indonesians tend to be comparatively wealthy and own consumer items like cars, which Dani rarely own. Even though Indonesian migration is associated with the spread of Islam in Papua (Richards 2015), there are Christian migrants too, and some of them live in Wamena. Because of their association with the Indonesian government and national culture, Indonesians in Wamena are differentiated from the Indigenous population (Butt 2005a: 164). Although there are indications of the emergence of Papuan elites in Wamena (Butt 2008: 118), it is still the case that most Dani men and women work in their gardens and sell produce to migrants to earn a living, while migrants who do not work for the government, the military or the police typically operate eateries, shops or market stalls. The streets of Wamena are usually full of Dani going about their business on foot, though possessing a motorbike is becoming increasingly common. Migrants tend to drive cars, motorbikes or ride in pedicabs (*becak*) driven by Dani youth. These are just some of the everyday manifestations of inequalities that give expression to racial boundaries between Indonesians and Dani, migrants and Indigenous people.

These distinctions have been raised and affirmed through violence, mostly towards Indigenous Dani at the hands of the Indonesian military and police, but on rare occasions amongst civilians. The time during which Dani students I describe in this book were abroad in North Sulawesi was perhaps a particularly difficult time to form bonds with Indonesians, learn from others or feel safe. Most of the students were in the latter stages of high school or had just left the highlands for university around 2000, shortly after the end of the 33-year Suharto dictatorship and at the height of subsequent reformation (*reformasi*) efforts. In Papua, critiques of Indonesian governance, expressions of independence desires and public talk about suffering were flourishing (Giay 2000). Papuans felt political change was coming, especially when leading Indonesian political figures conceded some political liberties to Papuans, including permission to raise the Morning Star independence flag. Others issued decrees denying such liberties. This, among other factors, contributed to a rare incident of violence from Dani towards Indonesian migrants on 6 October 2000. Police violently raided and destroyed a series of makeshift Indigenous community posts (*posko*) where the Morning Star flag was flying, killing one man, shooting ten others, and arresting and beating dozens (Human Rights Watch 2001; Mote and Rutherford 2001). A riot ensued, and by the end of the day, nine Indigenous Papuans were killed by Indonesian police and twenty-six Indonesian civilians were killed by Indigenous Papuans (Human Rights Watch 2001: 12). Octavianus Mote and Danilyn Rutherford (2001: 115) write that:

> Armed with spears, bows, and axes, local tribesmen set fire to houses belonging to traders, teachers, and bureaucrats from outside the Valley, then slaughtered their occupants as they fled. In a scene reminiscent of other Indonesian trouble spots, refugees flooded the police station, churches, mosques, and the airport. Most vowed they would leave the town of Wamena and never return.

Some Dani informants of mine were involved in the fighting, which they referred to as a battle or war (*perang*). Other people recalled hiding or fleeing home from school in terror to help evacuate their young and elderly relatives from the area.

Identity and ethnic categorization are inseparable from inequalities, violence and domination structures in Wamena. Shaped by these cultural, political and social conditions, Dani youth in this study set out on journeys to Manado, one of eastern Indonesia's most 'modern' cities, in search of new relationships, cultural connections and achievements. Their experiences reveal, among other things, new ethno-racial taxonomies and racialized challenges.

'Diminishment', Education and Racialization

Diminishment, as I use the term in this study, refers to Indigenous experiences of being rendered smaller (in land, in power, in physique or constitution, in confidence, and in networks and relationships) by processes and encounters that encourage people to question their cultures, commitments and capabilities (Clark 2000; Robbins 2004, 2005; Sahlins 1992; Tomlinson 2002). Matt Tomlinson's (2002: 237) work on Fiji, a context where there are some parallels with West Papua in terms of historical in-migration and resulting dominance of a non-Indigenous ethnic minority, explains that Indigenous perceptions of a diminishing *vanua* (land and people) are implicated in Indigenous politics to take back control, and in particular have been manipulated by elites in favour of military rule. In Papua New Guinea, Urapmin described in Joel Robbins' (2004) work feel racial, religious and moral failures in relation to colonization and globalization, but these feelings are very much based on their own moral logics and values. For them, diminishment inspires and shapes efforts at recovery and improvement, particularly Christian improvement and connections with global Christian moderns. Jeffrey Clark's (2000) analysis of Wiru 'madness' and narratives of 'shrinking men' in the southern highlands of Papua New Guinea suggests that Wiru are processing the inequalities and disjunctures of colonialism in their own ways, via their bodies. In a sense they are responding to, and taking back their bodies from, new forms of knowledge and power inscribed by colonial and missionary regimes.

In this study, I explore the contours of diminishment at different scales. To be clear, diminishment is the analytical frame I employ to make sense of interlinked Dani experiences, concepts and words that include, but are not limited to, reduced bodily size and clan numbers, newfound shyness and inadequacies, loss of power over population and territory, and limitations on relationships with Indonesians. There are diminishing hopes, as well as experiences of new feelings of inadequacy, including shame and a lack of confidence. These relate in part to the intense experience of being watched by Indonesians in North Sulawesi. Dani also express ways that they used to have better morals and stronger, healthier bodies, and how they feel they have changed because of Indonesian rule, especially the loss of control over land, goods and people (Munro 2019; Sugandi 2013). A deep examination of Dani understandings of the body, and how these have changed during colonization, is beyond the scope of this study, but in general Dani understand that bodies reflect social, spiritual and political conditions. The particulars vary among Dani from different parts of the Baliem Valley. Sugandi's (2013) work explores the collective social body and shows that in the highlands the body holds a prominent place in social relations. Bodies are 'made up by others' (Butt 1998: 115) and their wellbeing 'depends on a cosmological balance, particularly the relationship with the ancestors' (Sugandi 2013: 75). As bodies incorporate political inequalities, the issue of diminishing numbers arises – Dani students talk about the importance of pregnancy, for example, for avoiding Indigenous extinction. This comes up most clearly when they face the pressure to 'study first' and have children later, and they ask why not do both at the same time? Reproduction and education both 'save' Papuans. Diminishment might motivate education in the first place, and it certainly persists through experiences of education, but it also foments political critique and mobilization. Moreover, the sorts of diminishment at play shape what freedom looks like, and how and from where it can be sought.

Racialization is crucial to both the diminishment that occurs through becoming educated Dani and the forms of resistance that they most strongly articulate. Highlanders' sense of diminishment arises in relation to Indonesians and Indonesian rule, whether in face-to-face encounters, in their assessments of how they lost power, in the pursuit of closing the gap with Indonesians or in the assessment that they are losing a demographic battle. One of the pursuits of this study is to trace how racism operates towards Papuan highlanders today and to draw some conclusions about its effects. Floya Anthias and Nira Yuval-

Davis (1992) define racism as the discourses and practices by which people are inferiorized, excluded and subordinated. Naomi Priest and colleagues (2013: 116) describe the effects and operation of racism as:

> A phenomena that results in avoidable and unfair inequalities in power, resources and opportunities across racial or ethnic groups; racism can be expressed through beliefs (e.g. negative and inaccurate stereotypes), emotions (e.g. fear/hatred) or behaviours/practices (e.g. unfair treatment), ranging from open threats and insults (including physical violence) to phenomena deeply embedded in social systems and structures.

Observers, both foreign and Indigenous, have long described racism in West Papua. Indonesians tend to regard Papuans as 'primitive, stupid, lazy [and] drunk' (Koentjaraningrat and Ajamiseba 1994: 434). Racism underpins political violence (Butt 2012; Kirksey 2012; Kirsch 2002). The report *Stop Sudah! Testimonies of Papuan Women Victims of Violence and Human Rights Abuses 1963–2009* documents stories of sexual and political violence perpetrated by soldiers towards women as well as police violence towards intoxicated young men (see also Haluk 2013). Racism features strongly in acts of state violence, and relations between soldiers and Papuans are characterized by 'prejudice, distrust, disgust and frequently arrogance and hostility' (Hernawan 2015: 202). Racism, particularly police fears of angry Papuan males, has also been revealed in a number of recent shootings in the highlands. In Enarotali in 2014, Karubaga in 2015, and other places, reports suggest that police responded with deadly violence to the presence of an angry Papuan crowd (Human Rights Watch 2014).

While it is very difficult to generalize, Papuan women are racialized as objects of/subservient to Papuan men's passions, violence and power. For example, as I discuss later in the book, Indonesians in North Sulawesi spoke about young Papuan women who were pregnant and unmarried with a mixture of judgement and pity, and some young women described struggling with the expectation that they should be ashamed of their pregnancies (Munro 2012). Sexuality is always central to racialization (Stoler 2002), as Leslie Butt (2012) has demonstrated by looking at the state and political violence meted out to Indigenous highland women sex workers under the guise of health services. Racialization, put simply, produces desires for political independence from Indonesia and intensifies highlander identities and networks. In West Papua, the politics of cultural momentum are clear: as David Webster (2001: 508–10) proposes, West Papuan nationalists do not reject their own traditions; in fact, West Papuan political identity has always been shaped by cultural forms and local identities (see also Kirksey 2012: 179).

However, throughout this study I develop the argument that highlanders today also face 'technocratic racism'.[8] What I mean by this term is racism that is developed around, meted out through and more or less hidden behind the seemingly objective and neutral language of expertise, skills, capabilities and, in particular, the idea of human resources. Christoph Marx (2011) has used the term to describe how racism was produced and entrenched bureaucratically during apartheid in South Africa. Racial inequalities were hidden behind the seemingly rational and neutral language of social planning and administration; put differently, racial logics were 'rendered technical' (Li 2007) policy matters to be managed by siloed experts in the bureaucracy.

Sulfikar Amir (2013) argues that, in fact, high-tech bureaucracy is central to Indonesian state power. In Papua, and Indonesia more broadly, the concept of 'human resources' and the agenda of human resource development articulate young peoples' obligation to cultivate technical skills, expertise and knowledge. Gordon Means (1985) indicates that Indonesia's interest in human resource development started to evolve when international experts identified rural isolated populations as an impediment to national progress. The World Bank concept of human resource development locates 'the explanatory weight of why economies grow [in] personal qualities, social institutions ... or people's capacities, attitudes, values, and beliefs' (Toye 1987: 62), and 'human beings are understood as resources in need of modification, adaptation and change – in other words, development' (Du Bois 1991: 10). Looking after the human resources begins with having fewer children, which is promoted by initiatives on 'high-quality' families (*keluarga berkualitas*). Once they are born, babies become the human resources of the future. Even kindergarten children and their parents are called to this agenda.

In Indonesia, the concept of developing good quality human resources or SDM (*sumber daya manusia*) means more than the technical development of a skilled workforce. Achmad Yahya (1997: 43), for example, describes physical, mental and spiritual qualities of human resources such as discipline and having the right culture.[9] He describes good quality human resources as 'enthusiastic, tested, idealistic, productive, creative, and patriotic' (Yahya 1997: 43). He notes physical qualities such as 'health, posture, abilities, with a minimum height of 170 cm, well-nourished, energetic' (Yahya 1997: 44–45). Various threats and potential disturbances to the 'human resources' are also identified in government and religious discourse, including HIV, alcohol, traffic accidents and pregnancy, to name but a few. The notion of 'study first' (*kuliah dulu*), explored later in this study, is a moral construct that Dani students encounter in North Sulawesi that encourages youth to avoid marriage and sex until after they graduate (Robinson and Utomo 2003; Smith-Hefner 2005) for the sake of human resource development.

How young people should change, and what their 'inadequacies' are, relies on political and racialized interpretations of culture, lifestyle, intellect and capabilities. The ways in which outsiders have assessed highlanders' expertise and systems contrasts sharply with most ethnographic accounts and Indigenous perspectives on Dani society. Koentjaraningrat (1994: 288–89), an Indonesian anthropologist, asserts: 'There is no system of leadership.'

Throughout the 1990s and 2000s in particular, a great deal of commentary focused on explaining ethnic inequalities in West Papua through reference to a lack of technical skills and unemployability (i.e. Bandiyono 1996; Rusman 1998; Suparlan 1997, 1998, 2001). A government official (cited in Munro 2004) is quoted as saying:

> The weakness of the human resources in Irian Jaya [Papua] is the major problem faced by the local government. The lifestyle, ways of thinking, and a variety of local cultural practices have hindered their ability to follow the agenda of development ... Because of that, the local government must make bigger sacrifices to improve the human resources of the young generation. It is not easy to guide and educate the young generation of Irian Jaya [Papua], but it must be done.

Regarding the highlands, Koentjaraningrat (1994: 458) argues:

> The interior is the most 'poor' in terms of workforce, and is the area most difficult to develop. In the central highlands, there are no traditional skills and abilities or natural resources that can be used as a basis for development 'from below'. Thus, the most important effort for development in the area is the increase in the quality of the human resources, meaning increasing education and health of the population.

Representations of primitiveness in Papua are longstanding and always serve a political agenda (Ballard 2002; Kirksey 2002; Kirsch 2002). In West Papua, an alleged lack of human resources features in pro-Indonesia rhetoric that asserts that Papuan human resources are not yet ready for independence from Indonesia. Other arguments suggest that Papuans are marginalized because Indonesians are better-quality human resources. For example, a typical report on development in Papua concludes that migrants possess characteristics that are more modern than Indigenous Papuans in social, economic, demographic, physical and household environment dimensions (Bandiyono 1996). Suko Bandiyono (1996: 80) further concludes that:

> Non-migrants [i.e. Papuans] need to accelerate their self-adjustment in the process of modernization so they are not left behind. If they are incapable of eliminating their left-behindness then they will be increasingly marginalized in the city.

Towards the objective of clarifying Dani educational aspirations amid contexts of diminishment, in this study I track Dani understandings of 'human resources'. Tracking the 'human resources' concept reveals how technocratic racism, as a form of diminishment, originates in internationally sanctioned and ostensibly apolitical development perspectives, and becomes a prominent feature in relationships and encounters between Indigenous highlanders, Indonesians and the state. Ivan Karp critiques human resource development on the grounds that: 'These subjects are called to account in a discourse that defines them as failing to exhibit in their cultures or persons the qualities of developed persons' (Karp 2002: 82). This study goes further to show that 'developed persons' are expected to exhibit technical expertise and knowledge. It also extends our understanding of the possible range of moral and intimate interpretations of a technocratic agenda like human resource development. Technocratic racism is a different kind of diminishment from denigration that is rooted in religious or moral failures. This kind of diminishment encourages Dani to attain more skills and training to overcome alleged inadequacies that cannot be addressed through conversion, piety or even embracing certain cultural styles and tendencies that are marked as 'Indonesian'. Indonesians deploy these discourses about Papuans, but highlanders also apply some of the same assessments to themselves or other highlanders. Highlanders also grapple with what sort of 'human resources' they would like to become in ways that do not always align with, and in fact sometimes depart significantly from, dominant Indonesian perspectives. They question and consider what skills, values and attributes are needed in highlands Papua in ways that reflect the ongoing, perhaps even gathering, significance of Dani cultural values. These cultural sensibilities surrounding 'human resources' become clearer through students' experiences living abroad, feeling uncomfortable in Indonesian domains, facing up to Indonesian bureaucrats and professors, evaluating one another's habits and mistakes. These experiences promote a clearer sense of what moral, social and political principles they hope to foster back home.

If understanding diminishment is my main objective, and racialization is an important way that diminishment occurs, education is, in a sense, an important context in which diminishment occurs and is challenged. Formal education is a compelling but often overlooked social context, especially where schooling is a relatively recent development (Knauft 2005; Pomponio 1990; Sykes 1995, 1999). In Indonesia, culture and genetic heritage are widely seen as determinative of development levels, outcomes and achievements. These are not the only factors – piety and religious commitments are also considered important, and this is certainly the case in the Christian communities where Dani students become situated. In short, education promises to close the 'racial', 'stone-age' gap. Education is not just a project of improving knowledge but also a project of cultural and racial (or embodied) improvement. In fact, during the Dutch colonial period in Indonesia, 'education was the pathway through which native Indonesians sought to place themselves on an equal footing with their Dutch colonizers' (Nilan et al. 2011: 714). As President Yudhoyono implied, education makes Papua's children more like, and equal to, the rest of Indonesia's children. Education is a context for the testing of this proposition, where efforts at improvement and recognition, or the denial of it, are most strenuously contested and thus revealed.

Schooling also positions young people at the forefront of new forms of mobility that may entail living some distance away from home and their closest kin. Questions of education are also deeply gendered. Should girls and young women be encouraged to pursue education to the same extent as boys and young men? Should their objectives the same? What different risks are involved? Moral, cultural and religious concerns over women's independence, mobility, sexuality and marriageability come to the fore (see Stasch 2015: 80). In Melanesian societies, this also occurs at a time when new opportunities for women draw reactions from defenders of 'tradition', changing gender dynamics elicit forceful attempts to reassert men's control over women (Spark 2011), and women's mobility is morally suspect (Butt, Munro and Numbery 2017; Wood and Dundon 2014). At the same time, the commoditization of traditional norms may enable women to be violated even by those closest to them (Wardlow 2006). In Indonesia more specifically, Ariane Utomo (2016: 422) notes that 'the Reform era has also provided an opportunistic platform in both national and local politics, for the reawakening of traditional customary law, religious bias, and stereotyping heavily founded on a patriarchal perspective.' Pam Nilan and colleagues found that the vast majority of female university students expected to work outside the home, but that 'even working women focused primarily on their identities as wives and mothers' (Ford and Parker 2008: 9, cited in Nilan et al. 2011: 719), and 'neo-traditional ideals' of men as the breadwinner and women as secondary earners are prevalent (Utomo 2012).

Yet at another level, schooling is said to be constitutive of new identities and feelings of belonging or exclusion for both males and females, not least because it is linked to 'nation making' (Foster 1997), 'inculcating a national consciousness' and 'creating a common frame of reference for the young generation' (Jourdan 1997: 127). School is a place to learn, if not always take up, the rules, ideals and understandings of the nation-state (Bjork 2005; Parker 2003; Shiraishi 1997). Education in Indonesia is still strongly associated with processes of 'drawing in', 'homogenization', and 'national culture' (Parker 2003: 256). According to Nilan and colleagues (2011: 714),

> [E]ducation was the foundation for building the Indonesian nation. Even today, a well-educated person is respected for his or her assumed

knowledge and wisdom. The most commonly recommended remedy for widespread corruption and cronyism in the country is inevitably education. In other words, education is regarded as a social 'good' in itself. Education is understood as not only cultural capital that connotes the productive and authoritative citizen, but represents a means of ensuring ethical practice, order, harmony and consensus through the getting of knowledge and wisdom

Education teaches and elevates the national language, Bahasa Indonesia, as the language of modernity.[10] Related to this process, scholars suggest that education tends to deterritorialize or disconnect youth from their natal cultures and rural communities (Amit and Wulff 1995). Wayne Fife (1994) proposes that in Papua New Guinea, teachers promote a new moral order that celebrates the modern life of urban values and the cash economy at the expense of a village way of life. To the extent that students internalize this moral order, they are developing an urban consciousness (Fife 1994: 160). This makes it difficult for them to fit back into life in the village, but limited employment also keeps youth from achieving urban lifestyle goals. Dani students and the people they leave behind do experience some 'disconnection', 'discord' and disappointment (Powell and Wilson 1974; Sykes 1995, 1999; Weeks 1987). Disappointment relates to not finding a place amid an educated, modern, Christian population in North Sulawesi and not finding superior educational institutions or lessons. Disconnection is largely related to what is lost by not being part of social and economic activities in Wamena, but may become a matter of life and death if young people return home HIV positive (see Butt, Munro and Numbery 2017). Networks and partnerships develop, projects and funds are disbursed, and weddings and funerals (with pigs given and received) go on without students.

Educational opportunities obviously do not always translate into employment, prestige, social capital or political power, and instead generate rebelliousness, or even crime and 'anti-social' behaviour among disenchanted youth (Jeffrey et al. 2004; Jeffrey et al. 2005; Sykes 1995, 1999). But that education contributes to a growing sense of national identity, belonging and cultural cosmopolitanism is less questioned (although see Mains 2007, 2012). Where scholars agree is that formal education is always a political project and is itself a form of contact. Ann Stoler (2002), Edward LiPuma (2000) and Wayne Fife (1995), for example, by considering the colonial and missionary roots of formal education in Indonesia and Papua New Guinea, alert us to the ways that becoming educated is already racialized and politicized. The experiences of Dani students show that schooling abroad is racializing because it fosters a sharpening and politicizing of cultural and ethnic differences, and ultimately recommitments to the highlands social and cultural context. This is different from what Thijs Schut (2016), for example, finds for youth from another rural, but less politicized area of eastern Indonesia (the island of Flores), where unemployed, educated returnees are much less certain of the value of cultural forms of interdependence and collaboration. Still, like Dani graduates, they are nonetheless committed to volunteerism and community wellbeing.

Besides what education represents in the contest over 'modern' status, a close examination of Dani experiences reveals that education may also be an important site of regulation and surveillance – by Indonesians, Papuans and other Dani – and impression management. Schooling often entails living in dormitories that are divvied by cultural groupings, or in boarding houses where a 'house-mother' (*ibu kos*) watches over the inhabitants to ensure their morality and protect her own reputation by extension. Campus is a defined space with its own local government status, where the appearance of mixing and connecting glosses over the zoning of particular corners, fields and computer labs along ethnic, gender or cultural lines.

The Chapters

As the title *Dreams Made Small* suggests, I am interested in how the dreams (educational, political, social and personal) of university student migrants are refashioned, indeed constrained, in the face of multiple limits, and how they also test and push back against those limits. In Chapter 1, I begin the story not in North Sulawesi with Dani university students, but in Wamena with parents, schoolchildren and traditional leaders. In Wamena there are important social, political and gendered imaginings of education to consider. Education is at the centre of choices – marriage or school, gardens or town – that link to broader questions about identity, power, Indonesians, hope and the future.

Chapter 2 takes us to North Sulawesi, where both the anthropologist and Dani students are 'newcomers' (*pendatang*) relative to local 'masters of the land' (*tuan tanah*). This chapter situates Dani migrants within the local cultural, economic and political context of North Sulawesi Indonesian communities in Manado, the urban provincial capital, and in Tondano, the rural site of the National University of Manado (Unima). There are various ways that Dani students almost immediately stand out as 'strange' and 'backward' in their host communities, and may even distinguish themselves from other Papuan students. With minimum financial support from their relatives or from the government, Dani students live an exposed lifestyle, both in terms of the danger of quitting school and in the way that they traverse local communities on foot in search of jungle produce, towards taro gardens they tend, or to bathe and wash clothes in riverine areas. They live in the most haphazard of mixed-gender dormitories that are viewed with some suspicion by Manadonese as hotspots of sinful activity according to local religious morals, in huts they have built at the edges of rice paddies or in virtually abandoned housing complexes on university campuses. Experiences of social, economic and cultural difference become more acute as students enter into more intimate daily relationships with local Indonesians, especially authority figures.

Chapter 3 builds on this context by focusing on racial dynamics and constructs that occur in Dani encounters and relationships with Indonesians in North Sulawesi. Racial formations contribute to stigma and fear, as students are also branded as separatists and potential threats to local security. I discuss students' experiences with local communities as well as authority figures, police and intelligence agents. A particular focus of this chapter is the affective concept of *malu,* an Indonesian word which translates into shame, shyness and embarrassment. In addition to fear and anger, Dani encounters with Indonesians bring about feelings of shame, shyness and embarrassment. Through case studies, this chapter explores these situations in depth to understand what they tell us about broader racial formations. I find that when Dani students assert themselves, they challenge dominant views of them as 'dumb' (*bodoh*) and the hierarchy that puts Indonesians in positions of authority. The reaction from local society is largely to quash these assertions. In some cases the experience of stigma prevents students from wanting to assert themselves or speak publicly in front of Indonesians in the first place.

Chapter 4 focuses on the university campuses as sites of aspirations, educational goals, stigma and bureaucratic constraints where an economy of friends and favours dominates and largely leaves Dani students vulnerable to exploitation and dropping out. Racism is apparent, as university professors express that 'Wamena students are slow' and expect that Papuan students will not wear their hair in braids or dreadlocks. I show that ad hoc bureaucratic practices affirm experiences of differential treatment and the power of Indonesians to dominate and exclude Dani students from recognition as educated equals. Learning to navigate administrative structures and requirements, including paperwork and procedures, becomes an important part of a university education that is ultimately used back in Wamena.

If earlier chapters focus on how Dani students come into contact with local Indonesians, Chapter 5 delves ethnographically into the social world of 'Wamena people' that is a partial response to conditions of stigma and the myth of cosmopolitan mixing. Students relate to one another in ways that emphasize kinship and respect as well as hierarchies. Their student organization activities are a microcosm of aspirations for certain skills that are culturally valued and largely denied to them by society at large. But there are also divisions and deep challenges that students, who often come from backgrounds saturated by violence and alcohol (Munro 2014b; Munro and Wetipo 2013), are facing in North Sulawesi, where alcohol is cheap and flows relentlessly from local producers. This chapter examines the notion that in light of their experiences with local people and institutions, Dani students are drawn more closely into the dynamics of their own communities populated by 'Wamena People', that is, not only Dani, but also Lani and Yali students who originate from the western and eastern regions of the Baliem Valley and other subsidiary valleys. It examines what principles, activities and aspirations motivate, and sometimes disrupt, relationships and activities in the community. It draws attention to formal student organizations as sites where students seek to develop particular values, skills, expertise and morals associated with a Dani modernity in the absence of Indonesians, and yet also shows how these efforts sometimes falter in the face of difficult living conditions, including family conflict, altercations and alcohol abuse.

Chapter 6 focuses on students' experiences of sex, marriage and pregnancy/childrearing away from the watchful eyes of parents, amidst discourses that stigmatize Papuan sexuality and frown on starting a family while still at university. In this domain, Dani political views sometimes come together with cultural ideals that favour large families to push back against national and local admonitions to 'study first'. On the other hand, not having access to birth control limits their options and some pregnancies lead to a great deal of shame and disruption. In explaining the common occurrence of premarital pregnancy, students invoke the current political and cultural significance of reproduction and education in Papua, where Indigenous survival is understood to be threatened by violence and marginalization associated with Indonesian governance. Within specific parameters, some Dani women experience premarital pregnancies that are not dominated by feelings of shame or failure, but are seen as evidence of adulthood and as positive contributions to Dani cultural and political agendas. This chapter also shows that there are limits on the prominent experiences of humiliation and shame described by students. Confidence emerges somewhat unexpectedly against the backdrop of cultural, religious, national and local prohibitions on premarital sex and pregnancy.

Finally, Chapter 7 sees Dani students graduating and finds some of them back home in Wamena again to ask what their education has done for them, what has happened to their political and racial struggles, and how they are relating to their own kin as well as Indonesians. It explores how they struggle to do good things for others, even though 'Everything is back to normal', as stated by a male university graduate who returned to Wamena and found himself living again in a traditional hut with his family, eating sweet potatoes and bathing in the river. It contrasts ethnographic and personal accounts of graduation and hopes for the future with the political conditions that constrain graduates' achievements back home. It focuses on forms of employment, volunteerism and other social works that graduates engage in, particularly their roles as intermediaries between less educated and village-based Dani and

Indonesian institutions such as government offices, schools and public health clinics. Graduates use their education to help other Dani avoid experiences of humiliation, being judged uneducated or ignorant, and from having to see themselves in such negative ways. In doing so, they partially interrupt power-laden encounters that underpin marginality. Finding Dani at home again reveals some of the reorientations and rediscoveries that have occurred as a result of their education abroad.

This study shows the context of 'diminishment' that Dani students live with, including racial structures that they find confining and frustrating. It details what a lack of recognition from Indonesians looks like for educated Dani. It also documents affirmations of culture and identity in this context. There is a political critique, derived from feelings of inequality, oppression, injustice and being unfairly stigmatized, that cuts through 'diminishment' and inspires particular commitments. Feeling at best uncomfortable and at worst under siege amidst racialization fosters tenacity, a fomenting of highlander cultural values, and urgency around the notion that Indigenous survival is at stake as long as Indonesians are in control.

Notes

1. This book uses the term 'West Papua' to refer to the western half of the island of New Guinea, which is nowadays comprised of the two easternmost provinces of Indonesia (Papua province and West Papua province). West Papua is the English designation preferred by most Papuans, is the most commonly recognized term for the area internationally and conveniently distinguishes it from Papua New Guinea, the independent country immediately to the east. However, it should be clear that this research took place in the central highlands of Papua province, not West Papua province, as per Map 0.1.
2. I use the term 'Indonesians' to refer to non-Indigenous inhabitants of Papua. Some Indonesians are long-term settlers, while others are recent migrants. Indigenous Papuans are 'Indonesian' by citizenship, but in pertinent local cultural-racial designations 'Papuan people' (*orang Papua*) are differentiated from 'Indonesian people' (*orang Indonesia*).
3. I became interested in an in-depth study of Dani students' experiences in North Sulawesi after spending two months with Dani students in Manado in 2003 doing research for my masters' degree (Munro 2004). I had intended to go to Wamena, but in April 2003 the atmosphere in Wamena and the surrounding villages was tense. In raids by the military, at least seven people were killed, forty-eight were tortured and some 7,000 others were forced to flee after guns were allegedly stolen from a military base (Unrepresented Nations and Peoples Organization 2004). Manado was known as a common destination for Dani university students, so I went there instead. With students in Manado, I was intrigued by their seeming commitments to 'development', even dominant discourses that accused them of 'primitiveness', which were particularly evident when they spoke of how they understood the emergence of high rates of

HIV in Papua (Munro 2004). The students I met were also, it seemed to me, openly criticized by, and living mainly in silent avoidance of, local Indonesians. This situation was worth investigating. It was also more possible to investigate racialization in North Sulawesi because unlike Papua, it is open to long-term social research by foreigners (see Butt 1998: 41–47; Cookson 2008: 6–9; Rutherford 1997: 103–5; and Timmer 2000: 14–15 for discussion of barriers to research in West Papua). Living with Dani as a minority among the Indonesians of North Sulawesi thus gave me the opportunity to learn about racism, stigma and vulnerability based on long-term participant observation that is not yet permitted in the equally, if differently, racialized setting of highlands Papua. However, the continuity of racial formations across these diverse spaces is a key finding of my study.

4. The author of this internet post argues that once again, Papuan students have been terrorized by locals who take the law into their own hands to avenge the death or injury of Indonesian military personnel in Papua, and that this violence is covered up by the authorities, who accuse drunk Papuans of causing conflict with locals.
5. Article 1(t) of the Special Autonomy Law 2001 states that: 'An Indigenous Papuan is a person originating from the Melanesian race, comprising native ethnic groups in Papua Province and/or a person accepted and acknowledged as a Papua native by the Papua traditional community.' Retrieved 1 August 2017 from http://papuaweb.org/goi/otsus/files/otsus-en.html.
6. Yulia Sugandi's (2013: 36) work with Valley Dani elders suggests they prefer to refer to themselves as *Hubula* or people of the Palim, but in my experience with the younger generation, these other terms were also used and considered acceptable.
7. Colloquial Indonesian varies regionally, and people speak of a Bahasa Papua or a Papuan style (*logat,* dialect). The style is different in coastal versus highland areas. As discussed later, being able to speak Bahasa allows entry into bureaucratic, educational and Indonesian worlds. Yet there is tension in North Sulawesi between Papuans and Indonesians over which group speaks proper Bahasa. Highlanders, more so than coastal Papuans or Indonesians elsewhere, are likely to know their local language.
8. While it goes beyond the scope of this study, in other work (Munro and McIntyre 2016) I have demonstrated that international aid agencies also perpetuate technocratic racism in West Papua when they facilitate, or fail to challenge, the exclusion of Indigenous Papuans in development work on the grounds that they lack capacities or skills.
9. For more conceptualizations of human resources in Indonesia, see Danim (1995) and Tjiptoherijanto (1996).
10. In Jayapura, the capital of Papua province, a roadside sign from the government states: 'Let us prioritize Bahasa Indonesia and preserve local languages.'

1
Ethno-racial and Political Dreams of Education in Wamena

'Andy, get ready for school! Where's Andy?? Andreas, have you bathed yet?', called out Andy's older brother Laurence, home from university on holidays.[1] A forlorn-looking Andy appeared outside my hut, holding a garden spade that towered over his petite ten-year-old frame. 'Do I have to go to school? I'm helping with the garden', Andy implored. '*Nayak* [Dani language, 'friend', greeting used between males], you have to go to school. If you don't go to school we'll marry you off. Do you want to get married? You better get your pigs ready so you can get married', teased Laurence.

Rather than bathe in the icy, turbulent We River and go to school on an empty stomach, children like Andy become enthusiastic about labouring in the garden. Around them in Wouma village, women are in motion, collecting cabbage and sweet potatoes from their gardens and piling them into net bags (*noken* in Indonesian, *su* in Dani) to carry to the local Misi market. Older children are chasing younger siblings to get them to bathe and put on their school uniforms, while old men squat and smoke cigarettes, keeping warm in the chilly morning air. After the fog lifts, the sun will heat the rocks along the river to the perfect temperature for warming up after a lunchtime swim. Women who are not going to sell vegetables in town are washing clothes along the riverbank. A handful of children never make it to school; they run off with their friends, play in the woods, and regroup later at the river to swim with their aunties and sisters.

The conversation between Andy and Laurence seemed to capture important questions about how school fits into daily life for Valley Dani, and what social and political imaginaries inspire the pursuit of education. Going to school might seem like an obvious activity for a ten year old to undertake, but Andy's situation is not so straightforward. Andy's parents did not attend Indonesian school. His father went to Dutch school for three years in the late 1950s. Moreover, going to school is challenged by a lack of clean clothes, bathing facilities, breakfast and mothers who are available to coordinate the effort. Yet in their conversation, school is the 'modern' and appropriate activity for Andy to undertake, while getting married is the traditional, and amusing, alternative. Raising pigs, paying bridewealth and getting married, which are crucial parts of Dani sociality and social reproduction, are placed on a par with education as a pathway for Andy. Because Andy is ten years old, the option of marriage generates a laugh from Laurence, but what if Andy was seventeen years old? Or twenty-five years old? What if Andy was a girl? Their conversation asks us to think deeply about the meanings attached to education, and how schooling and educational pursuits mesh with cultural and social expectations, especially amid racial structures, poverty and violence. Going to school, as this chapter illustrates, requires persistent, daily and sometimes complex efforts, and it conveys certain capabilities, commitments and moralities.

I travelled to Wamena after living with Dani students in North Sulawesi for nine months. I wanted to better understand their seemingly immense dreams of both transforming their homeland and achieving personal success. These dreams appeared incongruous with their circumstances abroad: often, they had barely enough to eat, were plagued by stereotypes and suspicious government officials, were bogged down in administrative delays on campus and struggled to balance their sense of collective obligations with expectations of individual progress and achievement. In Wamena, I spent much of my time with rural parents and young children, those individuals who arguably make most of the sacrifices, and perform most of the labour, that goes into supporting formal education. This chapter is not about where Dani university students might be going, but rather about where they are coming from. Through the increasing proximity of 'modernity' in the form of school uniforms, roads, offices, shops and, critically, Indonesians, Dani are assessing themselves and others around them in novel moral and ethno-racial terms. Dani view education as a way to catch up with Indonesians and demonstrate modern commitments. The Indonesian governmental and bureaucratic system uses a lack of education against Dani, even those of considerable social standing in their communities. In their encounters with Indonesian bureaucrats, shopkeepers and teachers, Dani sometimes express feeling inadequate. Education conveys some status, though not enough to fundamentally alter relationships with Indonesians. Equally of interest are the ways in which education has come to matter in Dani families and marriage preferences, in judgements about sexuality, and gender expectations. Education dreams thus emerge in and through racial, political, gendered and sometimes violent dynamics.

Although it is only an hour's flight from the provincial capital, the Baliem Valley, like other mountain valleys throughout New Guinea island, has an entirely different atmosphere from the coast. Arriving on a morning flight, a blast of cold, crisp air greets passengers descending the stairs from one of the old Trigana Air ATR-72 to the tarmac. Until 2016, there was no baggage carousel at this airport; instead, baggage was placed in a corner of the arrival hall behind a wooden barrier. Passengers were required to climb over the wooden barrier and drag their luggage back over the wall. A chorus of *becak* (bicycle-powered pedicabs), a common form of public transport in Wamena city, surrounds the entrance to the airport. No flights will land at the airport after about 3 pm; by this time the clouds have descended from the mountains to obscure the only entrance to the valley, aptly named 'Pass valley'. On the ground, this is the time of day when what locals call the 'Kurima wind' (*angin Kurima*) starts to blow through town from the southeast. People without jackets chew betel nut and walk fast to stay warm.

Wamena and smaller towns in the central highlands can only be accessed by air from the coast, but a growing network of roads in the highlands links Wamena to towns like Tiom and Bokondini. While the local populations are certainly mobile from rural to urban areas in the highlands, there does not appear to be a large-scale outmigration for labour, and not much in the way of remittances is sent back to relatives in the highlands. If anything, Baliem Valley crops and pigs are used to help support relatives outside the region. Small communities of Dani live on the coast in and around Jayapura, enjoying the bustle of urban living and the tropical climate (see Farhadian 2001, 2005 for an ethnography of Dani in Jayapura). Dani relatives swap tropical and temperate produce by putting large packages of betel nut, vegetables, tubers, and fruit wrapped in used rice sacs or plastic bags on the daily flights between Wamena and Sentani airport in Jayapura. Those on the coast receive cabbage, tuber greens, avocado, sweet potatoes or taro; highlanders hope to receive a package of prized betel nut that can be sold for up to 2,000 Indonesian rupiah (about US$.20) per nut. While most of this trade occurs between Dani relatives, Dani people living on the coast might have arrangements with local Papuans or migrants with land to access the commodities in the first place. I met Dani students in Jayapura who worked someone else's betel trees and took their pay in kind to send betel nut up to the highlands. Some Dani men and women also fly to Timika, the city that serves the Freeport (Tembagapura) gold mine in the southern highlands, to search for gold pieces in the mine's tailings or to sell their produce at inflated prices. Within the central highlands, there is migration of young people to Wamena city for schooling as well as to seek cash by providing manual labour to construction projects. In rural areas, there are typically only primary schools, if that, so any students continuing their education must make their way to Wamena.

Indonesians and 'Wamena people' (Dani, Lani and Yali) share the streets of Wamena, but, with a few exceptions, are not deeply interconnected in each other's lives. Unlike coastal areas of Papua, intermarriage between Indonesians and highlanders is rare. During public celebrations surrounding Independence Day (17 August) and the visit of President Yudhoyono (July 2006), Dani and settlers flooded the streets but rarely interacted. Local relations between Indigenous and non-Indigenous inhabitants in Wamena are complex, rapidly changing and different in diverse parts of the city. Misi is very near to traditional villages and is considered a *rawan* or potentially dangerous, less 'civilized' part of Wamena. The We Bridge is an important symbolic and physical link between Dani settlements like Wouma, and Misi, the oldest part of Wamena city, where there are many Indonesians now. The bridge has several times had most of its wooden planks torn off by Indigenous men wishing to sever ties with the city, the state and the military, which now runs a base right next to the bridge in Misi. In 2015 a new concrete bridge was finished, positioned beside the old bridge, perhaps symbolizing that the Indonesian presence is permanent and will inevitably expand over the bridge into predominantly

Figure 1.1. Misi market area, Wamena. Photo by author

Indigenous areas. Dani and Indonesians watched the parade in this mixed, politically saturated space, and did not speak to each other. In this area, most Dani and Indonesians are not well acquainted, even though the same Indonesian shopkeepers open up the same rows of stalls each morning and the same Dani sell produce or transport people on pedicabs (*becak*) each day.

Schooling in Wamena is commonly disrupted not just by absentee teachers or principals, but also by violence and its aftermath of tension. When going to school means venturing out on foot or by bicycle through the centre of town or across a bridge to a rural area the day after a military rampage or a police incident, education becomes politicized not just as an idea, in terms of future aspirations or past injustices, but also because accessing it requires overcoming fear and hostile surroundings. Young people were explicit about conditions of fear, abuse and inequality in highlands Papua. For example, Benyamin said: 'The conditions on the ground in Wamena are terrible; people are chased like animals by the military.' Sam stated: 'People are afraid, there are so many soldiers, they do sweeping [search operations], sometimes they get angry for no reason . . . If someone says something, it will create big problems.' According to Lavinia: 'The Indigenous people have nothing, no clothes, sometimes they even starve. The "straight-hairs" have everything.' Anton (from Wouma) said: 'Indonesians never go into the villages, except for the military. Even in my village near the city, they never go there. We are here, they are there.'

Figure 1.2. A young girl ready for school in Wouma. Photo by author

Before moving into the local meanings of education, it is important to describe how and when schooling emerged in Wamena. Potent ideas of transforming and civilizing the Dani were enacted through foreign agendas of political control amid conditions of violence.

The History of Education in Wamena

Historically, the project of education in the Baliem Valley was inseparable from colonialism, violence, racialization and missionization. The bulk of the first formal education effort was in the hands of the missions, beginning in the mid to late 1950s, while the Dutch government provided financial subsidies (Naylor 1974: 198). Lessons in the missionary-run schools primarily involved Bible literacy and Christian ideology. The Christian and Missionary Alliance focused on spreading the gospel and training local people to become pastors. Charles Farhadian (2003: 55) suggests that evangelical missionaries, possessing unbelievable material wealth, focused on telling the Dani about the Christian heaven and spreading the message that Jesus would save them from their sins. Missionaries brought 'a new organisation with new rules and social expectations' (Farhadian 2003: 64), sometimes using forceful techniques. A missionary report asserts: 'If a group resists the Gospel, they should be roughed up, and then they will "find their hearts" and embrace the Gospel' (cited in Farhadian 2003: 56). Evangelical missionaries, like colonial authorities, had a particular vision for the new life they would create for the Dani.

The Order of Saint Francis, a Catholic mission, which established a station in 1958, was interested in development activities, such as animal husbandry, a housing resettlement project, an agricultural cooperative and a brickworks (Naylor 1974: 184–93). The Catholic missionaries opened the first schools. Formal education in this period consisted of two to three years of school. Graduates could carry on for another two years (Naylor 1974: 198). The prevailing perception of the Dani was that although they had many intricate cultural beliefs and practices of their own, they would have to abandon these traditions and learn 'everything' from foreign teachers. O'Brien (1962: 82) writes that schools were intended to bring 'a whole new conditioning and change in basic psychological attitudes'.

From 1963 to 1966, the Indonesian government worked to consolidate control over the Baliem Valley. From 1966, Indonesian soldiers filled the Baliem Valley in preparation for the 'Act of Free Choice' referendum, to be held in 1969. During this time, the inhabitants experienced great brutality and oppression (Naylor 1974: 13). In the Baliem Valley between October 1966 and January 1967, for example, Indonesian soldiers are alleged to have shot dead 103 Dani males and hanged a ten-year-old boy (Van den Broek and Szalay 2001: 78).

The presidential decrees passed with the Act of Free Choice in 1969 outlined plans for developing West Papua's 'inland' (*pedalaman*) communities (Naylor 1974). Indicating the importance of education in the occupation of the highlands, Karl Heider (1979) reports that the first thing Indonesian bureaucrats wanted to do after colonization was to send all Dani children to boarding schools on Papua's coast. Education was to be a core component of development and modernization, and it was to be carried out by Indonesians (including those from Christian areas of eastern Indonesia) and a handful of Europeans. Indonesia's first development agenda in the highlands was called the Koteka Operation. On paper at least, it came into effect in 1971. The main goals related to developing, educating and civilizing the Indigenous population, a radical change of their lifestyles and living patterns, and, obviously, getting Dani men to exchange the penis gourd for clothes. Not surprisingly, given the name of the agenda, it was to be led by the Indonesian military and included territorial defence goals (Naylor 1974: 149–50). The sentiments behind the Koteka Operation reveal what Jan Pouwer (1999: 178) calls 'a barely concealed scorn of Papuan cultures'. Education was thus racialized from the outset because it enacted existing racial hierarchies that placed Indonesians as superior role models for Dani to emulate. When the early days of government schooling in the highlands did not seem to modernize the Dani in the way that the Koteka Operation intended, this 'failure' justified and facilitated the government's transmigration programme on the grounds that Indonesian transmigrants would provide examples of 'modern men' for the Dani (Soepangat 1986: 330).

The Koteka Operation also illustrates the entanglement of violence, politics and militarism with educational goals and logistics. Indeed, in 1977, not long after the intervention began, the Indonesian military invaded the Baliem Valley on the pretence of ending a tribal war between the Dani and the Western Dani. It is not known how many Dani were killed in the subsequent napalm attacks by Indonesian forces (Bertrand 2004: 149). Today, Dani still talk about the need for resolution and compensation for losses they suffered in the 1977 war.

The Koteka Operation is thus one of the earliest examples of how Indonesians' thinking and perceptions of Papuans shaped what kinds of development and education would be offered to highlanders, and the ways in which race and violence would be inseparable from education. In the government's depictions of Papuans as completely devoid of modern attributes, it is easy to forget that educated Papuans were expelled from government positions they held during the Dutch era or were forced to leave during the crackdown on nationalist and resistant sentiments in the 1960s (Pouwer 1999: 177). Thus, education was always politicized and was intended to cultivate a particular sort of modern Papuan highlander who was acquiescent and who shared rather than challenged Indonesia's vision of development and the future. Of course, Indonesia's monopoly on violence and power over the narrative about highlanders does not mean that highlanders saw, or see, things the same way.

Controlling Efficacy and Regaining Power: Contemporary Dani Perspectives on Education

Dani describe education as new knowledge and experience brought by missionaries and the Dutch. These were opportunities that Dani took advantage of and that strengthen, or could be used to restore, traditional systems disrupted by Indonesian rule. Dani informants also portray education as a way to regain power from Indonesians who were able to colonize Wamena because of their superior education and knowhow. They hope that education will assist Dani to establish modern, Christian and prosperous lives in which they are equal to Indonesians. Dani informants describe how they and their parents saw the first foreign educators, namely Christian missionaries, as offering something that could change social status. For instance, Agus, a Dani government employee aged about forty, suggested the following history:

> When the first education started at the mission stations, some of the parents took their children to the missionaries. They left them there and the missionaries raised them. Almost all of those children were the children of big men. If they were good students the missionaries sent them to Biak or Jayapura to high school, otherwise after three years of school the students were able to lead church services and spread the gospel. Some of those first students are still alive. One of the men who went to the coast [later] became the Regent of Jayawijaya. The people who got this first education used it to their advantage and they got their children into education and so on.

In Agus' narrative, it is not clear why the 'big men' took their children to the missionaries, but it is clear to him that it resulted in long-term benefits. Viewed retrospectively, education creates positions of status and leadership, and the benefits are intergenerational.

Another informant, a Wouma big man, Molama, argued that he was among the first to be baptized as a Catholic. By his account, he took advantage of the funds that the Catholic missionaries were offering to build a house, which he used as the first church in the area. He still uses the building as his home, as a new church was built in later years to service the Wouma population. He explained his decision as follows:

> I saw what they were doing as a good opportunity for my people, and I thought we needed the right kind of place for this activity. We could

not do it properly in our traditional huts. Therefore, I asked them for money and built the house and we used it for religious services.

Molama indicated that he and others wished to take advantage of a new activity that appeared efficacious. Building the church helped him with his goal of doing good things for his community, and thus aligned with traditional forms of leadership. In the above perspectives, Dani take advantage of formal education. Agus Alua (2006: 171) and others remember things differently:

> [I] was born into a family who wore *koteka* [penis gourd] and *cawat* [fibre skirt] in the Kurulu region in Yiwika, Baliem Valley, Wamena. Because of this my exact date of birth is unknown, but it is estimated that I was born in late 1960 . . . A team of elementary school teachers on patrol at night time looking for new students captured me and I was forced to attend school by missionaries against the wishes of my parents.

Dani associate the entrance of formal education with their experiences of Dutch colonialism and Christianity. Looking back, therefore, formal education is associated with 'the word', 'the light' and becoming Christians.

While the older generation focused on the arrival of education via missionaries, for younger informants, school is associated with the Indonesian government. Markus said: 'School, clothes, these things are from the government (*pemerintah*). They are good things that we did not have before.' At the same time, sometimes school may not be associated with the Indonesian government because of the Christian-operated schools in Wamena that are preferred by Dani families. Informants said that the public schools are like Islamic schools because the majority of pupils are Indonesian Muslim children.

Although Dani may recall education as a process by which they engaged with missionaries and improved their social standing, other perspectives suggested that lack of education contributes to Dani marginalization today and thus schooling can reposition Dani as powerful once again. Nico, a gardener/farmer, explained:

> Some of my children will be farmers [*petani*], because not everyone can go to school and succeed. It is good if young people go to school because working on the garden is very hard work, and it is difficult to succeed. We work hard, but we still do not have anything. Why can other people do it but we can't? Everywhere we go now we run into *pendatang* [migrants], they have taken our land in the city and now we must fight with Westerners [Western Dani] who have moved into our area here too. We still have a war to fight with Indonesia. In the past, we did not know anything, so Indonesia was able to come in and to cheat us.

Nico's statement captures several important meanings of education. Education (or lack thereof) explains present-day struggles and marginalization. Gardening has not generated economic wealth or material possessions. In assessing this situation, Nico compares Valley Dani to Indonesians and other Dani who seem to him to have attained wealth. There is competition over territory and opportunities, and education might improve Valley Dani chances when competing against others. Nico felt that colonization was very much ongoing in Wamena and that Dani lacked the economic and educational power needed to keep Indonesians out. Education thus offers a chance to regain power and is shaped around a potent critique of the Indonesian system. In other words, education is not for becoming modern and like Indonesians; it is about becoming modern to challenge Indonesians. Hannah, a young educated woman, argued: 'Up until recently Indonesia gave us education-for-stupidity [*pendidikan pembodohan*] so they could cheat us and steal our lands', suggesting that the Indonesian system provides poor-quality education to Indigenous Papuans deliberately to further territorial ends. At least for Hannah, and likely others too, Indonesian agendas are not concerned with improving Papuans for their own sake, but rather they enact various ways of taking land and power.

Older Dani expressed feelings of dissatisfaction and disorientation under Indonesian governance, and hoped that schooling would offer some way for young people to gain confidence and knowledge that could be used to the benefit of Dani society:

> We used to have all of these clans, and we used to control this land. We had leaders for war, leaders for peace, leaders for the rain and natural elements, and we listened to them. We had the marriage festival. We had everything organized. Now under this government system, we do not know what to do. We do not come together as we used to, with all this splitting and dividing [*pemekaran*, a reference to new administrative districts being created in quick succession as part of decentralization]. The system now is chaos . . . It is too much for old people to manage. We just hope the younger generation will become educated and they will figure out these problems, these land problems, these organizational problems. (Molama)

Not knowing exactly how to succeed in the 'new' system does not prevent leaders like Molama from attempting to engage Indonesian institutions. But it is youth who are seen to have the potential for truly understanding the Indonesian system. Education is a way to foster this understanding. The development of young people through education enables an imagined trajectory in which they use expertise, skills and experience not only in Wamena, but also to help bridge a divide between Dani systems and Indonesian systems.

Although some Dani expressed views of education as a political strategy, others focused, like Nico, on how education could translate into improved economic circumstances and material comforts like those possessed by Indonesians and some Dani living in the city. As Helena, a gardener and grandmother who had two sons in university, explained:

> I do not really want anything for myself, except maybe a few cigarettes or some betel nut. I just want my son to be independent, and take care of himself and his family. I will keep taking care of these sweet potatoes until I die. I will take them to my son in his house in the city and we'll sit together and eat. His children will have an easier life than he did. It is cold in the women's hut and we cannot breathe for the smoke and the mosquitoes, and the dog has fleas. It is nicer in a house in the city, even if it has no lights or television.

Mama Helena's comments were echoed by many rural mothers and young people. Even though education is needed to take power back from Indonesians, it is not only politics writ large that influences the way in which Dani experience and understand education. Three ethnographic vignettes illuminate how educational status mediates racialized relations between Indonesians and Dani.

Literacy, Traditional Leaders and Technocratic Racism

A set of events in June 2006 reveals how educational status, expertise and skills generate enough power for some Dani to engage with Indonesian government officials, but not enough power to actually influence them. In a village near the city, Dani who were mainly gardeners were to receive cash from the government as part of nationwide payouts to compensate poor people for the rise in fuel prices in October 2005. The government-appointed village head (*kepala kampung*) allegedly corrupted several aspects of this process, which involved registering the names of eligible village inhabitants to submit to higher authorities and distributing cards that villagers were then to take to the post office to collect their money. He allegedly charged the inhabitants money to register their names in the first place. Then, after the amount owing was calculated by upper-level government offices, he altered the list of recipients so that some people found their names removed from the list of payees. In the end, the village head was said to have fled the area with most of the money anyway.

Throughout this process of corruption, certain big men, having heard about or experienced the official's trickery, became concerned and tried to find a way to intervene in the process. They held meetings and compiled their own list of payees and a list of names of people who complained of being charged money by the village head to register themselves for the government money.

These older men, and some younger men who were also gardeners, said they were building a case against the village head. However, they found themselves unable to get the attention of higher officials in order to get the information they wanted and catch the village head in his lies. One day in June, villagers gathered outside the Office of Statistics in Wamena, as these officials were responsible for determining who should receive the payments. It was a significant step because even small crowds of Dani gathering in the city can attract interference from the police or military.

The head of the Office of Statistics (BPS), an Indonesian, emerged to address the crowd of about forty residents. The women, dressed in typical attire – skirt, t-shirt, net bag and no shoes – were sitting in small groups scattered around the yard of the office. Some men squatted in one corner, while others squatted or stood just outside the fence around the office, many still wearing their tall rubber gardening boots. The official first shouted at the group to sit down. He asked who had received money and ordered them to raise their hands if they had. He instructed the crowd to create a team of villagers to investigate and document who had received money and who had not. Then the official went back inside the building. One of the big men, Molama, was carrying the list of names they had already prepared. Molama himself had written the names out by hand and discussed the list with other villagers. He carried the paperwork around town in between the pages of a tattered notebook. He approached the door of the building with some university students and a few other men, and they explained that they had already compiled a list. Then the students were invited inside to discuss the issue with the officials. Molama was left outside with the other older men. He later expressed that he would have liked to deal with the officials, but that he felt embarrassed (*malu*) to enter such a place, with such people, in his tattered old clothes. The students soon reappeared outside with further instructions to take the problem to the district head (*camat*).

On prior occasions, while the villagers approached other government offices in an effort to determine which government office should assist them, gardeners in knee-high rubber boots and cut-off trousers consistently hung back, often waiting in the street, while younger educated people 'wearing clothes', as the gardeners said, knocked on doors. These educated representatives explained that although the rural men can speak Indonesian, officials tend to 'talk in circles' (*putar-putar bahasa*).

Education complicates more traditional forms of authority, introducing social divides that may be uncomfortable in close-knit families and communities. Here, Indonesians recognize and prefer to deal with educated, usually younger, men who are more 'modern' in their style of dress and language, and are expected to better understand the government system and the bureaucratic spaces inhabited by officials. Government officials do not take local political

Figure 1.3. Dani gathered at the Office of Statistics. Photo by author

leaders such as Molama seriously, even though they may attempt to conform to modern bureaucratic expectations by using literacy to document important information and preparing written reports. Indonesians assume that traditional leaders lack the skills or knowhow to operate in the government system because of their age, cultural/ethnic background and how they dress. This is an example of technocratic racism. Seeing themselves from the perspective of Indonesian officials, the encounters leave Molama and others feeling that they are judged inadequate because of their clothes and language abilities, though it is not the officials' Bahasa Indonesia that confuses old men, but their circuitous bureaucratic ramblings. The pursuit of power, or even a modicum of acknowledgement from Indonesians, requires embracing education, but literacy is not enough to overcome technocratic racism.

Moralities of Sex and School

Being educated, or in school, may provide a degree of protection from dominant Indonesian views of Dani as 'primitive', 'dirty' and 'strange'. But being in school also has positive moral connotations. The experiences of a few young women and men from Wouma, a village near the city, show how being in school is seen by Dani as the proper orientation for youth, and that these moralities take shape in relation to the presence and surveillance of Indonesians. Indonesians are perceived to create a negative, risky environment for Dani youth in Wamena, but then also judge Dani who 'succumb' to bad urban influences. Education can be protective against negative influences and Indonesian judgements.

Wouma is located just over the bridge from Wamena city, Misi market, migrants' shops and a military base. Perspectives from Wouma are not generalizable to all Dani. In fact, even other Dani have said that people from Wouma are 'tough' and 'primitive'. As mentioned earlier, Wouma was a key spot where Dani defended their security post and Morning Star flag in the tension leading up to the violence of 6 October 2000. It is an intriguing village (divided into 'upper', 'central' and 'lower') where inhabitants are deeply engaged in living according to *adat* (custom) and also heavily affected by the modern installations across the river. The area itself is a dynamic settlement comprised of Dani with ancestral ties to the area, Valley Dani who relocated there after being displaced by the airport and urban developments of the 1950s onwards, and Western Dani migrants. Since I first visited in 2006, many changes have occurred in Wouma, but even in 2017, there were no Indonesians living there.

Sonia lived in Wouma with her grandmother. Sonia's grandmother was often ill, and was among the oldest women in Wouma who still gardened and sold sweet potatoes and cabbages at the market in Misi. Sonia's mother and father had her young and never married. Her father went on to university in North Sulawesi and then married and fathered two children. Her mother had been absent for much of Sonia's childhood, marrying, travelling and seeking her fortune in Jayapura and Timika. Sonia was raised by her maternal uncle and grandmother. Sonia had a bad reputation among people in Wouma village, including her uncle's clan. People in the area said she was only eleven years old, but that she was 'big' and 'already has breasts', which some argued was a result of smoking, sniffing glue and having sexual relations with men. In 2006, Sonia was about to go into her last year of elementary school, but she had not attended regularly. Her grandmother said that Sonia had not really been devoted to school (*tidak sekolah baik*). If her mother was in town, she often followed her around to socialize, work in gardens or help gather sand and rocks from the river to sell.

Lina, the younger sister of Sonia's grandfather, was one of the relatives who most frequently complained about Sonia. Each time she saw Sonia hanging around in the Misi market area of Wamena city, she told everyone in the village. Lina and others suggested that in this area of the city it is easy for Dani youth to get into trouble. Rumours are that the small family-run eateries (*rumah makan*) house Indonesian sex workers and that the televisions that young people pay to watch feature pornographic films. Moreover, it is an open environment where Dani easily observe each other's behaviour and are observed by Indonesian shop owners and military personnel. Lina asserted: 'It is embarrassing to see Sonia and others like that in Misi, hanging around with men. Our young men get drunk and walk around over there too. It is better to keep this activity in the village, I think, do not take it into the city. These youth have no shame.'

Clan members expressed similar thoughts about the behaviour of another family member, a young mother named Margaretta who had never attended school. Margaretta's father allowed her to move back home to Wouma after she left her husband, a man from a nearby village. Her family claimed that the relationship ended because Margaretta's husband believed he was not the father of her second child. When I first met Margaretta in 2006, people in the family complained that she was not a good mother because she left her children in the village with no one except elderly men and women to care for them. Three years later, Margaretta's relatives barely acknowledged her existence because she was accused of taking money for sex and spending her time drinking alcohol with men. This new behaviour was strongly associated with her tendency to be in Misi at all hours of the day and night. People claimed to see her walking around dishevelled and drunk. Her father began referring to her as a 'prostitute' (*perempuan sundal*).

By 2009, both Sonia and Margaretta had left Wamena and were living in Jayapura. Sonia was living with her mother, got pregnant with twins, and then was married to her Dani university-educated boyfriend. They returned to Wamena and lived there together for a time, but Sonia's husband hit her and she often fled to her father's house. She left her husband and returned to Jayapura with one of the twins, while the other was left in the care of her maternal uncle. Within the next two years, both of the twins died. Margaretta left her boys in Wouma and began living with her younger sister in a shack in Jayapura. Together they cared for her children and maintained a garden of banana and papaya, which they sold at the market.

All Papuans, especially Dani, are nowadays associated with 'promiscuous' sexual behaviour (*seks bebas*) in Indonesian state and popular discourses (Butt, Numbery and Morin 2002; Butt 2005a; Munro 2012). Nonetheless, supposed moral failures take on a new significance when they are exposed to others outside the village. Dani living close to town experience a pressing need to demonstrate proper behaviour in urban, public places, particularly where their behaviour may be observed by Indonesians (Butt and Munro 2007). It is common for male clan members to want to control the behaviour of female relatives and for kin to scrutinize one another's behaviour to assess wrongdoing. Criticism of Sonia and Margaretta begins in Wouma among relatives, but it takes shape in relation to how the women are acting in Misi. Being in Misi implies not being a school student, and not being in school facilitates getting into trouble in Misi. Being in school protects a young woman's reputation because she is out of the gaze of Indonesians in a morally appropriate modern space, as opposed to the modern dangers of alcohol, sex and pornography that Dani associate with Misi. Also, because pregnant young women or mothers are not legally or culturally allowed to attend school, there is an association of school with virginity and innocence. Marriage does not provide young women with the reputational protection that being in school can provide because men can leave the marriage, force women to leave through violence or deny parentage of children, leaving young mothers open to accusations of promiscuity and subsequent ostracism.

By contrast, in 2006, Viktor and Nelly were in their final year of high school. Everyone talked about their achievements, particularly that they would be graduating from high school soon and were making plans for university. People said Viktor was smart (*pintar*), good at school, diligent (*rajin kerja*), polite (*sopan*) and helpful to others. According to Viktor's neighbour, 'he does not go drinking, he does not chase women or get into fights, and he is a good boy'. Nelly was also highly regarded by people in Wouma. Clan members and neighbours praised her for offering her pocket money to help with their purchases and for bringing meals to sick people.

Nelly's identity as a good student was linked with her identity as a good Christian woman. Nelly did not smoke cigarettes like most of the other women in Wouma, although she did chew some betel nut occasionally, carefully so as not to leave visible traces of red on her lips. With her meticulous grooming, clean clothes and often some spending money in her pocket, Nelly did not look like she lived in a hut (*honai*, in Dani) amongst gardens, but rather more like she lived in a 'modern' house (*rumah sehat*, literally, healthy house) in the city. Still, I would run into Nelly's mother on the road to Misi, indistinguishable from other women going to the market carrying a net bag full of garden produce.

Nelly wanted to marry her boyfriend, Allan, another Wouma resident, but she also wanted to go to university. If Allan were also going to university, she said, they could get married and live together in Jayapura. Since Allan had dropped out of high school and was not going to attend university, Nelly's parents did not approve of him as a potential husband. Nelly encouraged Allan to become more suitable. She suggested that he try again to get his high school diploma so that he could go to university with her, and she encouraged him to get more involved in their local church. She wrote out Bible passages and taped them to the walls of his small garden hut.

Nelly left Allan in Wamena and went to Jayapura, where she finished one year of university before becoming pregnant and getting married to a Dani student. When I last saw her in 2015, she and her husband had built a new house, had three children and she was struggling with deep disappointment (her own and that of her family) that she had not yet been able to go back to university and that her educated, employed Dani husband was controlling and abusive.

These experiences show how Dani associate school with Christian, modern morality and propriety. Young people who are in school are also perceived to be doing 'good' things by Dani standards, such as sharing resources and helping others. Schooling is essential to the coproduction of good morals and cultural ideals, such as generosity and helpfulness schooling can, for a time, protect Dani from a gardening lifestyle characterized by young marriage and parenthood, but, more importantly, being in school shades Dani from judgemental gazes and novel opportunities for rebellion and victimization. Gardeners and people without much formal education idealize Viktor and Nelly, while Nelly and Viktor are concerned to live up to this image and to do their part to promote education and Christianity as proper activities for all Wouma villagers. That Nelly's parents disapproved of Allan as a husband for Nelly because of his lack of education also shows novel assumptions about what kind of spouse is preferred. It points to the potential for increased social stratification on the basis of education, but also to the fact that parents continue to value marriage for what resources and status can be gained through these new kinship connections. By attending school diligently and in spite of challenges and temptations, young Dani men and women can fashion identities for themselves that differ drastically from their parents' generation. At the same time, it is clear that they do not have much choice, if they want to avoid being judged as lacking by moral standards that have intensified and shifted as a result of the Indonesian colonization of Wamena. Not being in school leaves youth open to stigmatization as promiscuous, violent or primitive.

Mama Mateus' Daily Struggle to Get Ahead

The ideology of progress, modernization, or 'getting ahead' (*kemajuan*) is important for Dani families, and education is certainly a lynchpin in this struggle. In 2006, Mateus and Veronica were about nine and six years old, respectively. Their mother, Mama Mateus, as she is known, was about thirty years old, and was born and raised in Wouma. She was proud, she said, to be one of two females from her age set in Wouma who had graduated high school. Her family wanted to marry her off when she was young, but her older sister's husband supposedly asserted that she was intelligent and should go to school. Her husband Agus, forty years old and also a high school graduate, acquired a government job after many years of applying for a position. The family lived near the We River behind the busy Misi market. Their three-bedroom house was a patchwork of wood panels and woven fibres. Mama Mateus cooked over a fire in the outdoor kitchen, next to the pigpen. Birds, mice and puppies had taken over the semi-enclosed pantry where she stored cooking implements, plates and dry goods. Next to the kitchen, where the family bathed, a few planks of wooden fencing and a pile of old tyres offered a little privacy. The floor was made of thatched bamboo with patchy plastic laminate laid on top. In 2006, the home had no electricity and the children struggled to do their homework by candlelight. When I visited in 2009, Agus had connected the house to the local power grid. The main outlet was overflowing with a cascade of cables. The family had plugged in several mobile phone chargers, a television, a DVD player, a cable box, a water dispenser, an old computer and a large set of speakers. The lights in the bedrooms also had to be plugged in by extension cord to the main outlet, which dangled from the ceiling of the living room. Water was pulled up from a well in the front yard using an old cooking oil container on a rope. Besides Mama Mateus, her husband Agus and their children, a host of relatives came and went, staying for a night or a month. There were posters of the alphabet and Indonesian/Dani/English pronouns on the wall in the living room.

'Getting ahead' was a daily focus for Mama Mateus. She worked hard at home and she spent several hours a day over the bridge in Wouma tending sweet potatoes. She applied for government employment three times, including as a public servant at a new, remote regency, and criticized the local government for what she saw as nepotistic practices – she pointed out that most of the new government employees announced in the newspaper were relatives of the Regent (district head), a Dani man. 'It is really difficult for us here', she said:

> We heard about some scholarships to send the children to foreign schools when they are older. We wanted to put in our names but we could never get any clear information. Then someone showed us some photographs of children already in Australia at their new school. We do not know what happened, and we do not know who was behind this, *pendatang* [migrants] or the Regent [*Bupati*] and his relatives.

Her husband's salary was not enough to feed the family, partly because Mama Mateus had to share what they had to eat with hungry relatives who came to visit. Because of these obligations and insufficient income, she asked her uncle to pay for some expenses, especially school fees and uniforms. Because she asked for school money from her uncle, she was obliged to help his wife watch their children and do their cooking and laundry whenever they needed assistance, but this took her away from her own household, her garden activities and the other relatives she ought to assist. Moreover, Mama Mateus and Agus complained that these days, their Dani relatives seemed to be passing away more frequently than ever due to illness, accidents or disease, and this required them to constantly donate to funeral rites. A donation of a sack of rice, a box of instant noodles or a carton of cigarettes could cost half a month's salary, but a pig, the most prestigious sort of contribution, would cost many months' pay if they did not have one in their pen to give. To combat these conditions, Mama Mateus was usually out working or gardening all day. Her older sister's teenage daughter usually came from Wouma to cook dinner for Mateus and Veronica; if not, Mama Mateus boiled water for tea and roasted sweet potato over a fire at night when she had finished her other activities. Agus usually arrived home late as well. They huddled together for warmth and stayed up for an hour or two watching Indonesian soap operas on their small television set.

In 2009, Mama Mateus was suddenly offered a government job subject to a payment of 15 million Indonesian rupiah, about US$1,500, and equivalent to a two-year salary of a public servant in the highlands. Not quite believing this demand, Mama Mateus described going to visit the regent (*bupati*) to verify the request in person:

> I went to the regent's office after my friends started paying the money and getting their jobs. There were maybe twenty people waiting to see him for various reasons. The guards told us to sit on the floor outside his office. It was dirty, with garbage and cigarette butts strewn everywhere. I sat there most of the day. I was so hungry. Then an officer came out of the regent's office and started pointing to people, 'You, you, you', he pointed around and told those men they could go in to meet the regent. But I was not going to be stopped, so I jumped up and followed them inside. When I met the regent, I asked him if it was true that I had to pay 15 million rupiah to get an SK [*surat keputusan*, a letter stating the regent's decision to offer civil service employment]. He said yes. I told him I had worked as hard as I could, shovelling sand from the river for the past six months, and I had five million. I had borrowed two million, and I could not possibly get any more money. So he said okay, he would take my seven million and he would pay the remaining eight million so I could get an SK.

After paying the regent, Mama Mateus worked for about a year sweeping the city streets and picking up garbage at dawn. Then, at the age of forty, about twenty years after graduating from high school, she got a secretarial position at the local district office where she helped ration rice for the poor. She was able to get this job because her uncle became the head of the newly created district.

Mama Mateus had so many plans to get ahead: she wanted to make handicrafts and sell them, she wanted to start buying betel nut from friends in Jayapura and selling it in Wamena, and she frequently submitted proposals to the government to get funding for what she referred to as 'empowerment' (*pemberdayaan*) activities. The latest proposal she submitted asked for funding to open a doughnut stand in Misi. What she wanted, she told her children, was a big, solid house on a large piece of land. The house would have an indoor kitchen and she would not have to cook over fire anymore, which irritated her eyes. She said to her son: 'When you have done well in school, you can become an official [*pejabat*] and build Mama a good house.'

Mama Mateus insisted on sending her children to a Catholic elementary school, which was more expensive, but was seen as better quality than the local public schools. Her children frequently expressed a desire to skip school like their cousins in Wouma, but Mama Mateus argued that Mateus and Veronica were 'city children' (*anak-anak kota*), though they still participated in village-based activities like funerals and communal labour. She regarded the schoolteacher (a woman from Manado) highly and said: 'It is a good opportunity that we have her. She brings good influence to the children.' She explained that 'the teacher is from a modern (*maju*) place, she is a good Christian, and her husband does not drink or smoke.' She contrasted this with her relatives whom she said smoked or spent their paycheques on alcohol.

Mama Mateus and others associate high-quality private schooling, Christian development and clean living (no smoking or drinking) with getting ahead. Though their own education had not helped them get very far, she and her husband asserted that educating Mateus and Veronica was their most vital and pressing task, and was a marker of their progress as parents and the potential progress of their family. The strategies they invoked to get ahead reflect their complex positioning in Dani and Indonesian society. They try to earn money through employment, but also by selling garden produce. Garden produce becomes a back-up meal when money runs out. They try to get ahead using government-initiated strategies and by keeping strong reciprocal relations open with their relatives, especially those with money, like Mama Mateus' uncle. Though they might 'get ahead' more easily if they stopped spending Agus' paycheque feeding their relatives, they identify that obligation as something they cannot and, for now, do not want to forsake. This suggests that although Mama Mateus and Agus are very aware of the logic of progress in the Indonesian era, they also continue to value Dani notions of propriety and success, which oblige them to help others and contribute to funeral exchanges. She measures herself against the achievements of her Indonesian neighbours and articulates disappointment at her comparative failures, even though there is very little she could do to make her education translate into results. She tries many avenues and finds herself hampered by corruption in the hiring system that favours applicants with access to large sums of money, but she is ultimately able to save enough money from her labourer job to pay off the regent. Her education makes little difference in the regent's office, where she has to sit on the floor amid the garbage, waiting for a chance encounter. Frustration and disappointment characterize her experience as one of the first female high-school graduates from her village.

Mama Mateus' experience also shows the layering of intersecting alliances and hierarchies that defy simple categorizations like 'nepotism' or 'wantokism'. A longitudinal, ethnographic and gendered lens on her pathway to employment reveals that networks and relationships are as essential to overcoming exclusion and discrimination as they are to perpetuating these social and sometimes racialized formations in the highlands. Women like Mama Mateus cannot depend on achieving anything by virtue of education alone; they must maintain favoured connections with Dani men and with Indonesians who facilitate modern identifications and the state's 'empowerment' agendas.

The Meanings of Schooling in Wamena

Educated youth may be seen as possessing a novel kind of superiority that elders must acknowledge, especially if government officials favour younger educated people over established community leaders. People without education express feelings of inferiority, while those considered to be educated, like Nelly and Viktor, are defined by this status and the need to uphold expectations. Parents like Mama Mateus fear judgements from Indonesians and other Dani. They may judge themselves according to standards of wealth and moral displays that are hard to achieve, as Mama Mateus finds when she tries to ensure that the school fees are paid on time, the children are not late for school, the electricity at home is working, there is a television to watch, there are books to read and that her husband does not go drinking with his friends after work. This feeling takes shape not just in relation to the chance for modern jobs, but also in relation to Indonesian power, success, systems and norms. Going to school is a modern, moral expectation. Schooling is embedded in concerns about family appearances – not looking poor, not looking like bad Christians or drinkers, and not seeming to be ignorant of the value of education. In this moral matrix, women and girls clearly experience more pressures, while men and boys have more opportunities to prove themselves.

Older Dani, particularly men, are adamant that young people have, or may acquire, the capacity to regain power and authority, in part by succeeding in the Indonesian system. They find that Indonesians do not recognize any of their capabilities or authority as elders or big men, even if they are literate. In other words, Indonesians in offices do not see past garden boots or tattered clothing. In relation to these experiences, including historical violence and invasion, moral judgements among Dani centre on what is appropriate behaviour for whom in relation to Indonesians and the spaces they dominate. Old Dani men want to be seen in town, engaging with Indonesian officials, but should not be seen drinking alcohol with them. Young Dani women should not be seen in town, amidst Indonesian shops and men in general, unless they are there to sell vegetables to Indonesian customers or are on their way to school. Whatever actually takes place in school, as a potent symbol of modern life, being seen to be in favour of education, and actively participating in it, provides Dani people with some reprieve from the moral, ethnic and political scrutiny of 'primitiveness'. School provides some shelter, a clear moral path, even as it also necessitates deeper and more intimate forms of engagement that can increase feelings of inadequacy, or at least generate self-questioning.

Besides moral framings in relation to new vulnerabilities and expectations, there is also an emphasis on using education to do good things for others, whether these 'others' are parents, children, communities or the Indigenous population as a whole. Mama Mateus wants to use her education to provide her children with education so that one day her son will build her a proper house. Molama wants to facilitate education for his people so that the next generation can regain control of social, political and economic life. It was a community effort at justice that saw villagers painstakingly track subsidy payments and present this data to Indonesian officials. The theme of using one's expertise for others surfaces for Dani students in North Sulawesi and becomes very important when they return home and try to demonstrate what they have achieved, as well as come to terms with what sort of transformation is possible, and valuable, in Wamena. This understanding of education also reveals that what Dani are imagining for themselves goes far beyond their (and others') statements about 'human resources'. The human resources of World Bank derivation undergo individual transformations to benefit the nation, mostly by working in paid jobs in urban settings. They do not achieve success by helping their neighbours or building homes for their relatives, and certainly not through political revolution. So while Dani have been criticized as lacking 'human resource' capacities, and sometimes use this language themselves, the idea of education being used for local social benefit exemplifies one way in which 'people reinvent the civilizing process by making it partly their own' and live with themselves in a world that has been severely problematized (Lattas 1998: 314). This is not to say that Dani do not pursue less collective, sacrificial or more commodity-oriented goals, but the broader project of education is deeply entangled in cultural and political agendas.

The links between ethno-racial hierarchies, power and education in Wamena shape what students anticipate will happen in North Sulawesi and also help situate their dreams of transformation. In North Sulawesi, Dani youth hope to mix with more cosmopolitan Indonesians and develop modern skills and qualities while at university. They expect that they will be admitted into the elite category of 'university student' (*mahasiswa*). From there, they anticipate they will gain some ground in relation to Indonesians and perhaps feel respected, or be treated as equals. They could become powerful and return to Wamena and dominate others, or govern as they please.

Despite feelings of being colonized, cheated and duped, there is a desire for 'progress', modernization, and development – agendas that may be shared with Indonesians and could offer the possibility of deeper forms of belonging. The meaning of education in Wamena takes shape in relation to the presence and activities of Indonesians, and it is a recognition of their importance, whether as oppressors, role models or something in between, that leads Dani youth to seek expertise and qualifications not just from textbooks or lectures, but also through new relationships with other Indonesians in a different place.

Note

1. All names of informants are pseudonyms.

2

'Newcomers' and 'Masters of the Land' in North Sulawesi

In West Papua, Indonesians are newcomers (*pendatang*), while Papuans are Indigenous (*asli*), sons and daughters of the place (*putra daerah/putri daerah*) or masters of the land (*tuan tanah*). In North Sulawesi, Papuans become newcomers, and so did I, as a white female anthropologist. This chapter gives an overall picture of the social world of North Sulawesi through three categories of subject positions in relation to 'primitivism' and stigma: the locals ('masters of the land'), myself as white female foreigner and researcher, and the Dani students. This provides the basis for understanding racial formations and interactions that are revealed throughout the rest of the book, and that ultimately constrain, reorient and further politicize students' educational dreams. It first sketches out some of the ways that locals think of themselves, especially feelings of cosmopolitanism, foreign heritage and 'whiteness', and social stratification that occurs along the lines of wealth and 'whiteness'. My entry into this scene brought new questions of racialization to the fore. Methodologically, locals anticipated that I would use existing racial hierarchies to my advantage in my research rather than turn them upside down by fitting myself into the stigmatized social world of Dani students. For many local Indonesians, the ways in which Dani students live – in co-ed dormitories or dilapidated houses, growing gardens or cooking outdoors, and waiting for cash from Wamena – are important, if contested, affirmations of 'primitivism' and racial distinctions.

Tuan Tanah (Masters of the Land)

If Papuans are problematized by dominant discourses that allege backwardness and underdevelopment, by contrast, the local inhabitants of North Sulawesi are supposedly predisposed to being modern. Helmut Buchholt and Ulrich Mai (1994: 6) write that: 'Minahasans have developed a distinctive bias in favour of modernity.' Locals in North Sulawesi celebrate their education levels and cosmopolitanism, and express cultural and religious pride. In 2006, North Sulawesi province was home to approximately two million people, of whom over 600,000 claim Minahasan ethnicity (*suku*, literally, tribe). Duncan (2005:

28) describes a long history of regional movement among the peoples of North Sulawesi, Gorontalo, the Sangir archipelago and the Maluku Islands. Migrants have long been attracted to the North Sulawesi's stability and prosperity and have typically settled in the provincial capital, Manado (Duncan 2005: 28). North Sulawesi comprises a mix of ethnic groups from eastern Indonesia who may also trace Dutch, Chinese, Japanese, Portuguese and Indian heritage.

North Sulawesi is approximately 70 per cent Christian, though Minahasa regency that surrounds the capital city of Manado (population 434,000) is estimated to be 90 per cent Christian (Ananta et al. 2004: 15). Since the province of Gorontalo seceded from North Sulawesi in 2000, Minahasa Christians have become the dominant ethnic and religious group in the province (Jacobsen 2002: 36). Michael Jacobsen (2002) proposes that this has led to a revitalized interest in Minahasa as a 'race-nation-people' (*suku-bangsa*). He asserts (2002: 55) that Minahasans are struggling to define themselves as a group without drawing on the historical interventions of missionaries and Dutch colonialists who inaugurated the concept of *bangsa Minahasa* (Minahasa nation/people). I found the opposite: local people confidently engaged these histories to assert

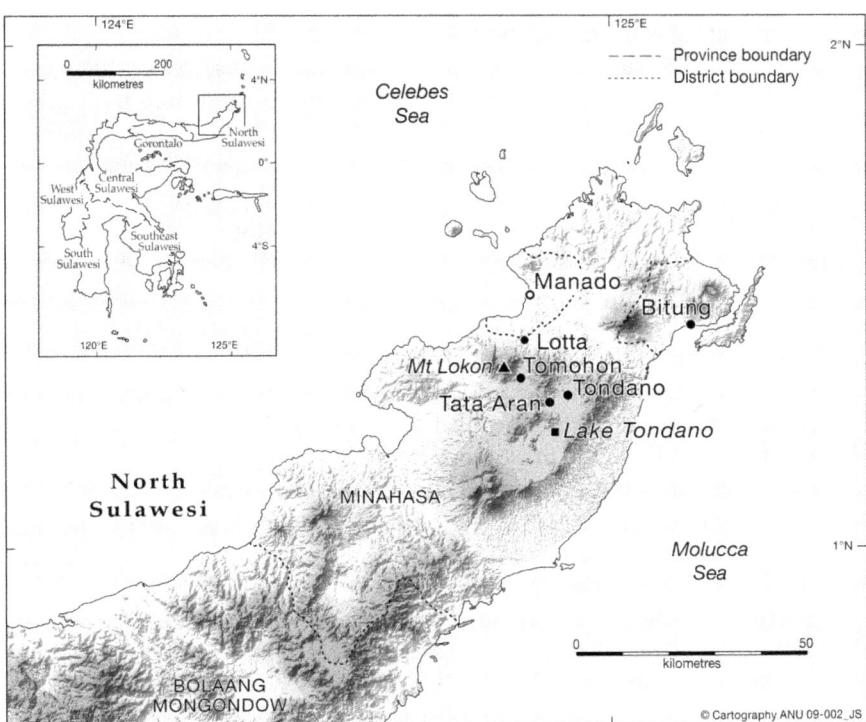

Map 2.1. North Sulawesi province. © The Australian National University, College of Asia and the Pacific, CartoGIS

superiority and to explain their distinction from other Indonesians. Locals described North Sulawesi as a province blessed by God with high levels of education, prosperity and stability; these features, in their views, distinguished the area from the rest of Muslim-majority, extremely poor Indonesia. These conversations took place during my first few months in North Sulawesi, in the homestay where I first lived, at the churches with Manadonese ministers that I attended, on campus with university professors, and with some Manadonese students who I met early on in my research. As I will describe later in the chapter, local people who knew me (as opposed to those who saw me walking down the street and called me names) were very welcoming, at least until I began living with Dani students. They were eager to have me recognize their education, expertise and status, especially given that they did not have many opportunities to interact and converse with white foreigners. I found that local people were equally proud to identify themselves as Minahasan, Tondano people, by their linguistic heritage, or as Manadonese. Any of these labels could be used to identify oneself with the majority – typically described by Minahasans themselves as a kindred community of educated, forward-thinking, open-hearted, Christian people with local heritage (and diverse ethnic roots) who tolerated others (including Muslims) using the kinship metaphor of *saudara* (family). Duncan (2005: 28) suggests that Minahasans pride themselves on their willingness to incorporate newcomers from other ethnic groups into their urban centres. 'We are all family' (*torang samua basudara* in Manadonese slang) is a local ideal that people often referenced when describing social, religious and ethnic dynamics in North Sulawesi. A sign carved and painted by students at the National University of Manado tells us that this ethos requires people to 'Be good to one another, love one another.' Perhaps as evidence that this ethos prevails, locals cited the fact that North Sulawesi had not experienced ethnic and religious conflicts that enveloped communities to the south (Poso, in Central Sulawesi) and east (in Maluku) in recent years.

During the Dutch colonial period, Minahasans were the first people in Indonesia to experience formal education from missionaries, and for a time the region was home to the most literate population in the country (Buchholt and Mai 1994; Jones 1977). The Dutch established an early presence in North Sulawesi to support the trading activities of the Dutch East India Company, which was primarily based in the nearby Maluku (also known as Molucca) Islands (Henley 1989, 1996).

Northern Sulawesi is described as modern and well-integrated into the Indonesian state (Weber 1994: 199). The area is not rich in natural resources, but has a history of producing agricultural commodities. Visitors arriving by plane will notice the sea of coconut groves, a well-groomed plantation landscape. During the Suharto era, the region benefited from government investment. These funds were used to help produce a good communication network, electrification, a water supply, and to improve the educational system and the road network (Buchholt and Mai 1994: 10). Even in the 1970s, according to Jones (1977), low-level public servants had to hold four-year tertiary degrees to be competitive in the job market.

Minahasan Christians are predominantly Protestant, members of the Christian Evangelical Church in Minahasa (*Gereja Masehi Injili di Minahasa*). As in other parts of Indonesia, Church and state have a tangled history. Proselytizing continues to be infused with a modernization platform, encouraging villagers to participate in state projects, and religious rhetoric informs local evaluations of progress and success (see Aragon 2000: 275; Weber 1994). Christianity is seen as cosmopolitan, as people identified it with prosperous, developed countries like America, Singapore and Korea. Manado has its own television station – Pacific TV – which frequently broadcasts Christian services and other programming from around the world. Christianity is not the only link to modernity or 'the foreign'. Manado's Sam Ratulangi International Airport provides direct flights to Singapore, the Philippines and Taiwan. North Sulawesi is described as belonging to an international 'growth triangle' because of its economic ties to the southern Philippines, Brunei and East Malaysia (Jacobsen 2002: 35). Locals asserted that they saw manifestations of their own level of modernity in stores such as 'Golden', and were aware of their global connections:

> We never used to have plastic things like these, colourful plastic toys and clocks, spoons, dishes and buckets. But this area is very modern and we get these things imported directly from China now. If we go to the market, to the used clothing stalls [*cabo, cakar bongkar*] we get clothes directly from Korea. See these, these are Korean peoples' clothes! (Nancy W., Manadonese housewife)

Manadonese people like Nancy suggested that the term 'Manadonese' identifies people who have lived in Manado for a long time. Manadonese value their urban lifestyle and consider the relative peace and prosperity of their area to be a reflection of their progressive, open and sophisticated nature. They say they are doing better than most Indonesians in terms of modernization, prosperity and living in harmony. Many point to Christianity, arguing that their living conditions are a blessing for being of the 'right' faith. Generally speaking, Manadonese say that they do not get enough credit for the level of development in their area because they are Christian and therefore ignored by the nation-state, which centres on Java and, in their views, favours Muslims over non-Muslims. As a result, Manado may be one of only a few places in Indonesia (besides Papua) where visitors might see American flags or Stars of David pasted proudly around town, particularly on the back windows of the public transport buses (see Myrttinen (2015) for Papua). These symbols are markers of Christian identity. Here, people sit around in the afternoon drinking tea and expressing hopes that America (especially its evangelical Christian leaders) might take over Indonesia so that the nation could finally experience true economic, cultural and spiritual progress. Other Manadonese explain their region's progress more in terms of innate cultural characteristics that give Minahasans advantage over others and allow them to be high-quality human resources. A.J. Sondakh (2002), for instance, argues that the Minahasan people are more cosmopolitan, educated and successful than other cultural groups because of their ideology of 'Man lives to educate others' (*Si Tou Timou Tumou Tou* in the Minahasa language). He argues that ST4, as he abbreviates it, foreshadows democratic principles, a strong work ethic, appreciation of scientific knowledge and self-confidence among Minahasans.

Light skin colour (*putih*, literally, white) is highly valued in North Sulawesi. Following L. Ayu Saraswati's (2010) argument, it is not necessarily 'Western' white skin that is sought-after, but cosmopolitan white skin, a transnational whiteness that could be Korean, Singaporean, Western or some combination. In North Sulawesi, informants focused more on European heritage in producing light skin rather than Asian heritage. Whiteness and wealth/status are mutually constituted, as light skin belongs to (or is seen as the purview of) upper-class Minahasans who are perceived to possess these historical, genealogical and cosmopolitan connections.

In official terms, Manado appreciates its diversity, captured in the descriptor *kota tinutuan* (literally, stew city) – a reference to the spicy local stew (also called *bubur Manado* or Manado porridge) with many ingredients – rice, fish, tubers, corn and leafy greens. Although they described themselves as modern (*maju*), Manadonese also described themselves as farmers: 'pegi kebon' (the Manadonese way of saying 'going to the garden', *pergi ke kebun* in standard Indonesian) is a common feature of many people's lives beyond the city. Many Manadonese maintain rural roots in the Minahasa hinterlands, where they travel to visit relatives during holidays. Although some expressed confidence in the 'modern' character of their region, others, particularly poorer inhabitants I met living on the fringes of the city in precarious housing settlements subject to landslides, joked about choosing to own traditional furniture, housing, toys and kitchen implements. The way in which Manado is imagined by some people – prosperous, developed and blessed – is certainly not how it is experienced by all.

North Sulawesi is not the Indonesian nation writ small. Local people considered themselves quite different from other Indonesians. Yet they criticized Papuans in ways that parallel mainstream views, using the dominant language of the nation-state and invoking racial stigmas parallel to patterns described in the previous chapter. They expressed that eastern Indonesia is typically associated with backwardness, poverty and tribal populations, but that Minahasans are modern and cosmopolitan, having been 'civilized' quite some time ago. While this sense of cultural advancement underpins local views of Papuans, there are also countersentiments of Christian kinship and care around which newcomers and masters of the land might build connections.

'You'll Get Raped': The Anthropologist as Newcomer

Most anthropologists have the experience of being an outsider in their fieldwork, no matter how closely related they are to the community in question. What was interesting about my fieldwork was that I was an outsider studying other, different outsiders, and none of us were 'local'. Students, locals and I all came from different cultural, ethnic and 'racial' backgrounds. Where Dani were stigmatized as primitive and violent, I was stereotyped by dominant Indonesian perspectives as sexually available to local men and in need of protection from Dani men. My presence provoked discussion of racial dynamics as locals analysed my relationships with Dani, and Dani observed my encounters with locals and reflected on how locals were responding to my presence. There is nothing new about the principles of building rapport and trust in ethnographic fieldwork, but I recount some of these dynamics here because it sheds light on the racialized local social context, and because building rapport is not as straightforward as it seems when it necessitates choosing sides, showing loyalty to a minority group that is treated with suspicion and avoiding everyday social invitations from the majority.

North Sulawesi attracts modest numbers of foreign (mainly white) tourists who like to visit the islands off the coast for diving and snorkelling. Most do not spend much time in Manado or the rural areas. The city also attracts foreign entrepreneurs and investors, particularly from Asia. According to the chart on the wall of the police office I visited in 2005, approximately 15,000 foreign tourists land at Sam Ratulangi International Airport each year. However, walking around the city of Manado, I rarely encountered other 'white foreigners', referred to as *bule* (or literally 'albinos'). In the beginning, I was overwhelmed with expressions of concern, astonishment and curiosity that I was *sendiri* (alone). Strangers at roadside eateries learned I could speak Indonesian and were much more interested in understanding how and why I came to be alone in Manado than where I was from or what I was doing. Most people seemed to find the idea of being alone horrifying. It was also not, I got the impression, how *bule* normally operated. White foreigners usually travelled with friends or associates by car, stayed in hotels called 'Ritzy', dashed in and out of the international supermarket, and otherwise remained out of sight.

In Manado people of all ages and positions seemed to be reminding me that a female *bule* is associated with sex, stereotyped as hypersexual. In public, people on the streets called out to me 'Bule!', 'Miss!', 'Hello!' and 'You like sex?!' Dani friends and acquaintances who walked around Manado with me were surprised and shocked at the amount of mostly derogatory attention I received in public places.

It was not only people on the streets who apparently held these views. A local preacher introduced me to a neighbour, Mr Rumroken, a professor at Unima (National University of Manado). The professor invited me to visit one of his classes, which I did. The next week, he stopped me on the street on campus to ask if I wanted a ride down the hill to our neighbourhood. With his young son between us on his motorbike, we stopped by an office where he introduced me to someone. He showed me photographs of him with some foreign supervisors from a course he took overseas, and said that he enjoyed talking to someone like me and hoped we could meet up again. He said it would be best if we kept this relationship secret from his wife and the neighbours. I thought he was joking until he stopped his motorbike and dropped me off two blocks from our neighbourhood. He came knocking on my door several times over the next month, but I pretended not to be home.

My research sponsors (from Sam Ratulangi University in Manado) were, by contrast, polite, professional and exceptional, but the notion that as a white woman I was open to sexual relations with any male of status made it difficult to establish a professional rapport with potential research informants in the universities and in local government institutions. Their perspectives appear in the book in informal ways and perhaps my research would have been enriched by improved access to institutional materials and interviews. Being racially profiled as such sparked questions about how Dani students experience these same authority figures and institutional settings. It also alerted me to the ways in which my research was structured by the way I was perceived by not only Dani students, the focus of my work, but local Indonesians as well.

In my early weeks in Manado, interactions with local Indonesians dominated my time as I visited government offices with my research permit, spoke to police and immigration officers, and sorted out my accommodation while staying at a homestay near the centre of town. I was soon saturated with local perceptions of Papuan students every time I mentioned the focus of my research. I wearied of hearing things like 'The Papuans are drunks', 'You'll get raped' or 'They only eat *ubi kayu*' (cassava), which is rejected as inferior to the Manadonese preferred diet of rice and fish. I doubted Dani students would trust me if I had anything to do with local Indonesians, even though they owned the comfortable homestays where I probably could have avoided getting dengue fever and typhoid. As a result, most of what I learned about Indonesian perspectives came early in my fieldwork, before I moved in with Dani students, or via the Indonesian individuals who form an ongoing presence in Dani students' lives, like university professors and church ministers.

I soon met some Dani students and was invited to live in their dorm on the National University of Manado (Unima) campus, located about an hour's drive up into the mountains south of Manado near the town of Tondano. Known as the Yepmum dorm, it was built and partially funded by the Jayawijaya regency in the central highlands of Papua. I lived in the Yepmum dorm in Tondano from November 2005 until April 2006. I then spent June to September in Wamena, and then lived in Manado city with Catholic students from Sam Ratulangi University (Unsrat) until December 2006. Where the Yepmum dorm housed only Dani students, Dani students were a minority in the Catholic dorm in Manado, which mostly housed students of Manadonese and Javanese heritage. We became friends, cooked together, cleaned together, watched television, hunted for vegetables in nearby gardens and waterways, went to church, went to campus and visited friends in other dorms. I had to prove to them that I was able to live with them, eat what they ate, and that I was not ashamed of any of it, nor would it do me physical harm, which was a popular rumour going around. I found that their early expressions of shame at their living conditions waned over time. In those months, the dorm saw sickness (not just mine), it slept four to a room during events and fundraisers, it was empty on lazy Saturday afternoons, the electricity came and went, a volleyball court was built and went back to weed, it was raided in the middle of the night by the local Headman, it had a visit from 'Intel' agents from Indonesia's central intelligence bureau that sent students scrambling up the hillside behind the dorm, and it was nearly washed away in four days of torrential rain in February 2006 that caused a deadly landslide in Manado.

Because of my presence, students confessed, the dorm had Indonesian visitors for the first time, as other students came to investigate me and, as they sometimes stated upfront, to be friends with me. At first, I was uncertain how to avoid these visitors and did not want to create negative feelings among local Indonesians. It was not my intention to become the unfriendly white woman. Still, after several visits from Indonesian students who quizzed Dani students about how I managed to adjust to their supposedly primitive lifestyle, I accepted my role in the wider Tondano community as the strange *bule* who only had time for Dani students.

Because I lived in their dormitories and participated in as many activities as I could, I was also permitted to gradually, and often indirectly, learn about more sensitive topics, such as dropping out of school, physical violence, pregnancy, alcoholic behaviour, stress and conflict. I made frequent visits to dormitories, boarding houses and other residences around Manado and Tondano to hear students' stories of recent events, political demonstrations, conflict with local authorities and gossip.

Some members of the local Indonesian community disapproved of my methods (participant observation, living with my informants) and ethical stance (favouring relationships with Dani over non-Dani and Indonesians). This rejection had a racial component, as locals in Tondano and Manado drew on various negative constructions of *orang Papua* to convince me that I should be afraid of being too close to Papuans. They questioned my need to participate fully in students' lives, to live and eat with them, and to treat them as equals. One particularly assertive man argued:

> You do not need to live in the dorm. You already know Anton [one of the Dani students], and you know his supervisor on campus. Anton would be embarrassed and afraid not to help you. So, just ask Anton to bring you students to interview. If you want five males, ask for five males; if you want females, tell him to bring you females.

Trust or rapport was not, in these views, necessary, and living in the same residences with Papuans was not a legitimate way of obtaining data. Even several months into my research, local Indonesians living around campus in Tondano repeatedly asked students from the Yepmum dorm what I was really doing there, even though I had initially explained to everyone I met (including local authorities) that I was studying Dani culture and experiences of education abroad. These continual questions I interpret to be a reflection of two issues: first, that my way of doing research was seen as very unusual and strange; and, second, that Dani students are seen as strange (poor, of lower intellect and troubled) and anyone who wished to immerse herself in that environment must be quite abnormal.

Across much of my research period, I was in trouble with the local government official in charge of Unima District (*Kelurahan Maesa-Unima*) because I did not have an official letter of explanation for him and his boss, the Mayor of Manado. The Indonesian research office (*Lembaga Ilmu Penelitian*) gave very specific instructions about reporting to local authorities and created letters for me to take to the pertinent institutions. There was no letter for this man, locally referred to as *Lurah* (the person who runs the local administrative area, *kelurahan*), which I translate as 'Headman'. I arrived home at the dorm one day to a message from some of the students: the Headman had come by and he wanted my 'data'. As it turned out, he was not after my research data but my 'biodata': my name, age, marital status, address, nationality, passport number and the details of my research permit. However, the extent to which the village Headman tracked me around Tondano and turned up at what I thought were fairly impromptu discussion groups convinced me that he just might turn up one day and demand my research data. He and other government officials I met expressed that they were very interested in knowing about the activities of Papuan students, and students' experiences of surveillance affirmed this level of scrutiny.

The local understanding of what it means to be engaged in research in North Sulawesi demanded that I display my superior education, work in formal ways in formal settings, and use my influence to get data, ignoring the feelings, preferences and level of comfort of my informants. I was encouraged to be unethical. When I relied more on informal methods in casual settings, I was not simply trying to achieve a rapport with Dani students, I was refusing to occupy a place in local racial and cultural hierarchies that I could or, in some people's views, ought to claim. When I refused to do research that was 'proper', according to some local people, they began to question my motives. My intense focus on a stigmatized minority created questions in the first place; my rejection of the dominant local understanding of research cemented the view that I was doing something other than what I claimed to be doing.

Pointing out my own uncomfortable experiences of being stereotyped as a *bule,* being scrutinized for choosing to be with people labelled black and poor over those considered white and rich, and having to take sides at all is one way of situating this book in the local politics of race of which I was certainly a part. When I visited Wamena for the first time, nine months into my research, I felt some of the same kinds of vulnerabilities I had in North Sulawesi because of dealings with police officers and soldiers, but I certainly faced fewer incredulous questions about why on earth I would be interested in Dani students and their experiences.

Dani Students as Newcomers

This section explores the everyday ways in which students sustain themselves, maintain certain forms of contact with relatives and others back home, and connect with their new place of migration. Living in dormitories, cooking Dani food (*bakar batu,* a way of cooking pork and sweet potatoes under hot rocks) in the forest, waiting for cash from the highlands and embracing Christian churches run by Indonesians are also lived practices of difference and cultural affiliation through which identities and racialized categories become fleshed out and revealed.

Some Dani students found the bustling urban life they imagined in the North Sulawesi capital, but a significant number of others found themselves studying in locations outside the city:

> My relatives took me to the docks in Jayapura [Papua]. It was night time, around 8 pm. I had a small bag of clothes and some fruit – bananas and avocados, I think. I had my last *ubi* [sweet potato] with me, for the boat ride. I had about 500,000 rupiah with me, too. When I got on board I found some other Wamena people [*orang Wamena*] and we stayed in the same part of the ship for the whole four days. It was late afternoon when we docked at Bitung [a North Sulawesi port]. My 'uncle' Etinus met me there. He took me to Tondano. I woke up in the morning and looked outside, and I said, "Where's the city?!" All I could see was green fields and trees. (Minke)

Minke had awoken in a relative's tiny brick shack on the campus of Unima. Locals said the campus location was chosen by a wealthy Tondano person (*orang Tondano*) who wanted to see some development in his area and who later became the first Dean of Unima.

As mentioned earlier, students who call themselves 'Wamena people' originate from one of three dominant cultural groups in the Papuan central highlands – Dani, Lani and Yali. These cultures have many similarities, but also some differences. Within the group called Dani, there are 'Valley people' (*orang lembah*) or 'westerners' (*orang barat*). These Valley people and westerners speak different dialects and originate from different areas of the central highlands around Wamena. Students also belong to different Christian religions and to different political units. The proper names for these administrative areas, called regencies (*kabupaten*), are sometimes used to denote identity.

There are no clear-cut historical flows between the populations of Papua's central mountain valleys and North Sulawesi that can be used to explain the particular movement of today's youth. Coastal Papuan populations were involved in flows of people and goods with the Islamic kingdom of Tidore in the Maluku islands prior to European exploration and contact (Rutherford 2003). In the Dutch colonial period, the Dutch used educated eastern Indonesians as teachers and administrative staff in coastal Papua. The missions in Papua employed Christians from eastern Indonesia as teachers and missionaries, including people from North Sulawesi and Toraja (located in South Sulawesi) (McGibbon 2004).

The majority of Dani people in Manado and Tondano are in fact students. There were, and are, only a handful of nonstudents. These are mainly former students who married local Indonesian women and never returned to the highlands. Male students far outnumber female students, though this also varies according to where they come from. Female students from Puncak Jaya regency, for instance, appeared to be numerous, while female students from Yahukimo regency were few in number. In 2006, there were no new female Valley Dani students starting school in North Sulawesi. Overall, there were more Wamena students in Tondano, but there were more female Wamena students attending Unsrat in Manado. This was partly explained by the fact that in Manado there is a women's dorm (albeit a ramshackle one) for students from Jayawijaya, and so sponsors and relatives were said to prefer to send their female relatives to Manado. I was also told that as a general principle, Dani parents would not send their daughters abroad unless they felt certain that they could send them satisfactory amounts of money regularly. To not sufficiently support a female student is to make her vulnerable to 'marrying' as a strategy for financial survival. This might be true in theory, but there were certainly women students in both sites who struggled to have enough money for tuition, food and transportation. Most of them did not get married, but a fair few did (see Chapter 6).

There are more Papuans in the rural area of Tondano than there are in Manado. If you ask Manadonese about Papuans, they will direct you to visit Tondano. Approximately half of the Dani students in my research did not live in Manado at all, but lived in the Lake Tondano area adjacent to the National University of Manado (Unima). Tondano is not a cosmopolitan place. Most locals are in fact 'Tondano people' born and raised, or at least from other parts of Minahasa regency. Tondano has an urban area, but it is some distance (and two bus rides) from campus. Thus, what passes for urban near the campus is the settlement of Tata Aran II, at the intersection of the road into Tondano town and the road up to campus. Occasionally students would make their way to this market zone, two blocks of kiosks selling instant noodles, soap, withered farm produce, simple meals and mobile phone credit, but more often, they were on the streets walking to other friends' residences, to and from campus, or to and from the buses that take them down to Manado. Wealthier Papuan and Indonesian students regularly went to the market area on Friday and Saturday nights to eat, drink or hang around shops chatting and spending time with friends. Because of the large groups of Indonesian youth hanging around the area after dark, sometimes drinking alcohol, Dani students said the area is a place where they are likely to get into conflict with Indonesians and thus they do not spend much time there.

In Manado, Wamena students regularly visit the crowded street markets, but said they never go into the shops, supermarkets or the 'Megamall' where young locals hang out and are said to 'show off' (*pasang gaya*). They said they have the sense that they do not belong in the mall, even if they had just been sent money from home and could afford to buy items or food inside. As Ana, a confident Lani girl in hip-hugger jeans and pink lipstick, explained to me when I arranged to meet her and some other girls in front of the mall before heading to another location: 'I never get close to this place, I never stand in front of the mall, let's go, I'm scared!' As she commented: 'People have been staring at us non-stop.'

Dormitory Living

From the outset, Dani students distinguish themselves, and are seen by Indonesians as different from the local populations in Manado and Tondano. There are dormitories for other migrant students, such as the dorm for students from Ternate on the Unima campus, but by far it is Papuan students who most inhabit dorms. A smaller percentage of students in Tondano live in crowded thatched huts or rundown old houses. Living in dorms helps segregate Papuans students from the rest of the Indonesian population, while the highlanders' practice of living in makeshift huts promotes the perception that *orang Papua* are inferior. Because they often lack money to pay for bus fares, which is the most common way of getting around the hilly area, Dani students tend to walk wherever they go. Their activities and whereabouts are visible for others to see and to scrutinize.

Dorms are funded by regency governments, so students live with others from the same regency. They also form student organizations based on these regencies. Not all affiliations are determined by regency, as some students live with members of their clan and others live with members of the same Christian religion.

Many migrant students (not just Papuans) live on campus grounds or in Tata Aran II, a small urban settlement about a kilometre from the campus housing area. Housing choice reflects income levels and is thus stratified by ethnicity, with Minahasan students and other Indonesians living primarily in boarding houses. Indonesians suggest that a small, gender-segregated boarding house with a friendly 'house-mother' (*ibu kos*) is the most stable, pleasant and protected place to live. As a second choice, or for those who desire and can afford more independence, students may live in the campus-housing complex (*perumahan*) in a small brick unit. These units have no ceiling, only angled roofing positioned atop walls, so they are accessible to many rodents and mosquitoes. The electrical power is only sufficient to turn on a single light bulb. The bathroom is located behind the house. The housing complex is for university staff, but staff members rarely inhabit the unfinished units, which tend to flood when it rains. Instead, lecturers sometimes allow students to rent their unit for 100,000 rupiah per semester (about US$10) or allow them to stay free in exchange for taking care of the place.

In 2005–06, there were Dani students living in three different dorms on Unima campus, namely Yepmum, Fransiskan and Kaonak, but there were other Wamena students (Lani and Yali) living in three other dorms. Yepmum is the main dorm on the Unima campus for Dani students from Jayawijaya regency. It is located at the bottom of the first short, steep hill upon entering campus from the south side. The Jayawijaya regency government built the dorm in 1998. Though the government covers the electric bill and students do not pay rent, residents are responsible for buying water that flows through a pipe from Lake Tondano into holding tanks on campus. If there is enough water in these tanks on campus, the water flows to Yepmum dorm and other student residences. The dorm is two levels, with five bedrooms on the bottom and six bedrooms on the top. At any given time between ten and twenty students live in the dorm. There have been Catholic Dani students living in the dorm in the past, but the vast majority have been Protestant students from the northern and western parts of the Baliem Valley. During my research, Protestant Dani from the Wolo Valley dominated the dorm. These students call themselves Walak people: there were ten Walak students of the seventeen at Yepmum. Three other students were from Pyramid, north of Wamena, and the Pass Valley, northeast of Wamena.

In 2005, every room in Yepmum dorm held at least two students, but some students moved to new dorms after Jayawijaya regency was divided. This newly created Yahukimo regency leased two residences on campus in Tondano. One of these had a few Dani students, while the rest were Yali. Puncak Jaya regency paid for another residence; just one Dani student lived there. Students suggest that the newer regencies have the most funding to offer them because they have large 'start-up' budgets from the provincial government. The new Yahukimo residences had kitchens equipped with more than one kerosene stove and a good supply of plastic dishes and cooking implements. One of the Yahukimo residences also had a television and DVD player, carpet, plastic chairs, a computer and a colour printer.

Off Unima campus but still near Tondano, approximately ten Catholic Dani men lived in a two-level house rented using a private trust fund set up by a Dutch priest who once worked in Papua. Another Dutch priest who lives just outside Manado city administers the trust fund. Amidst the paddies and farmland, there were several other Catholic Dani students living in small thatched houses with their young children. Normally, if students have children, they live with their spouse in a boarding house or a thatched house. Another house with a dramatic view over rice fields held ten Lani students who are members of the Baptist church.

In Manado, the residences of Dani and other 'Wamena people' are dispersed around the area; one small house is even on the outskirts of the city far from the university. Sario, the name of the area around Unsrat, was home to approximately ten Dani students in boarding houses. Slightly further from Unsrat, the dorm for women from Jayawijaya regency (inhabited by eight Western Dani women and two Lani women), a four-bedroom house for Walak Dani men from the Wolo Valley, the dorm for men from Jayawijaya regency and a large co-ed dorm for students from Yahukimo regency are located in an area called Batu Kota. The Kamasan dorm funded by the Papua provincial government is also in the area. Closer to the centre of Manado city, five Catholic Valley Dani men shared a dorm operated by the Union of Catholic Students of Indonesia (PMKRI) with seven Indonesians. Four Valley Dani lived in a small house leased by the Archdiocese of Jayapura-Timika on the edge of the city. There were also Dani students living in several of six residences leased by the Yahukimo regency government.

Dorms exhibit various states of disrepair. In 2006 the original women's dorm (*asrama putri*) leased by Jayawijaya regency located in Sario was abandoned so that the owners could rebuild it. The indoor squat toilet had stopped functioning some time ago, the ceiling was falling in, strangers were getting into the dorm through a broken fence that led into the backyard where the house had no walls, and the corrugated steel door on the temporary outdoor toilet and bathing area was falling off its hinges. Women simply bathed out in the open after dark. The new dorm is in much better shape, but with ten women and an infant sharing four small, fan-less bedrooms, half of the inhabitants sleep on the tile floor in the living room. Students use bedrooms for storing clothes and toiletries. Another dorm supported by the Dutch priest's trust fund is located on the northern outskirts of Manado in a landslide prone area that students call a 'danger zone' (*daerah rawan*), implying that both the geography and the human occupants of the area are wild and uncivilized. Built from woven tree fibres, mosquito-ridden, without electricity and 15 minutes' hike from the nearest paved road, four male students live there because they do not have to pay rent and because they attend institutes close by. They say they are in frequent conflict with the neighbours, who do not acknowledge that students lease the location and consider it their property.

'Wherever We Go, We Garden'

For sustenance, Dani students require garden produce such as cassava, which they plant and tend on land borrowed from local farmers in Tondano, as well as green, leafy vegetables (*kankung*) collected from the irrigation ditches amongst Tondano's rice paddies. They also fish amidst the rice paddies. To my knowledge, Dani are the only students around Unima who collect food in this way, leaving students like Jhon to assert: 'Wherever we go, we garden.' Once the tubers are dug up, they are roasted over a fire. Indeed, cooking outside over a fire is the most common way that students in Yepmum dorm prepare meals, as kerosene is usually in short supply. One day, a few students repositioned the fire pit further behind the dorm so that, as one student explained, the pit (and the students sitting around it eating tubers) would no longer be visible from the street. Jally, the dorm leader, said that students were embarrassed to be seen cooking tubers on the fire by the Indonesians who walked by on the street in front of the dorm. Cooking tubers over the fire is only one way in which students' consumption practices distinguish them from the local population. *Bakar batu* pig feasts are common and closely identified with the culture of 'Wamena people' by students and by Indonesians in the area. Heading off to the jungle around Unima campus carrying a dead pig and a few net bags of tubers is not the mainstream way of celebrating the end of the semester. Shaking the soot off a roasted tuber and tearing at large chunks of pork with one's bare hands, sitting on the ground in the forest, is also not the local norm. When students create a *bakar batu* for Indonesian guests, they take the food out of the ground and bring it into a house or dorm, where they serve it on plates and offer spoons to eat with. Creating a cleaner and more civilized pig

'Newcomers' and 'Masters of the Land' in North Sulawesi 71

Figure 2.1. Bakar batu, Unima campus. Photo by author

feast practice is one way that students attempt to shield themselves from local judgements while maintaining an important culturally valued practice.

In urban and urban-fringe locations, students are unable to tend gardens or collect vegetables for sustenance. When Minke and I would ride the bus

Figure 2.2. Final examination celebration, Unima campus. Photo by author

down from Tondano to visit her relatives in the women's dorm, we would bring raw and roasted tubers hidden in our backpacks. While we grew bored of eating roasted tubers, the women in Manado saw these as a treat and as a sign that they would not have to worry about buying rice, kerosene and vegetables for dinner. Similarly, when I returned to Manado after visiting Wamena, Minke's relatives took a large duffel bag of carrots, cabbage and tubers that I had brought from the highlands back to their dorm. Without gardens, students in Manado are even more dependent on their sponsors in the highlands than are students living in Tondano, and the kinship system of responsibility and reciprocity is more important for everyday living. At the same time, in the 'big city' it is more acceptable, and possible, for students to go off in groups of two or three and spend money furtively. These experiences of freedom and danger in urban Manado relate to the economic circumstances of Dani students.

Sponsorship

Not many highlanders get to university, but this does not necessarily mean that university students are from an elite class. Like staying in primary and high school, going to university requires cash injections at critical moments. It means being able to pull together resources. Students depend on money sent from Wamena to finance their education, and this money comes mainly from horticultural activities. Family members tend to send large amounts of money sporadically (maybe once or twice a year) rather than small amounts on a regular basis. Families may sell some pigs and send their sons and daughters off to university, and they do. Students then eke out an existence until another cash injection comes from somewhere. At critical moments like examinations and graduation, students have more power to pull resources out of Wamena.

Students are expected to share what they receive rather than hold on to it and spend it bit by bit on rent, food and school fees. Daily life for students is thus 'characterised by the informal flow and mutual aid between households linked by kinship ties' (McKeown 2006: 374), except that students also produce kinship ties out of hierarchical, non-kinship relations. Any senior student becomes an 'older sibling' (*kakak*) to a junior student, who is termed a 'younger sibling' (*adik*), regardless of gender. The point is that reciprocity underpins students' survival abroad and contributes to the feeling of being poorer than other non-Dani and non-highlanders. They assert that other Papuan and Indonesian students receive regular dependable financial support from their parents who have urban employment, while they depend on what their sponsors (often but not exclusively their kin) can earn from selling sweet potatoes and cabbages. In reality, students also have relatives with jobs in the government, but many of these salaries are too low to support junior relatives abroad in any regular fashion, and the same rules of reciprocity apply to remittances procured from urban employment.

Besides money sent from Wamena, students may also receive government scholarships. Representatives from the local highlands governments (and, to a lesser extent, the Papua provincial government) normally visit students in North Sulawesi (and other locations around Indonesia) to distribute these scholarships to students in their final years of study. They often give the money to student treasurers from the various student organizations to distribute, which may lead to conflict amongst students if the money goes missing or the amount received is less than what students were expecting. It is also possible to receive a scholarship by creating a letter of request and submitting it to the local regency government in Wamena. Scholarship money comes infrequently and often in large amounts, similar to government funding for development activities (or, even more generally, for governance), and so students get accustomed to the benefits and pitfalls of managing large, unregulated and sporadic amounts of money.

Difficult living conditions and cash shortages frame students' campus experiences – both in terms of how they perceive themselves in relation to other students and in terms of how they are able to relate to campus figures. Besides limited support from Papuan governments in the form of dormitories and scholarships, agricultural work supports students in North Sulawesi. Their relatives acquire wealth in Wamena by selling vegetables or pigs, or through gifts that are given on the occasion of a birth, marriage or death. For example, upon marriage a groom and his relatives will be expected to give pigs and other valuables to the bride's family (Hayward 1983: 8–9; O'Brien 1969). The agricultural basis of support is an important part of students' sense of being 'Wamena people' (*orang Wamena*) and highlanders (*orang gunung*), even though some students have the financial support of a family member employed in the public service (see also Farhadian (2005: 57) regarding highlanders studying in Jayapura, Papua). Students are quick to emphasize the garden work their families do to send them money, even though some have relatives employed in the public service.

In Wamena, a relative takes cash to the bank and fills out the transfer paperwork to send money to the student's account abroad. Not every student has a bank account and sometimes money is sent via someone else's account. It is challenging to convince relatives to send money regularly, as university students are often considered to be adults who should be taking care of themselves. Nonetheless, they are family, and thus it is possible to gain support even into adulthood. When students want to leave Wamena to start their education, they can draw on obligations and relationships to get money together. Potential sponsors include people who are likely to have money, or with whom aspiring students have a close emotional relationship. A favourite uncle may not have money, but if he loves his nephew, he will do his best to get some money from other people by drawing on his own social network. An older cousin who works for the government may not feel obligated to help a 'younger sibling' in Manado, but he or she, having been a student, feels sympathetic and also understands the possible rewards when the 'younger sibling' eventually comes home grateful and indebted.

During their time abroad, students' sense of purpose waxes and wanes with the flow of money from Wamena. Students argue that they experience a feeling of belonging and connection when sponsors send them money because it means that someone is thinking of them or working on their behalf. When I met students' rural relatives in Wamena, they often asked about the progress of the students they were sponsoring. For instance, in July 2006 I was called out of my friend's kitchen to visit Taddeus' mother. When I arrived at her house, she poked her head out the kitchen door and asked about her son. She was not entirely certain where he was studying and, at first, nor was I, but we managed to place him by the family names of some of his friends from Wamena who were also studying in Manado. The last I had heard of Taddeus, he was unofficially married to a local Manadonese woman and was not actively attending his university, but I was not certain and did not want to spread such bad, and possibly incorrect, news. Therefore, I said that he seemed well and I had seen him at the students' Easter celebration, which was true. Taddeus' mother's voice cracked as she told me that she had been longing to know of her son's progress, but since she had no money to send, and had not had any money to send for some time, she felt he was certainly disappointed with her. She asked me to tell him that she was thinking of him and she had not forgotten about him, even though she had not sent him money. What Taddeus' mother told me corresponds exactly to the way that students say they feel if no one sends money: forgotten.

More than cash for fees and snacks, a blessing (*berkat*) from Wamena, as students sometimes refer to these electronic bank deposits, is a gift wrapped in a poignant net of social and political relations. If financial support deteriorates, it is a sign that sponsors (who are often relatives) and other members of the family are no longer thinking of students. The implication is that relationships have deteriorated. While students are physically absent from the highlands, they are unable to give, or be good kin to people in Wamena in typical ways. They cannot raise and give pigs at funerals, earn money for funeral payments or medical expenses, help with gardening or with other projects, lend support and influence, or even spend small amounts of money on gifts such as rice or cooking oil. They cannot sit together, chew betel nut, smoke a cigarette and sympathize with someone's plight. Instead, they hope others will reciprocate on their behalf by helping and otherwise acknowledging the assistance provided by the sponsor. If no one sends money, it is as if students are cut out of exchange relations and the family. This is certainly the impression students give when they say they experience great stress when no one sends money. To avoid being severed from the family, for some students, the solution is to 'show one's face' (*taruh muka*) in Wamena, or at least show one's face to relatives in Jayapura. Being at home again allows students to help others and to remind sponsors and others that their generosity is still needed. Showing one's face back home is so successful a strategy for securing financial assistance that students will take a small remittance and use it to ride the ship back to Papua or use a scholarship (or portion thereof) to travel home to the highlands, rather than using the money directly for school fees and living expenses in North Sulawesi.

Students from the Wolo Valley have an organized, formal system for 'showing their faces' in the highlands: when students are in year three and they are required to conduct a research project, they return to Wolo, where a community fundraiser is organized. For the price of travel by ship and airfare to the highlands (perhaps totalling US$150), two students I met in 2006 were able to each secure approximately US$2,000 or 20 million rupiah from their community event. The event centred on a typical highlands pig feast at which village men and women donated tubers and pigs, except there was a village leader sitting at a table counting money and recording the amounts in his book. This type of arrangement is a bit like a traditional 'prestation' whereby a large amount of wealth is given and received publicly and ceremonially to demonstrate the generosity of the giver and the connections amongst the group. The giver also gains social and cultural standing for the ability to create wealth (in the case of pigs, for example) or the ability to elicit contributions from others (see, for example, Lederman 1986; Ploeg 2004; Strathern 1971).

In other words, sponsors typically send large amounts of money, perhaps double what a student might need in a year (five million rupiah, for example) on an irregular basis. If a student receives five million rupiah, he or she will likely not receive money again for a year or two. All Wamena students know, however, that trying to hang on to their money is not a strategy that will last. There will not be enough money for a year, or a semester, because they are obliged to share with relatives and friends, both to be 'good' kin and 'Wamena people', and to reciprocate to others whom they have relied on in times of need. Many students try to be cautious with their money, but strategically spend money on themselves and others in order to foster relations that they can draw on when they inevitably run out of money or food. However, this is not a perfect system and there are periods of time during which no one seems to have any money. There are students who never seem to have money and rely on others for daily meals, while there are others who have reasonably regular support from home.

Although they say they prefer to live with other Wamena people anyway, students express that they wonder if living together and being obliged to take care of one another is conducive to the kind of quality development they are seeking. As Jhon asked me one day: 'We want to ask you something Jenny. You have seen how we live. We all eat or nobody eats. But do you think we would be more successful if we went out on our own?' Some students do decide to go out on their own. Mainly they live in shanties or in rundown campus housing that they cannot afford to rehabilitate. Jally, who lived this way for a time, explained to me that he wanted 'to live independently' to see if he could manage 'on his own'.

A Spiritual Place

One of the reasons students usually say they go to North Sulawesi is because it offers a supportive Christian atmosphere. The majority of local Indonesians are Christian, and students create groups based on church affiliation to support their religious development. There are approximately six churches located on Unima campus within walking distance of the Dani dorms, and more churches are situated in Tata Aran II and in Tondano city. Protestant Dani living on Unima campus typically attend the small Eben Haezer Bethel Tabernacle Church, led by a preacher originally from Java who, he said, 'wanted to go to Papua, to the place that is really in the dark [*gelap*]', but while still in Java he became ill and felt he could no longer pursue that dream. Thus, he reflected, it must be God's plan that so many of his churchgoers are highland Papuans. At Eben Haezer, 'Wamena students' make up approximately 60 per cent of the congregation, which usually totals around fifty people. The other members of this church tend to be student migrants from Maluku and Central Sulawesi, and a handful of local Indonesians who live near the church on Unima campus grounds. This church and the Pentecostal churches on campus tend to attract poorer residents, especially farmers. Wealthier and more prominent Indonesian locals attend the New Life Minahasa Evangelical Church. This pattern is repeated throughout North Sulawesi. Though Pentecostal churches do attract some wealthy individuals, the Christian Evangelical Church in Minahasa (*Gereja Masehi Injili di Minahasa*, or GMIM) churches attract the area's most prominent citizens. Small Pentecostal and other evangelical non-GMIM churches proliferate in neighbourhoods all over Manado, funded by community donations and projects, attracting followers to their strong ideological emphasis on the end of poverty and rewards that good Christians will experience. Students are often drawn into these personal, intimate groupings, dominated by Indonesian preachers and ministers, where they take up an intense schedule of daily worship.

The Catholic churches in North Sulawesi are made up of large congregations where small numbers of Dani may go unnoticed. Religious activities are not as intense among Catholic Dani as they are among Protestant Dani.

The messages from Catholic clergy are, overall, less critical, and large groups of worshippers make it difficult to personalize the messages in the way that evangelical ministers do in small neighbourhood churches. When I attended the Eben Haezer church from November 2005 to March 2006, there were three occasions when Dani students in the congregation walked out crying in the middle of the minister's preaching about immoral behaviour and sinful actions. Students expressed feelings of affiliation with local Indonesians of the same denomination, but these bonds did not exist very far beyond church settings and seemed to do little to alter negative preconceptions held by many Indonesians.

Racial ideas are prominent and sometimes publicly expressed in North Sulawesi. Dani students find a population that considers itself to have achieved modernity and cosmopolitanism due to inherent cultural or ethnic traits, Dutch blood and longstanding Christian influences. Upon arrival, and as students get to know the place, there is still the possibility of developing the connections they desire. Although there are local concerns about maintaining peace and stability, there are also expressions of compassion and support for diversity.

Living in dorms, attending churches, gardening, waiting for cash from home and trying to build relationships with locals are Dani strategies of survival, but they are also ways in which identities, distinctions and hierarchies are revealed. The tension between how Dani students see themselves and how locals see them is already building before they interact with one another. Most students see themselves celebrating in culturally appropriate ways, delving into the local Christian atmosphere, supporting one another, promoting hard work and being grateful for the sacrifices that allowed money to be sent from Wamena. Some Indonesians see them as strange black people heading off to cook in the dirty forest, living in dilapidated co-ed residences with their infants and, possibly, myself. This tension gives rise to ever-intensifying questions about whether aspects of Dani culture are 'right' for the modern context, and whether there are values and practices that might be holding them back. What students do elicits and feeds into racial formations, especially notions of primitivity, setting a challenging context in which to conduct deeper interactions and relations with Indonesians. Moreover, a lack of money in North Sulawesi might mean that, particularly in Tondano, some students are gardening for the first time, washing clothes in a stream (where they might have had piped water in a house in Wamena), and sharing food and resources with non-kin. Ironically, these new social and economic arrangements may reposition them as poorer and more rural or 'backward' than anything they previously experienced in Wamena. Thus, their education abroad begins with a process of being stripped of achievements and elevated status, the pockets of cash and high confidence they arrived with fading fast.

3

Stigma, Fear and Shame
Dani Encounters with Racial and Political Formations in North Sulawesi

Dani aspirations for new relationships and experiences with Indonesians are constrained by stigma, tense relations, surveillance and novel forms of shame. For Erving Goffman (1963: 3), stigma is 'an attribute that is deeply discrediting'. Similarly, stigma is a 'special kind of relationship between an attribute and a stereotype' (Yang et al. 2007: 1525). Stigma marks people as different and leads to devaluation. It is dependent on relationship and context – that is, stigma is socially constructed.

At the level of resistance politics and criticism, experiences of stigma seem easy for students to pinpoint and describe. Sometimes these are not their personal experiences, but form part of the *memoria passionis*, or collective suffering (see Giay 2000: 55) of Papuans under Indonesian rule, and they make up part of an agenda for independence from the Indonesian state. But stigma operates in less overt ways than the racialized battles that they are engaged in as part of their political struggle (*perjuangan*). Technocratic racism comes up, as Indonesians are particularly critical of Papuans' supposed intellectual and 'human resource' weaknesses. However, racialization of Dani students goes much further than Indonesians' furtive conversations or name-calling. Educated Dani youth are confronted with Indonesians' novel expectations of submissiveness and may either rebel against these expectations or shy away from encounters that could be humiliating. Racialization is the underexplored social process that fills in the contours of Dani–Indonesian relationships, underpins everyday interactions and explains awkward tensions. Racial and political formations are entangled, and Dani students may be denied experiences of belonging and security by Indonesians who take it upon themselves to keep a close eye on students and protect the 'community' and the 'nation' from recalcitrant Papuans.[1]

'We Came to Study, Not Play Politics'

Students interpret their new experiences abroad in terms of ongoing racialized colonial relations that position Papuans against Indonesians. Dani informants, both men and women, located political power and possibilities in a racial critique and felt that political moves are needed to save Papuans from elimination:

> They want to get rid of the black people, the Melanesian race, so they can claim all of the riches of Papua for themselves. They want the land, not us. *Orang putih* [lit. white people, a reference to Indonesians] regard Papuans as the most primitive of all people. They look down on us and they would be pleased if we all were taken into custody or just died. But we do not want this, so we continue to struggle. (Petrus)

> Indonesians touch our black skin and look at their fingers and say its black but it is not dirty, they are surprised. Indonesia does not want black people, so that is why we need our own country for black people. (Mika)

In students' perceptions, colonialism is racialized and so is its opposite, independence. Dani students are racialized as dirty, primitive and unwanted by Indonesians, who see themselves as white and advanced. Comments that Indonesians do not want Papuans, or Indonesia does not want black people reflect the important political belief among Papuans that Indonesian colonialism is operating to eliminate Papuans through overt as well as covert means (Munro 2019). Papuans' sense of colonialism is intimately tied to the understanding that the world's largest gold mine operates on their land, that the Indonesian state profits immensely from the mine and that the discovery of gold determined their political fate (Leith 2003; McKenna 2015). Commentators ranging from politicians to journalists to student activists complain that Papua has abundant natural resources and yet Papuans remain considerably poorer than most other people in Indonesia (see Munro 2004). Of course, the idea that Papuans are unwanted by Indonesia and that their presence inhibits external actors from accessing the natural wealth is also derived from the understanding that Papuans continue to be killed, tortured, raped, imprisoned and neglected. Papuans also point to the flourishing of illegal sex work amid an HIV epidemic (Butt 2005b), and the surge in alcohol amid government bans, as evidence of Indonesia's 'refined politics' (*politik halus*) (Munro 2019). Thus, many Papuans and some outsiders suggest that genocide is taking place, and the concept of the 'Melanesian race' referenced by Petrus takes centre stage in these understandings (Wonda 2007; Yoman 2007). Commenting on the pace of Indonesian in-migration, thirty-odd years ago, the first Indigenous Papuan governor, Isaac Hindom, reportedly stated that within a decade all Irianese [Papuans] would have straight hair (cited in Webster 2001: 521).

The politicization of 'black' as an identity around which Papuans can resist racist colonialism has emerged in complex ways, but this phenomenon has not yet been studied in detail. Sarah Richards (2015: 146) describes how Papuan youth are embracing American hip hop because it associates black identity with being 'attractive, stylish, talented and potentially wealthy' in direct challenge to the negative connotations associated with being black in Papua. Even before urban Papuan youth were on the internet via their mobile phones accessing Rihanna and Kanye West (Richards 2015: 146), black political identities have been available through reggae music (of South African, Caribbean and Papua New Guinean origins) copied onto audio tapes and compact discs. Among Dani students, the black South African reggae artist Lucky Dube is a particular favourite, and songs like 'Is This Freedom' and 'Remember Me' were often playing in dormitories. As mentioned earlier, in North Sulawesi there is considerable local emphasis on 'whiteness' and local Indonesians consider whiteness to be common amongst them. Dani express frustration at the consequences: in a competition for progress, Papuans are accused of being backward and at the same time, students argue, are prevented from 'going forward':

> We cannot advance because we are always oppressed [*tertindas*] by Indonesia. It must be true because we see black people in all these other countries, they can progress, be talented at music, acting, or sports and we think, why can't we? (Lavinia)

As Lavinia's comment indicates, there is a clear subtext of racialized competition with Indonesians over the process and achievement of advancement, although in this statement it is interesting that she mentions creative and athletic pursuits, not scholarly, technical or intellectual pursuits per se. Artistic and athletic pursuits, not scholarly achievements, are racialized in the United States, for example, as 'natural' domains of African American superiority. President Yudhoyono's assertion that 'all of Indonesia's children . . . including children of Papua' have the same chance to achieve success can be read not only as a promotion of education as an ethnic equalizer but also as a reflection of the prevailing racial logic that Papuans are being marginalized by the presence of better-skilled Indonesians. While Lavinia and other students draw attention to the structural violence that constrains their life chances, Indonesian views focus on Papuan 'weaknesses' and how they can catch up with Indonesians.

In spite of this critical dialogue, students are genuinely seeking new dynamics, new relationships and new possibilities in North Sulawesi, which they see as peaceful and stable compared to Papua. Colonialism, they figure, is confined to the land of Papua (*Tanah Papua*). They make commitments to education as a way of 'joining in' with Indonesians. Jally explained: 'Bad-mouthing people is not good behaviour . . . even if they do it to us, we must hold back, and do what is right. If we talk about these things everyone [Indonesians and Papuans] begins to feel unsafe. We always have to remember, we came here to study, not to play politics.' The relationships that they would like to have are ones in which they learn from locals, they exchange assistance with locals, they are accepted by locals and are invited to become part of the community. Relationships and belonging are an important part of Dani dreams that are made small by oppressive racial and political formations. Moreover, interactions with Indonesians lead to new feelings of shame, shyness and embarrassment, leaving some students with the sense that their very constitution has changed as a result of Indonesian colonialism.

Racial Stereotyping and Hidden Feelings

During a graduation ceremony for Dani students held at the Yepmum dorm on Unima grounds, the local government official gave a speech:

> I am happy to see so many Papuan kids [*anak-anak Papua*] graduate. Papuans are good-hearted [*baik hati*]. Minahasa people like to think of themselves as being white [*putih*] but I think Papuan students are black-skinned but with white hearts. I have only one bit of advice: students should value their parents' money, and not go straight to the nearest road-side stall and spend it all. Some of you also have a problem with drinking. Except for the time when one of the kids stole from a shop, I am happy to have Papuans in the neighbourhood. Congratulations on your graduation.

There were a few laughs in the audience of students, but most looked at their neighbours, perhaps wondering, as I was, if the official was trying to be critical or funny. Was he paying them a compliment or being racist? Were Papuans to feel good about being black with white hearts or did he mean that Minahasans think too highly of themselves when Papuans are just as good? Was he saying that Papuans are black, but they are still good (to his surprise) – though not all of them? Perhaps above all, the speech seemed to reveal something normally unspoken in the relationships between Papuans and Indonesians, namely that there is a 'Papuan' racial category, that there is some judgement by local people on the character of Papuans, and that skin colour, as a racial marker, forms part of local hierarchies. These normally hidden assumptions were publicly revealed and acknowledged because the government official perhaps thought he was paying the students a compliment.

For students, it is obvious that Indonesians hold stereotypical views of Papuans. They draw these conclusions from snippets of conversations, from actions and inactions, from euphemisms, and from feelings of being judged and scrutinized:

> Before you [Jenny] came none of them ever visited or wanted to hang out but now they all want to come. All straight-hairs [Indonesians]

> look down on us [*gengsi*] Papuan kids. Whether they are from Java or Toraja, they are all like that. They would never eat with us. (Albert)

Nina, a Yali student, said she came to North Sulawesi to have new experiences and to meet people from other cultures. However, she argued that overall 'the local girls do not want to hang out with Papuans'. She has a few friends from Sangir and Toraja (regions of Sulawesi), but she only sees them on campus. They do not come to visit her dorm and she does not visit their boarding house. Nina's explanation for her lack of Indonesian friends is that Indonesians think that Papuans are not good: 'They have heard that we get drunk, that we are promiscuous, we do not have money, I think that is why they are not friendly.' Gigi, like Nina, articulated that she does not have any Indonesian friends, partly due to the racist name-calling of some local Indonesians in Tondano:

> The ones who try to cause trouble are the kids of the bosses, who have the big houses down by the lake, they usually just yell out bad names like monkey or dog. I do not usually associate with straight-hairs [Indonesians] around here, except for my friend Siska, who is really open and friendly with everybody.

I was, for a time, in a position to hear what locals say about Papuans in their absence. Jerry, a Unima professor, said: 'Papuans have low SDM [quality], so they usually have to study for a long time.' Mrs L., wife of a church minister, said: 'The Papuan students are very poor, but good, polite, hardworking. If they come asking for work we usually give them some grass-cutting or laundry to do.' Mrs C., wife of a Unima professor, said: 'The students are really quiet, very shy, they are slow-thinkers, like you know "James" and "Donald" – they have been here for maybe ten years already but they are still students! Their minds are not yet, not yet ... good.' Arthur, the twelve-year-old son of a Unima professor, said: 'A Papuan and a monkey went to the zoo to join the exhibit. When they got there the boss asked, which one is the monkey?!?' Sonny, a car salesman, said: 'They still have low "socio-economic" [status], they are below us, so just be careful.' Papuans are thus stereotyped as having low intellect, sometimes using the term 'SDM' (human resources). Other particular alleged characteristics include a tendency towards negative behaviours such as intoxication and promiscuity. Poverty is part of the stigma, but it is seen as stemming from the various inadequacies in terms of skills, capacities and the ability to achieve financial success. Papuans are said to be irresponsible in a variety of ways, including being unable to handle money. They are accused of being poor because they spend all their money without thinking, an example of how their living situation and reliance on sporadic, large sums of money from home enlivens racial stigma.

Local understandings of poverty play a role in this stereotype. The Christian Church's interpretation of poverty is particularly important. I attended Pentecostal church services with Dani and Indonesians church members at least once a week in Tondano for six months, and through sermons and more informal discussions, ministers and others revealed an understanding of prosperity as a blessing or, rather, reward from God for good behaviour, leading a proper Christian lifestyle, serving the Lord and so forth. People who struggle in poverty are said to have inadequately embraced Christian values and practices. While it is not the case that all poor people are stigmatized as having inferior values and low morality, the dominant local perspective on poverty interacts with other stereotypes about Papuan values and inabilities, adding to stigmatization.

This matrix of beliefs and perceptions forms the backdrop for interactions and relationships, creating instability and mistrust, and amplifying the effects of stigma. Whenever a problem arises, local Indonesians may resort to assertions about Papuans, and students argue that they are prejudged by Indonesians. Nina is not certain why she has not yet experienced close relations with any Indonesian students, but since they seem unfriendly, she thinks they believe stereotypical views of Papuans. In a stigma-rich atmosphere, being ignored or avoided creates feelings similar to being criticized, called names or otherwise rejected in an outright fashion. Students thus suggest that stereotypes are actually extremely widespread and may prevent them from trying to establish good relationships. Rather, they spend almost all of their time with other Wamena people.

Stereotypes are 'powerful social myths' (Pickering 2001: 49) that may deny status, position and belonging to others. Stereotypes allow some Indonesians to treat Dani as 'others' who do not belong. This legitimates differential treatment. Students also experience difficult relationships because local Indonesians tend to hold prejudices that are revealed in times of conflict.

Brittle Relationships with Indonesians

Some students asserted that they develop good relations with their Indonesian neighbours, but if a conflict arises, the relationship quickly deteriorates and negative constructs of *orang Papua* are invoked by Indonesians. A common remark about relations was that 'if we are good, they are good'. Students cannot expect good treatment automatically; rather, if they go out of their way to create positive relations, then they may receive some friendship in return.

One incident illustrates some important points about relations with locals. In the village of Tata Aran near Unima, Dani students were holding an end-of-year celebration and a birthday party for a student's daughter. After supposedly consuming too much alcohol, two junior male students, Markus and John, went to rent a motorbike from one of the Indonesian neighbours. A few hours later, Markus returned looking nervous and said that they had scratched up the motorbike and when they went to return it to the owner, he demanded a very large sum of money. Senior students were very upset. They said that Markus and John should have asked a senior student who lives at the dorm to go with them to rent the bike because some of them had positive relations with the some of the neighbours. The dorm leader, David, who had just graduated, outlined that the neighbours around the dorm were safe, while the neighbours further down the street in Tata Aran and near the intersection of the main Manado-Tondano roads (which students refer to as the *pertigaan*) were not safe: 'We know some of the neighbours around the dorm, we can deal with them, but in Tata Aran or at the intersection, we do not know them. Sometimes they call us names. We have to be careful there.' Had John and Markus been more careful, they would have been able to negotiate a fair payment to fix any damage to the bike. In addition, senior students said that they should have been more careful because causing a problem with a few people in the neighbourhood may result in many more locals taking sides against Papuans. When some students and I went home that night, we were accompanied on the walk to the bus stop by some longtime student residents to deter any attacks or other angry exchanges. Students were serious about the possible threat – similar events in the past had resulted in innocent students suffering at the hands of vengeful neighbours, who, if not violent, were rude when they tried to purchase items or meals at the small roadside stores. As David explained: 'They do not know who caused the problem, they just know he is Papuan, and we all feel unsafe.'

While students can develop positive relationships with locals, relations easily break down. Local Indonesians who may not otherwise always get along themselves quickly form a unified front against students, who may be viewed as outsiders or troublemakers. Just below the surface of friendly relations, there are deep divisions. In developing positive relationships, students must continually negotiate safe and dangerous areas – areas where racism is more overt and aggressive.

A few students create quite strong relationships with Manadonese, but most have a few acquaintances or casual friendships. Jally, for instance, is an extroverted, confident engineering student. Although he says he became a heavy drinker after he arrived in North Sulawesi, a relative took him to church and this inspired him to change his life. He went to his professor's house in Tondano and asked for work. He started by asking Franky, the professor, if he could help build his house in the campus housing complex. For 30,000 rupiah (US$3) a day (paid in lump sums whenever Franky decides to pay), Jally levelled the dirt in the yard, carried wood, threw away trash and tiled the kitchen floor. After the house was built, Jally began visiting each day to turn the outdoor lights on and off and to make sure the property was secure. (Franky has another house in Manado where he and his family live. The Tondano house is used for holidays.) Franky offered him more work tending the garden at his Manado house. Jally occasionally spends a few days at Franky's house, playing with his children, cutting the lawn and cleaning. He stays in a spare room in Franky's house during these visits. Franky has invited Jally to spend Christmas with the family and has promised to give him some money if he returns to Wamena for a visit during the summer holidays. To date, there is nothing specific that Franky has done for Jally to aid his academic progress, but the friendly relationship puts Jally's mind at ease. He said: 'I really like living here now. I am in semester ten but I probably will not finish for a few years. I am not worried.' Although Franky and his family seem friendly, when Jally is not around, they make jokes about his appearance, saying that he looks like an ape.

Partly because of his relationship with Uncle Franky, Jally has forged relationships with other Manadonese for whom he sometimes does odd jobs. Relations are mostly based on work, although Jally may be invited over for socializing on special occasions, which provides him with a free meal and probably leftovers to take home too. Jally's various Indonesian friends and acquaintances shout greetings to him when he walks around Unima campus. However, when the local village headman raided Jally's dorm (discussed later in this chapter), the fact that Jally was 'friends' with some of the men and had gone out of his way to be friendly and helpful to local government officers did not improve the treatment of him and other students.

Benyamin, a Lani man from Bokondini, north of the Baliem Valley, described being one of the first Papuans in Tondano in the mid 1990s. He argued that he came to Sulawesi in search of a more modern life, but found himself alone, isolated, homeless, hungry and rejected by locals around Unima campus. He also said that students have become better at establishing relationships with local people in the last ten years. Although locals do look down on *orang Papua*, it 'depends on us, on our personal charisma, whether we can relate to them or not . . . We had to learn how to talk to them, and show them that we can be honest and trustworthy'. Benyamin suggested that if students have negative relationships, it is probably their own fault: 'If we are good, they are good.' Yet he admitted that he did not have any close Indonesian friends, despite having lived in Tondano for eleven years. He did consider members of his church to be people with whom he has a good relationship, even if he only interacts with them at church. I first met Benyamin at this Pentecostal church, one of four located at Unima campus. Among his acquaintances at church, he was always extremely deferential and helpful, taking on chores around the church such as cleaning duties, painting, stacking chairs and so forth. Like other students, he nearly always sat near the back of the church and never put himself in a prominent position amongst the other churchgoers, even other students from coastal Papua and eastern Indonesia. He described the people at church as 'good' (*baik*) and he considered this an example of a successful relationship between Papuans and Indonesians.

Lastly, despite initial claims that North Sulawesi is 'safe' and 'peaceful' (*aman*), students have concerns about their safety:

> Whenever there is political trouble in Papua, we find ourselves in trouble here. Papuan students in other cities report the same thing, especially for Wamena students. The security forces come to our dorms; we get chased, interrogated, hit with the back of their rifles. In Sulawesi here it was very serious when Manadonese people were killed in Wamena. The people here wanted to take revenge on us. (Laurence)

Students advise each other not to go walking around alone, especially at night. They fear that local police or state spies will detain and question them. They fear that if this happens, the police will gain information about where they live, their full name and other identifiers that would allow the police to find them again during operations against Papuan students that usually take place following incidents in Papua. Another fear is that they will encounter intoxicated Indonesians who may assault or intimidate them. In the event that this happened and Papuan students fought back against assailants, the assumption among students is that they would become targets for other Indonesians looking for revenge, that conflict would escalate out of control or that they would be taken into police custody. Students' concerns about their safety can be linked to not being allowed to build supportive relationships with local Indonesians. In the event that Papuans were, for instance, targeted by police for questioning, students suggest that local Indonesians could intervene and speak to police or government officials on their behalf, but do not. Power is associated with having a strong social network with links to individuals in various positions in society who could offer assistance and protection. I frequently heard the expression: 'We do not have many people here.' In North Sulawesi, Dani do not have local Indonesians in their social networks, just other Papuan highlanders. They have difficulty building good-quality relationships because of stigma and discrimination. Students' sense of themselves as already vulnerable to the assumptions of Indonesians is reinforced when they are treated differently by people in positions of authority.

Being Treated Differently

Even though Manado is a city with a population of 400,000 inhabitants, people tend to live in close-knit neighbourhoods (*kampung*) that operate much like the small neighbourhoods in Tondano. People coming and going are noticed and greeted, local residents talk about each other and share gossip, people shop and eat in the *kampung,* and the *kampung* is overseen by a government official. Herbert, a senior Dani student living in Manado, angrily described a common scenario in his neighbourhood:

> The people on this street are difficult. A few weeks ago one of the [Dani] students, Yohannes I think, was drunk and they were taunting him, the neighbours, calling him *Ale, Sobat* [literally, friend or buddy]. It really pisses me off when they call us *Ale*. So Yohannes got angry with them, he did not punch anyone, just told them off. Then they told the *Pala* [*Kepala Lingkungan,* neighbourhood government official]. The *Pala* got angry at Yohannes about it. The *Pala* came to me and told me to keep the younger kids in line, and to tell Yohannes to go and apologize. I did not tell Yohannes to apologize though because the neighbourhood kids [*anak-anak kampung,* referring to young men] make a ruckus [*ribut*] constantly, they are always drinking and making a racket, but if a Papuan kid makes trouble they come and say we are disturbing local security.

Ale and *sobat* are names that some Indonesians call Papuans, and some Papuans call each other; the words literally mean 'friend' or 'buddy'. Whether or not they are perceived as offensive depends on who is speaking and the context for their words. It is up to students to interpret the context. Still, it is a term used exclusively for Papuans. As students describe their interactions with Indonesians in Tondano and Manado, they argue that Indonesians sometimes attempt to incite conflict, that disagreements tend to escalate and that they are insulted by the use of special names for Papuans. Herbert's story also shows that Papuan students are asked to do humiliating things (like apologize to neighbours who start conflict with name-calling) in order to be accepted in the neighbourhood. Senior students may be called upon to support the discriminatory 'security' approach of neighbourhood officials by disciplining junior students.

Another example students give of discriminatory treatment relates to the assumption that Papuans are always the cause of social disruption:

> In about the year 2000 in Tondano a group of us played volleyball against a group of Manadonese guys and we were winning but one of them got angry and came over and punched one of our guys in the head. This caused a big fight. But we thought it was over. Then they came back with more local men [*orang sini*] carrying sticks and started hitting us. We tried to fight them off and then we ran away. After that one of our friends took a bow and arrow to their dorm

to scare them. They reported this to the *Lurah* [headman]. Because of this incident the *Lurah* says we are a threat to security and so he 'sweeps' our dorm to look for weapons whenever he likes. But we were not the source of the problem. The behaviour of the Manadonese was ignored. (Laurence)

These descriptions of some common experiences reveal that forming relationships based on trust and mutual understanding is important for Dani students. Having no relationship is experienced as similar to having a bad relationship. Lawrence Yang and colleagues (2007: 1530) write: 'Stigma, we hypothesise, threatens the loss or diminution of what is most at stake, or actually diminishes or destroys that lived value.' It is possible to argue that for Dani students, stigmatization and racialization most threaten their ability to form relationships with Indonesians, other Papuans and, as explored in Chapter 6, even other Dani. Relationships are the ultimate source of provision and protection for Dani students. The relationships they most privilege are gift relationships – webs of obligation never to be closed (Lederman 1986). They argue that they feel powerful obligations to care for each other and to thrive together. Requesting assistance and being obliged to provide in return is not a debt that is to be feared or avoided, it is the sign of kinship. Stigma prevents students from achieving the kinds of bonds they hoped for with Indonesians in Manado and Tondano, for the most part, but it does not threaten everything that matters most. They simply remain focused on other 'Wamena people', trusting few others. These experiences mean that stigma entrenches, enables and enlivens the already politically charged typologies of 'Papuan' (*orang Papua*) and 'Indonesian' (*orang Indonesia*). Stigma is the everyday experience of Papuans amongst Indonesians and it amplifies segregation.

Lex and the Headman: A Midnight Raid on the Dorm

Lex, a 25-year-old social sciences student in his ninth semester at Unima, argued that it is important for Papuan 'kids' (*anak-anak*) to get out of Papua and see how things are done elsewhere: 'Even though the Papuan "kids" have to be careful with the locals, here we can meet with and talk with Indonesians. Here we can also join organizations and mix with other Papuans and Indonesian students.' Like other students, upon arriving Lex was advised about the local environment, the temptations to be wary of and how to get along with the locals. Although the locals sell alcohol to Papuan students, Lex commented: 'they also talk badly about them for drinking ... in general we students feel that the locals are quite impolite, and we advise new students to be careful especially if they are drinking, not to get into fights with them. We have to be extremely polite to them', he said, clasping his hands together and bowing his head a little. Alongside these views, however, Lex was a leading supporter of West Papuan nationalism and took prominent roles in student demonstrations in North Sulawesi.

In January 2006, a local *Lurah* (Headman) and several of his friends (whom students refer to as *anak buah,* or protégé, but who are not actually government employees) raided the Yepmum dorm where I lived with Dani students on Unima campus around midnight. Students who answered the door reported that the men said they had come to search for weapons. Jally, John and Ally discussed the matter with them and tried to convince them to come back another time. Some students in their bedrooms upstairs heard the voices as I did and came out to peer down the stairway at the men. There were never visitors this late at night. After a few minutes, two men came upstairs, banged on doors and made everyone open their bedroom doors so they could look for weapons. Most were alarmed and shaken at the events. Students telephoned their friends at the other Wamena dorms in the area to warn them. We all stayed awake talking after the incident until everyone's nerves had calmed down.

A few days later, Lex was told to appear at the office of the Headman. Coincidentally, or not, I was also called to appear before the Headman that day, and Jally and I heard the entire conversation while we sat in the waiting area outside his office door. In the office, surrounded by the same men who had raided the dorm, Lex was berated because, according to the men, Dani students had been telling their friends and Indonesians in the area that the men who came to the dorm were intoxicated. The Headman argued that Lex had no proof and that this was slanderous. One of the men asked Lex if he was stupid. At one point, one of them announced that he was 'very upset [*ganas sekali*] about this' and threatened to punch Lex in the head. Lex tried to argue that the dormitory is under the protection of a former Wamena regent (*Bupati*) who lives in Manado and cannot be entered into forcibly as it was that night. He also asserted an argument I heard among students after the incident, namely that the Headman should have brought a letter of explanation signed by higher authorities or the police to legitimate the late-night search. Lex also argued that the men should not have come in the middle of the night, frightening students and disturbing them from their sleep. Jally and I could hear the emotion in his voice. The heated conversation continued on, with the Headman and his men repeating their accusations and threats until Lex conceded that he agreed that it had been wrong for students to say the men were drunk and that the Headman was within his rights to raid the dorm. The emotion in his voice suggested tears. At this point, the Headman further asserted that raiding the dorm was necessary for local security and was therefore in the students' best interests. 'We know there have been a lot of problems of separatism in Papua', he stated. He also referred to previous conflict between Manadonese

90 *Dreams Made Small*

youth and Dani students that resulted in injuries on both sides. Lex mumbled in agreement.

Lex emerged from the office and averted his eyes, suggesting to Jally and I that he was ashamed that we had heard this humiliating encounter. As we left, the Headman demanded to know when the students were going to come and help with the construction of his house-office. Jally promised to get some

Figure 3.1. Dorm room poster. Photo by author

students organized to assist with the labour. Jally tried to make light of the situation on the walk home. He said it was better not to speak at all or just to agree with everything because otherwise 'they just go on and on'. Lex did not laugh. When another student joined us in the street and asked how things had gone, Lex just said: 'These people are difficult [*susah*] and I am sick and tired of talking to them.'

For the rest of the day, Lex stayed in his room. Jally and others argued that Lex was feeling ashamed (*malu*). He was supposed to be the leader of the dorm and speak on our behalf, but instead he was unconvincing and uninfluential in his encounter with the Headman. Lex was in fact normally a strong leader, articulate, organized and authoritative. Before the encounter with the Lurah, he expressed that he wished for new experiences abroad, and advocated politeness and submissiveness as the best way to get along with locals, though he disagreed with allowing wrongdoers to get away with their actions. The dorm raid and humiliating confrontation demonstrated for him and other students that whatever expertise and status he had achieved among Dani students were of little use amongst Indonesians.

Shame is only one part of Lex's experience. Dani students are also singled out for treatment as 'security threats' by local officials and are made to feel that they have no rights or status, and that local Indonesians harbour negativity towards them. Students talked about the incident with their friends for many weeks, mostly astonished that even when drunk men come crashing into their bedrooms in the middle of the night, they are still wrong to criticize or challenge this treatment. It would be nice to be able to say that Lex recovered from his shame and continued on as an authoritative dorm leader, but in fact his confidence and strength seemed to wane around this time. He spent a few weeks living with some Dani friends in Manado and allowed other students to take more prominent positions in the dorm leadership. However, he did retain his commitment to political issues and was one of the leading organizers of a protest staged by Papuan students in Manado opposing the operation of the Freeport mine in February 2006.

Surveillance and Intimidation: A Meeting Interrupted

On 4 February 2006, students held a meeting at the Yepmum dorm in Tondano to discuss a demonstration they wished to hold in Manado on the following Monday. The issue was the Freeport copper and gold mine at Tembagapura, outside of Timika, in the southern highlands of Papua. According to news reports heard in Manado, Indigenous protestors had recently blocked the road to the mine, and demonstrations by Papuans subsequently erupted in key cities across Indonesia in support of closing Freeport mine until it could be operated in a just fashion, controlled by an independent Papuan government. Papuan student protesters in Jayapura were attacked by security forces.[2]

At one point during the discussion, a minibus pulled up in front of the dorm. The room quietened. 'No, it's okay', said a student sitting near the window. Lex and Sam, the local leader of the Association of Central Highlands Students of Papua (*Asosiasi Mahasiswa Pengunungan Tengah Papua Indonesia,* or AMPTPI), described various aspects of the planned demonstration, such as the roles that would be assigned to participants, the need to keep the demonstration calm and peaceful, and the need to focus on the 'Close Freeport' message without bringing up other issues, especially independence from Indonesia.

As the discussion waned, I went to the kitchen at the back of the dorm with some of the women. After a few minutes, the happy chatter in the kitchen suddenly went dead. 'Intel', Minke said. We saw Lex and Sam rushing out the back door of the dorm, clutching papers and other belongings. I heard unfamiliar voices. Minke went to investigate and ordered me to stay in the kitchen and keep the door locked. Approximately ten minutes later, Minke returned and showed me a text message from Sam asking Minke to please bring Lex's shoes up the steep hillside behind the dorm to a house where they were hiding out. After she delivered the shoes, we rejoined the students who had been present when 'Intel' arrived at the front door and heard their version of events. Jally said that the Intel authorities were looking for Sam and Lex, who had identified themselves as the planned leaders in an application for permission to demonstrate submitted to authorities in Manado. The authorities wished to identify Sam and Lex in person and, supposedly, to tell them that any students who wished to participate in demonstrations had to obtain individual letters of permission from the local government officials in their areas. Tondano-based students needed a letter from the Village Head, otherwise they would be doing something illegal and would be arrested.

Jally, uninterested in political activism, was angry with Sam and Lex for drawing attention to the dorm and then fleeing instead of taking responsibility. Jally said to the group: 'We had better all know exactly what we are doing here and what these political actions are about, because we will all have to answer questions about what we are doing.'

When I talked to Lex later, he said he and Sam ran away and hid because they were afraid of being arrested or taken to the police station, or anything that might result in the demonstration being cancelled: 'I have friends who have been intimidated, punched, or worse, by police in other cities. Once they know your name, your face, where you live, they never leave you alone. You can never live normally again. You always fear being taken in every time there is any political trouble here or in Papua, they will come and ask you about it.'

Political and social activism is a longstanding tradition for university students (*mahasiswa*) in Indonesia (Aspinall 1993, 1999; Douglas 1970) and in

West Papua. In West Papua, students are at the forefront of political activism and criticism of the Indonesian government. University students hold public rallies, speeches and demonstrations in Papua, effectively becoming the faces of separatism. When news of political action in Papua leaks out to the rest of Indonesia, it contributes to an impression amongst local people in North Sulawesi that Papuans are violent, are not good citizens, and are worthy of suspicion and mistrust.

Indonesian students in North Sulawesi from groups such as the Union of Catholic University Students of Indonesia (PMKRI) and the Indonesian University Students Movement (GMNI) regularly hold demonstrations in accordance with national and international days of action, such as International Workers Day and National Education Day. They raise issues concerning state policies, social injustice and current events. Papuan students also participate in these activities, but for many Dani students, fears of detention and reprisal may keep them from participating in such events. Students say that police and 'Intel' agents do not just watch, but may also question, interrupt, intervene, detain and intimidate them. Even if students have done nothing 'wrong', they are reluctant to face 'Intel' for fear of ongoing repercussions and because confrontations are uncomfortable, frightening and sometimes humiliating. Certain Dani student activists, such as Sam, who produces leaflets with political messages and tries to organize demonstrations, report receiving threatening phone calls and text messages, and being followed around the area. Others say that Intel agents approach them on the street and question them about their identities and activities.

Students advise each other not to travel alone, particularly after dark, because they fear being confronted by Intel agents. In January 2006, a group of Papuan asylum seekers arrived in Australia by boat seeking protection from Indonesian state violence, action that stirred emotional reactions across Indonesia. Shortly thereafter, a rumour spread through town that Papuan students were planning to seek political asylum in the Philippines travelling via Manado, and several students said that police picked them up off the street and put them into a jail cell. They were interrogated and released unharmed.[3]

So far, students in North Sulawesi have managed to escape physical violence and punishment from the police, but the fate of fellow student activists tortured and murdered in detention in Papua is never far from their minds (see Human Rights Watch 2001). In March 2006, I was with Dani students in Tondano watching television reports of street demonstrations in Abepura, Papua that resulted in the deaths of three Indonesian police officers (and the subsequent detention and torture of alleged Papuan student participants in police custody). Students expressed concern that they would be subject to increased surveillance and possibly detention by local authorities in North Sulawesi, especially if any of the officers killed in Abepura were from North

94   *Dreams Made Small*

Sulawesi. Older students stated that relations with local people in North Sulawesi were not good following the 2000 Wamena incident, when a number of Manadonese migrants were killed in Wamena. At the same time, as some of the images of dormitories indicate, there are ways that students may push back against surveillance and intrusive authorities, such as by displaying political posters or independence-related imagery in the dorm.

Staying out of Sight at Eben Haezer Church

Eben Haezer Bethel Tabernacle church, located on Unima campus in Tondano, is part church, part house. The minister (Javanese) and his wife (Minahasan) have lived there with their two children for two years. The front room in the house takes up some of the space for the congregation, such that people sitting too far to the right face the minister's front door and living room. The space accommodates approximately fifty plastic lawn chairs and a small band of singers, their guitars and amplifiers.

The minister and his wife are among the poorest religious leaders in the area. Their house-church remains unfinished, the kitchen and bathroom are outside; they are young, and just starting out. Outside of worship times or Bible reading groups, they wear casual, even torn t-shirts and cut-off trousers.

Figure 3.2. A Dani student is baptized by a Pentecostal minister in Tondano. Photo by author

They are certainly the least intimidating church leaders that I met and they appear to work very hard to establish good relations with the students in their congregation, half of whom are *orang Wamena*. Not only does the minister make his sermons about them and youth-oriented issues and struggles, he and his wife take their worship sessions to the dormitories, where they sit on the floor, eat simple snacks of bread or juice, and make jokes and regular conversation. They act in a way that is friendly and egalitarian; they seem aware that Dani students experience discomfort in certain settings and go out of their way to make them feel welcome. Still, as the minister explained to me: 'We try and we try but they are always shy.'

During church services at Eben Haezer, it is common for members to stand in front of the congregation and 'bear witness' to God's presence in their lives. In the six months of Sundays that I was there, Dani students gave witness only twice. During the service, worshippers are asked to raise their hands, expected to sing loudly, clap and generally express their love for Jesus with abandon. Despite the congregation being at least half Wamena students, the vast majority of students are quiet, stiff and do not raise their hands when instructed to do so. My informant Mina said that she was not yet courageous enough to speak up in public in mixed company. Some students said that they were not committed enough Christians to do so, but others said they were ashamed and embarrassed to stand up in front of everyone.

Dani compete for seats at the back of the church. At church events, students create more rows of chairs at the back of the church if all the seats are taken. At a Christmas event, students moved chairs into the shadows and hidden parts of the church where they could not see the minister. This type of avoidance is interpreted by the minister and students to be a result of shame, embarrassment and shyness, captured by the Indonesian term *malu*. Students say they feel embarrassed to sit at the front near the action. Still, even in small groups, such as when the minister comes to the dormitory to lead a worship session, students will distance themselves from the minister. During a postbaptism feast in December 2005 the minister and his wife attempted to sit with a group of students on the living room floor. Students gradually and subtly moved out to the yard.

When students are alone with the minister and his wife, such as during a worship session at an all-Dani dormitory, most students are still shy, but not to the extent they are in front of other Indonesians at church. At the dorms, some students have to take a more active role in the session because they have invited the minister to help them worship.

When Dani students hold their own religious gatherings, or when they run an event for their student groups, participation is lively and uninhibited, if still usually respectful or serious depending on the situation. They are actively involved in the service, they act much more confident and they sit in the front rows.

Thus, students are reluctant to accept the advances of friendship offered by the church leaders and put up strategic barriers (including physically distancing themselves) to keep the relationship impersonal. Put another way, students prefer the company of other Wamena people. In addition, despite the efforts of church leaders to be welcoming and approachable, Dani students still claim to be shy and ashamed in front of them, and continue to try to stay out of the centre of attention, especially in more formal, public events dominated by Indonesians. Students make an effort not to be noticed by Indonesians and would rather not interact. Even though the religious setting may influence feelings of shyness and discomfort, these behaviours are similar in other nonreligious settings and are different from how students act in religious activities with other Papuans.

The Limits of Quality: Stigma, Scrutiny, Shame

In their interactions with Indonesians, Papuan youth may confront stereotypes that are derived from racial and evolutionist thinking. Cecilia McCallum (2005: 100) writes: 'racialization takes place when differences between human beings are simplified and transformed into Difference, overvaluing particular bodily differences by imbuing them with lasting meaning of social, political, cultural, economic, even psychological significance'.

Although students reject the content of stereotyping, the practice of being marked as 'other' translates into experiences of awkwardness, shyness, shame and discomfort (*malu*) amongst Indonesians. Recent analyses of *malu* in other Indonesian social settings depict ways in which individuals may experience *malu* in relation to living up to national values and expectations or in relation to threats to perceived national values. Johan Lindquist (2004: 503) found that young urban migrants were ashamed of their lack of economic success. Because economic success is linked to national ideals of modernity and development, '[i]n this context *malu* appears as an emotion that describes the failures to live up to the ideals of the nation'. Similarly, in Tom Boellstorff's (2004) analysis of violence against gay men in Indonesia, those who perpetrate public forms of violence are said to be lashing out as a result of feeling *malu*. *Malu* in this case arises because a particular kind of nationalized masculinity is at stake, and the nation is perceived to be in imminent danger of being represented by non-normative men (Boellstorff 2004: 469).

When Dani students say they feel *malu*, they seem to mean shyness or embarrassment rather than shame because in their descriptions, the opposite of *malu* is courageous or confident (*berani*). Yet at other times their expressions of *malu* also mean shame, particularly if we follow William Reddy (1997: 347): 'Shame derives from thoughts about how one is seen by others ... thus, shame can lead to withdrawal coupled with action aimed at managing appearances.' All of the above case studies refer to 'situations in which one's dignity and status are on the line' (Keeler 1983: 160). What Dani students describe as *malu* arises at the intersection of Melanesian constructs of shame, stigma, and local cultural and racialized hierarchies they encounter in the context of university migration. In Melanesian cultural contexts, Andrew Strathern (1975: 350) describes shame as 'a notion of a loss of prestige or inadequacy caused by a confrontation with the power of the community'. Albert Epstein (1984: 32) proposes: 'Shame tends to be elicited when one's shortcomings are exposed to the concentrated gaze of others.' Dani have their own culturally defined understandings of shame (*nekali* and *nayuk* in Dani language) that emphasize concern over appearances, reputation and privacy. Shame is said to arise if private behaviours or personal weaknesses are exposed, or if someone fails to live up to exchange obligations, such as not having pigs to give at a funeral or marriage celebration. Traditionally, how one is seen by others comes into play for men who wish to publicly show capabilities and hide shortcomings as they jostle for authority and status in the group, while women might be said to be concerned to show their capacities for garden work and childrearing, or to appear demure and submissive in the context of traditional marriage arrangements (Alua 2006). Today, what counts as shameful is increasingly shaped by new cultural and political forces that lessen the potency of traditional norms and engender novel expectations and judgements (Butt and Munro 2007).

Feelings of *malu* can be linked to locals' refusal to acknowledge any of the achievements of the young Papuans in their midst and, rather, an insistence on seeing and treating them as primitive, labour-ready and potentially dangerous. A powerful sense of local hierarchies, and students' positioning near the bottom, contributes to awkwardness and silences amongst normally critical and confident young people. Following Jeffrey Denis (2015: 220), the 'racially stratified settler-colonial context and small-town dynamics breed divisions and silences that shape the forms and meanings of contact in ways that sustain group position prejudice'. These findings affirm the need to consider *malu* at the intersection of racial politics: 'Interactions with whites are more potently minimised by defining or experiencing the relationship itself as one attended by shame and hence by avoidance and/or other restrictions on behaviour' (Kwok 2012: 39). Discomfort, awkwardness and the feeling of being scrutinized by Intel and government officials are significant effects of stigma, and they place limits on students' ability to assert themselves and take prominent positions. As Denis (2015) argues, in colonial encounters between settlers and Indigenous people, contact reinforces rather than alters existing inequalities and racialized divisions.

Submissiveness is a key understanding of *malu* described by Ward Keeler (1983), and public gestures of submissiveness by Dani students seem essential for maintaining relationships of tolerance with Indonesians. Assertiveness by students can create open conflict. It is clear that it is more often male students who defy these expectations and may react with both shame and anger. Considering the gendered forms of propriety that *malu* usually entails (Boellstorff 2004; Collins and Bahar 2000; Lindquist 2004; Slama 2010), the public shaming of Dani men raises questions about emasculation and its role in sustaining racial hierarchies.

These experiences, and the politics of submissiveness that they evoke, should give us pause when considering mobility as a trajectory primarily characterized by opportunity rather than vulnerability. Students have developed a new awareness of dominant perceptions and expectations associated with new relationships and cultural contexts in North Sulawesi. Awareness is grounded in encounters 'where racial ideas and representations were enacted, reworked, or forged' (Douglas 2013: 14). The confidence that allows Lex, for example, to take action when he feels that local authorities have treated Dani students unfairly, is based on a sense of being educated and living in a place where it is more possible to express discontent. On a more positive note, for every student like Benyamin, who is more tolerant and satisfied with the terms on which he relates to local Indonesians, there are other students like Lex, Markus and their supporters, who seem to expect more respectful recognition. How they are seen by others fuels anger and ambition, not just shyness or shame.

Considering that Dani students approach their time in North Sulawesi with a certain amount of humility and openness, acknowledging that they are not 'masters of the land' (*tuan tanah*), the relationships they achieve and the submissiveness they are expected to show exemplifies the 'confrontation with the power of the community' described by Strathern (1975: 350). That new relationships, cultural understandings and networking with Indonesians cannot take place even amongst those who call themselves 'kin' (*saudara*) united by Christianity in a region characterized by peaceful stability raises questions about whether Papuans may achieve a sense of belonging anywhere beyond their lands. Colonialism is more mobile and fluid than students had imagined.

Lindquist (2004: 498) suggests that young urban migrants feel *malu* because they find themselves outside national propriety, and amiss of personal expectations, when they apparently fail to live up to ideals of progress (*kemajuan*). Dani university students' experiences illustrate a different possibility, in which a stigmatized cultural and ethnic minority begins to achieve national ideals and expectations, at least in terms of education, skill development and mobility. In doing so, they pose a critical challenge to powerful national precepts concerning development potentials and inherent cultural and ethnic traits. By their educational successes, Papuan youth may offer convincing proof that cultural minorities deemed backward in the Indonesian national imaginary are not, and maybe never were, held back by their ethnic and/or racial constitution. These challenges do not, and will not, go unnoticed.

Notes

1. With permission, this chapter draws on material previously published in Munro (2015a).
2. Retrieved 20 December 2017 from https://www.youtube.com/watch?v=EX5ajS4ZFbI.
3. As someone involved with Papuan students, I also became a person of interest to 'Intel'. I only became aware of this when I was in Jayapura in 2009, where I had the opportunity to meet with Agus Alua, then leader of the Papuan People's Assembly (*Majelis Rakyat Papua*, or MRP). Upon arriving at the MRP office, I was asked about myself by a security guard. Another security guard in the room answered before I could speak. He informed the senior guard that he remembered me from when I met with Markus Haluk, the secretary of the Central Highlands University Students Association (AMPTPI), at their head office in Jayapura in 2006. The guard was right; I had met with Markus to discuss the student organization three years earlier.

4
'Discipline Is Important'
Aspirations and Encounters on Campus

> Study Motto
> I come to learn, not to enjoy
> I come to listen, not to reject
> I come to accept, not to deny
> I come to succeed, not to fail
> I come to suffer, not to have fun (get drunk)
> Discipline is important
> (Declaration written on notebook paper and pinned on
> a student's dorm room wall)

On campus, Dani students aspire to become good-quality 'human resources' (*sumber daya manusia*) and develop technical skills, but they also hold on to less technocratic renderings of education, hoping for real-world knowledge and capabilities that can help them ameliorate conditions of poverty and hopelessness back home. They also hope to improve upon, or develop, a range of personal and collective characteristics like confidence, leadership, honesty and generosity that reflect Dani cultural and political aspirations. Yet students are singled out by Indonesian students and lecturers in ways that emphasize their supposedly inferior intellectual and linguistic capabilities, attempt to embarrass them or put them ill at ease, and racialize them as being of the 'stone age'. Students face technocratic racism that emphasizes their supposed inability to successfully gain 'human resource' skills and knowledge and is perpetuated through bureaucratic structures, procedures and personnel. For example, prevailing racial formations inhibit students from creating alliances or networks with Indonesian lecturers and staff, which forces them to struggle on their own through bureaucratic procedures and also renders them more vulnerable to administration 'fees' as well as financial demands from some lecturers. There is tension between views of education – are Papuans just at university to 'buy their diploma' (*beli ijazah*) and return home quickly to 'fill up' positions in the rapidly expanding public service?

This chapter adds to my discussion of 'diminishment': first, we can see that students' alliances with Indonesians that are essential to successful navigation of university are hampered by racialized stigma. It is not just a matter of students experiencing feelings of inadequacy, but networks in which they would like to participate are also made small. Diminishment can shape social relations and networks, not just experiences. Second, diminishment has been mostly discussed by other scholars in relation to historical, foreign-led encounters like colonialism and missionization (Clark 2000; Robbins 2004, 2005), but this chapter shows diminishment in the context of contemporary Dani encounters with the Indonesian state. Unlike the occasional foray that occurs in Wamena, like the villagers' visit to the Office of Statistics described earlier, the bureaucratic campus environment presents an intensive, daily context for the formation of, and confrontation with, racialized hierarchies. Dani networks are consolidated through this shared experience, but ultimately, money for fees, bribes and other supplies may be the only way for students to overcome racial barriers and get their degrees. Third, in this chapter we see a range of affective experiences related to encounters with Indonesians, not just shame/shyness (*malu*). Racialized hierarchies also generate feelings of frustration, stress and anger.

The Universities

As I outlined earlier, the National University of Manado (Unima) is situated amidst banana palms, cornfields and Lake Tondano, 40 kilometres uphill from Manado past the volcanic Mt. Lokon. In the local social geography beyond the campus, horticulturalists dominate the hills while rice-growers surround the lake; on university grounds, a small population of local Indonesians operate shops, boarding houses and churches.

Unima was originally a teacher-preparation college (*Perguruan Tinggi Pendidikan Guru*) built in 1955. From 1965 to 2000, the institute was called IKIP Manado. It became Unima in 2000. In 2005, according to government records, it had a student population of just over 11,000, with 900 academic staff. Since 2000, Unima has offered a variety of nonteaching degrees, but it still maintains some teacher-oriented programmes. Students choose whether they want a bachelor's degree in Education (in their chosen faculty) or a 'pure' bachelor's degree.

Some students at Unima are from rural areas of North Sulawesi province, but most students from Minahasa regency prefer to attend more prestigious institutes. Besides Papuans, significant numbers of migrant students at Unima come from nearby regions such as the Sangir-Talaud Islands, Central and Southeast Sulawesi, and the Maluku Islands. The student population is more diverse than the staff population. Most of the lecturers and other staff at Unima are locals or Minahasan.

The campus of Sam Ratulangi University (Unsrat), by contrast, occupies a hillside not far from central Manado with views of the beach and its newly developed boulevard of shops and eateries. Spacious, multilevel buildings with glassless windows house many of the faculties at Unsrat. Rooms are furnished with heavy wooden chairs and desks. White tile and stucco predominates. Around campus, enthusiastic players occupy soccer fields. Banners proclaim upcoming events, offer motivational slogans or welcome visiting conference attendees. Many students live in the hilly neighbourhood that surrounds Unsrat (Sario), where trudging up slippery dirt tracks yields majestic views of the city and the ocean.

In 2005, Unsrat had over 1,700 academic staff members, 800 administrative staff members, 15,000 students and ten faculties. Using statistics provided by the university, it was possible to estimate the number of student migrants and their province of origin based on where they graduated high school. Based on 2008 figures, just under half of Unsrat students were migrants from outside North Sulawesi. Approximately 700 students enrolled at Unsrat completed high school in Papua province. The next most common provinces of origin based on high school graduation were Central Sulawesi (347 students), North Maluku (317 students) and Gorontalo (224 students). These figures corroborate the estimations of my Dani informants.

Academic and administrative staff members at Unsrat are primarily people from North Sulawesi. The ethnic composition of campus is relevant to experiences of discrimination described by Dani students later in this chapter. At Unsrat, it is not as if Dani students are the only migrants in an environment thoroughly dominated by local students from North Sulawesi. Dani students join significant numbers of student migrants from around the region, particularly the Maluku Islands and Central Sulawesi. Yet what Dani students describe is far from a celebration of diversity or a cultural exchange among educated, enthusiastic youth.

Most students are engaged in four-year bachelor programmes, though there are also some in shorter diploma programmes and a handful in graduate programmes. Students are required to complete courses, undertake a community service component, prepare a research proposal and present it for examination by a supervisory panel, conduct research (which many decide to do back in Papua), write up their data in a thesis and pass final oral examinations for graduation. These are the mechanical (and bureaucratic) milestones through which students seek to achieve educational goals.

Good Hands, Good Heart: Dani Human Resources

Education goals are shaped by current political conditions, stigmatization and highland cultural ideals. Minke, a female Dani student from Wolo who was studying Economics at her brother-in-law's behest, gave political, cultural and structural reasons why education is essential and challenging:

> Because of all the new regencies coming down we have to fill up the positions. We have to provide a good example for others. Everyone in Papua is disappointed, regretful [*menyesal*]. The young ones do not want to go to school, they are unemployed, and they drink too much. We have to impress upon them that they cannot do this, and they must go to school. We have to progress them [*kasih maju*], they still wear *koteka* [penis gourd], but people must go to school. We have to go forward in order to achieve independence [*merdeka*]. (Minke)

As this comment suggests, the overwhelming reason why students say they undertake higher education (*kuliah*) is to contribute to transformation back home. Students say they feel very strongly that their families and friends live difficult lives in a difficult (*susah*) place. She also mentions new regencies that have been created through government decentralization agendas. Under special autonomy, Indigenous Papuans are supposed to have greater access to employment opportunities, such as in the new regencies to which Minke refers. Filling up the positions in the new regencies does not exactly convey a transformative political agenda, though for Minke and others, taking up employment is part of a broader project of Indigenous advancement that leads to independence from Indonesia. Education is a cultural and political agenda that reflects dreams of collective progress and amelioration of Indigenous disappointment with current conditions. The need to 'fill up the positions' in administrative roles reflects a technocratic rendering of education that is in tension with these other ambitions. Minke's explanation also speaks to the racialized funnelling of Papuans into public service roles rather than entrepreneurial or professional work that is typically done by Indonesians.

In line with the dominant technical renderings of development, one of the specific concepts that students employ to describe their educational goals is 'human resource development'. However, they extend and reshape the concept, incorporating pertinent political and cultural agendas:

> We want to become the human resources [*sumber daya manusia,* or SDM] for Papua. We want independence but right now there are not enough human resources. It's like this: if we have an exam, we have to prepare first, right? So if we want independence we have to prepare first. If people's SDM improves they will be more prepared. (Jally)

Jally's statement reflects a complex mix of technocratic racism and Papuan nationalism, as he implies, following dominant Indonesian views of Papuans' low 'SDM', that Papuans are not yet sufficiently skilled or knowledgeable to run their own country. At the same time, Indonesia envisions human resources who are patriotic, not machinating for independence. For Dani students, to be high-quality human resources means to have been educated at school, preferably beyond high school. A good human resource has good prospects for employment. The field of employment students most commonly associate with higher education is the public service. Within the public service, they predict that if they are good human resources, they will become high-level officials. Being good human resources also means being knowledgeable about subjects that can have a direct and positive impact in highlands Papua, such as economics, technology, social science, administration, agriculture, law, education, medicine and biology. Good-quality human resources, students say, are able to 'go into the field' (*turun lapangan*) and actually make progress happen. Those who are good human resources also understand and have experience with the state system of governance and can work on villagers' behalf to talk to officials, to get problems solved and to get state promises delivered. More broadly, good-quality human resources have particular personal characteristics that allow them to attain positions of high status in society. They are organized, polished and sophisticated. Good human resources are able to organize 'development', manage groups of people, organize large-scale events and speak eloquently in public meetings.

Both Indonesians and Papuans describe Papua as the most underdeveloped province with the poorest-quality human resources in the country. Rhetoric on human resources criticizes everything from Papuan cultures to alleged

Figure 4.1. Dorm room decorations may depict political views, represented by the Morning Star flag drawing, and Christian commitments. Photo by author

sexual habits. These terms and allegations have become part of the fabric of race relations in the highlands. From students' perspectives, they sometimes agree that Papua is low in human resources (SDM), saying, for example, 'People do not know anything', 'They are left behind' (*terbelakang*) or are simply 'lower' (*di bawah*). Polygynous marriage, clothing that is too traditional or too tattered, feeling afraid of authority figures or lacking confidence to speak in front of others, and lack of skill in the Indonesian language are all examples of practices and beliefs that are described by students, at times, as evidence of low human resource quality. Dani and other highlands students in North Sulawesi state that they are part of a movement of educated people who are aware of the SDM problem and are committed to improving the SDM. Even though they toy with ideas of highlanders' supposed cultural and other inadequacies, they are also adamant that the Indonesian government is responsible for poor-quality human resources in Papua. Indonesia, some explain, has employed a system of Education-in-stupidity (*pendidikan pembodohan*) to keep Indigenous people powerless. Dani students may even argue that they, not the government, are the true proponents of human resource development in the area because they have motivation, morals, ethics, discipline and a strong desire to help highlands communities.

Students associate education with improving their capacities to make good things happen for themselves and others:

> We want new experiences here, so we can take what is good back to Wamena. The human resources in Wamena are not good yet, and people do not know anything. We want to do everything, there is no electricity, people have no shoes, and everything is expensive because there is no road. (Laurence)

The education students want is also results-oriented, which is in tension with so-called 'opportunities' to fill up the bureaucracy back home. Students frequently say they want to go home with results (*hasil*) and expect to prove to others what they have learned by taking action 'in the field' (*di lapangan*). Among students, it is very common to talk about 'going into the field'. As they often remind each other, if they do not actually learn, it will be very obvious back in Wamena, where, as they describe it, they are expected to act as agents of transformation for rural villagers with high hopes. As Jally summarized, 'if we get out into the field [*turun lapangan*] and do not know anything, the people are going to laugh at us. They will say, look at this guy, he has a degree [*sudah sarjana*], and he cannot do anything'.

Specifically, they wish to learn about their chosen subjects and become experts in their respective disciplines. If they take more than about four years to complete their studies, many say their families will give up on them, hence they try to keep delays a secret. Although they have not completed their education, some express that they miss (*rindu*) West Papua so badly that they go home for a visit, but do not go to the highlands because they have nothing to show their families and other sponsors. Diana Glazebrook (2008) discusses similar feelings among Dani refugees living in Papua New Guinea who are reluctant to return home without results. There is a strong desire to deliver tangible benefits in Wamena and these desires are often situated in relation to the affective states of people back home:

> Over here we can learn more about managing time and discipline. Later on we can make things happen in Wamena. Like here at the dorm we built this volleyball court, well, it's like that, we get everyone enthusiastic and we just work hard and do it. We do it together so it's fun [*ramai*]. We put music on and roast some cassava. People back home work very, very hard but they do not see any results, they give up hope, the men just wander around. We want to see development in Wamena. (Edward)

> I want to finish quickly and try to become a civil servant because they are the only ones with a salary in Papua. My parents also want this. I am the only one from my village who is going to be a 'graduate' [*sarjana*] so I feel responsible. All the people in the village want a 'graduate'. (Lex)

Students feel responsible for transforming conditions of hopelessness. Lex's and Edward's statements also indicate that their dreams of education are shared among kin, villagers and others. Morality, technical skills and expertise, and democratic principles are not enough for Dani human resources; they must also demonstrate generosity, put the interests of the community above their own interests, be readily available to provide assistance 'in the field' and be honest about their capacities. In expressing a desire to create benefits for themselves and others, Dani students demonstrate the ongoing importance of certain values in the highlands. These values are associated with traditional leaders, who gained standing in the community in particular ways. Alua (2006: 154–56) identifies these as 'leadership qualities' associated with 'influential men' (*ap kaintek*, Dani language). Influential men, or big men, possess a 'good heart' (*etaiken hano*, Dani language), 'good hands' (*eki hano*, Dani language) and 'good voice' (*ane hano*, Dani language). As Jally suggested, students want to actually be able to gain skills and demonstrate their knowledge, not just manipulate perceptions to cover up a lack of knowledge. The desire to use education to benefit others is also the mark of a leader, and shows the ongoing importance of generosity in Dani culture (Hayward 1983) and the pursuit of status through 'making good things happen for others as well as for themselves and their children (or at the very least, making a good appearance of doing so)' (Zimmer-Tamakoshi 1997: 110). These aspirations challenge technocratic renderings of development that have so far been used by Indonesia to exclude and criticize Papuans.

Dreams of transforming conditions in the highlands are also dreams of political independence. This is another way in which students' education ambitions are different from those articulated by government officials. Students have a powerful sense of coming from a place where Indigenous rights are neglected, where only Indonesians are able to succeed, and where Indigenous people are treated with violence to such an extent that they may become extinct. Thus, it is political conditions that need to change. Etinus expressed this hope, saying: 'We need independence [*merdeka*]. It is the only way to survive and to create prosperity.' Students such as Etinus hope that through education, they will be able to transform political conditions, take power from Indonesians and some day achieve political independence so that Papuans may survive.

Trying to achieve these objectives is much more difficult than students initially imagine. An extensive, hierarchical educational bureaucracy promotes paperwork and patience more than scientific knowledge or intellectual development. Technological skills and expertise that professors demand are often not available to students. Superficial kinds of quality on offer do little to realize students' hopes of doing well 'in the field' back home. Graduation signals successful navigation of stigma, corrupt practices and shifting formal procedures, but not successful development of values and capabilities typically associated with quality SDM and modernity.

A Typical Day on Campus

The Yepmum dorm is rarely fully quiet, with all of its inhabitants asleep, and the front and back doors locked. Students may depart for classes as early as 7 am and return home as late as 7 pm. During the evening hours, students work in pairs or small groups on their assignments, watch the news on the small television in the living room or attend prayer meetings elsewhere on campus. For those without early-morning classes, late-night movies are a popular option. Before dawn, around 5 am, joggers depart for a morning run around campus. At dawn, just before 6 am, window shades begin creaking open, a radio is turned on and someone starts sweeping the floors. Shortly thereafter, brave students with early classes are dousing themselves with pails of cold water in the bathroom. Shrieking helps ease the discomfort.

In a typical day, most of the students living in the Yepmum dormitory eat, bathe, change out of old shorts and t-shirts into trousers and a clean, ironed shirt, and attend classes. Even though the dorm is located on campus, it takes

30–60 minutes to walk to some of the faculty buildings around the hilly terrain. Students typically arrive early and socialize while waiting for their lecturer. On average, once or twice a week students wait and no lecturer arrives to teach. Often this happens because not many students turned up to the previous class, so the lecturer cancelled or changed the time and place of the next class on the spot. Those students not in attendance find out by chance if they meet up with someone who has heard the news. Classes go on for one to two hours; often students are given an assignment to work on in the second hour. There are clearly periods of peak activity on campus, around exams and assignment deadlines. There is much more time when attendance is variably important, when assignments drag on and when the term comes to an abrupt end. Students typically say they are on holiday several weeks before the official end of the term.

At certain points during their degree programme, students experience a great deal of pressure to complete requirements, such as when they must prepare and present proposals for the research component of their degree or when they are preparing for their final examinations. Still, throughout their schooling, many are able to devote time to extracurricular student organizations, religious groups and political activism. In fact, for some, it is these activities that take up most of their time, lie at the heart of their schooling and fill in the contours of self-improvement when classroom lessons fall short.

One day, like many other days, I accompanied Minke and Ina to campus. The young women study in the Economics department, which is located in one of the buildings closer to Yepmum dorm, so our walk to class was only about half an hour. When we got there, we went upstairs to the second floor of the building, which is built around a large central courtyard. From this vantage point, we could see friends coming and going. There were approximately one hundred students in the courtyard; the hallways in front of the classrooms were also crowded. Minke and Ina called to their friends, who joined us where we waited. As 9 am approached, the crowd seemed to thin out, as students presumably went into their classrooms. Minke found some of her classmates waiting together for their instructor. No one was in the classroom yet, but, tired of standing, Minke and Ina went to sit down inside. The room was sparsely furnished with heavy, dark wooden desks. At around 9:30 am the instructor arrived. By this time, about ten students occupied the desks. The lecture began and students pulled out their notebooks. The instructor wrote notes on the chalkboard for students to copy in their notebooks. After about 30 minutes, the instructor asked the students to write her an assignment related to the lecture. They were given 30 minutes to write a business letter following the format provided. The teacher left for a while, then came back and sat at her desk. After about 45 minutes, the instructor asked the students to stop working on their assignments. She requested volunteers to tell the class how they had introduced their letters, what the main content was and how they had ended their letters. Some students said they were not finished, so she told them to finish at home and bring the letters next time. A few students gave examples using their letters. The students were told that class was over and we migrated to the canteen for fried banana with hot chili sauce (*sambal*) before walking home again.

Based on what students express, this is a very typical class at Unima. It is common to listen to the lecture, write notes and work on an assignment in class. Students also receive assignments to complete as homework and they undergo written examinations at various times throughout the year. At Unima, when students are in their third year of studies, they develop a research proposal that they present to a panel of professors for review. They spend a month or two preparing these proposals. Though they are supposed to field questions from the panel about their proposals during the review, based on what I observed, students do not answer questions or respond to professors' comments; they just listen to the professors and keep quiet. After the review, they carry out their research projects, which may be based on library research or on original field research. Preparing a thesis takes six months to a year. Theses must be submitted to the supervisor and approved by him or her. Once the thesis is submitted, students are scheduled to take part in their final programme examinations, normally held twice a year. After these examinations, they are permitted to apply to graduate and attend a graduation ceremony.

Figure 4.2. Examination panel, Unima. Photo by author

Figure 4.3. Student with his professor after his thesis examination, Unima. Photo by author

This is the process as it ideally should be, according to students and the university administration. However, Dani experiences are not characterized by steady academic progress, professional, productive interactions with campus staff or the sense that they are acquiring the skills and expertise that they seek.

Racialization on Campus

Dani students describe discrimination and stigmatization in a variety of ways. David Mellor (2003: 479) proposes that 'underlying all racism is an element of differential treatment of people because of their race'. One element of differential treatment that they frequently mention is the claim by professors that frizzy Papuan hair is not 'neat' (*rapi*), so it must be kept short. Nelly lamented: 'I used to have fabulous hair, it was long and my sister would braid it but I had this professor and she hated it and told me to get rid of it.' Albert, a Dani student, explained:

> You can tell who is actively studying and who is not based on their hair. All these guys with braided hair, they are not studying. Everyone who is studying must cut their hair off.

These students report being told by professors to cut their frizzy hair short, though I gather from others that sometimes this expectation also goes unstated. Wearing it in little braids or dreadlocks, known as *anyam* or *lingkar,* is not acceptable, even though students say that this is a tidy way to wear their hair. However, Indonesian students (male and female) are commonly seen with long hair. Comments directed at Papuan hair are likely to raise emotions, as hair has historically been asserted as a marker of racial difference between Papuans and Indonesians. Though Papuan hair does not resemble the shiny straight black hair seen on Indonesian television, Dani students express pride in their hair and often spend much time combing, oiling, braiding and otherwise 'caring for' (*pelihara*) their hair. A female student expressed to me that some Indonesians are envious of Papuan hair because Indonesian hair is too slippery to braid. Ina said: 'They pay a lot of money at the salon to get their hair done like ours.' It is thus considered insulting to have lecturers tell students to cut their hair short, a violation of a personal attribute that students argue is important to them and an example they often cite of how they may be treated differently from Indonesian students.

Students also experience discrimination from campus figures who assert that Papuans are 'backward' and slower than non-Papuans in their learning and study progress, an example of racism that operates through bureaucratic hierarchies. Edward, a Unima student, described one experience as follows:

> In my experience, they make comments about Papua but they do not actually know anything. The lecturer posed the question, 'Papuans own Freeport, Freeport is in Papua, so why is there no development, why is it so backwards there?' She asked for a Papuan student to answer. I said that Freeport is in Papua but it is more like Indonesia owns it, actually foreigners own it and the money goes to the headquarters. And she said, 'Oh so it's like that?' But I could tell she did not believe it, she was laughing a bit. I was confused, and then I just felt angry.

Lecturers, most of whom are local Minahasan people, stereotype Papuans as backward, even in front of other students. Edward suggests that the lecturer was trying to intentionally put Papuans down and to humiliate him personally. Lecturers and staff on campus do frequently question Dani students about how long they have been studying and encourage them to finish quickly. Edison added: 'They say we take too long to finish our studies because we are dumb. The lecturers are always saying this, on campus, and telling us not to waste our money, to finish quickly.' On one such occasion that I observed, an official in the main office at Unsrat asked a student what business he had being in the offices on campus, what semester he was in and what part of Papua he was from. Upon hearing that the student was from Wamena, he replied: 'Wamena students have the most difficulties. They take a very long time to finish.' Informants say that this type of exchange is typical. The way that the student mumbled a response while averting his eyes suggested that he was uncomfortable with this line of questioning.

Students also experience racism from other students, who act out myths of alleged intellectual inferiority and body odour. Local Indonesian students make it obvious that they do not wish to sit next to Papuans. They laugh and whisper, which makes students uncomfortable. Dani students are denigrated or teased by other students. Herbert recounted: 'Once a student brought a penis gourd to campus and laughed at us. They asked us if we eat humans and all this sort of stuff.' In a different example, Jill reported: 'I had a fistfight with these girls because they said that Papuans are dumb and do not know how to speak Indonesian.' Students say this kind of assertion makes them particularly upset because they regard their Indonesian language skills as quite good compared to the way Manadonese and others speak colloquial Indonesian. Bahasa Manado, as we have seen with phrases like 'Torang samua basudara' rather than the standard Indonesian, 'Kita semua bersaudara', comes with different words, accent and style of speech. Moreover, the Indonesian language is relatively new in the Papuan highlands; most students' grandparents know a few words only and converse entirely in Indigenous languages. With the exception of a few males who were the first to experience formal education in the highlands, most of the first generation did not learn the Indonesian language in school, but learned it from their children as they progressed through the school system starting in the 1980s. Students know from their older siblings and cousins that it was difficult to learn Indonesian when few of their parents could speak it. Learning Indonesian is symbolic of a particular commitment to modernity, alongside formal education more generally, and for students is an example of the desire for progress among highlanders. When students are accused of not knowing Indonesian, they experience this as another critique on their level of progress and a denial of the structural conditions that they and others have struggled against in order to learn to speak proper Indonesian. Indonesian students from outside North Sulawesi may experience similar instructions from lecturers to learn the particular Indonesian slang spoken locally, but assertions made about Papuans link language skills to alleged poor intellect and racial inferiority.

Another way in which students experience discrimination is when they are stereotyped as separatists who are not loyal to the Indonesian nation. For example, Petrus reminded me:

Yesterday, you saw Jenny, after the exam one of the professors just came up to a group of us and said so do you support [Papuan] independence? We just looked at him and did not know what to say. He laughed a little bit and then he walked off.

I witnessed the encounter described by Petrus. A smiling professor had approached a small group of Dani students and immediately demanded to know whether they supported independence, using the gloss 'M' for 'merdeka'. His demeanour was conversational, even friendly, but students looked stunned at his boldness and nervous about his question. Although the professor seemed to be joking, teasing or looking for a reaction (perhaps like the government official mentioned earlier who gave a racist speech at a graduation ceremony), students and the majority of authority figures they encounter in North Sulawesi take the issue of having potential 'separatists' in their midst quite seriously. Students do not want to be stigmatized as worthy of suspicion, as perennial outsiders, or for refusing to conform to Indonesian values of patriotism, regardless of their actual feelings about independence. They say they want to form good relations with local Indonesians during their education, but being stigmatized as separatists because of their racial appearance as Papuans positions them as outsiders deserving of scrutiny and suspicion. Stigma challenges the image they want to build of themselves as good students who deserve to be treated like everyone else.

'[R]outine questioning and disparagement of black people's intelligence' (Foster 2005: 493) are common experiences for Dani students. Kevin Foster (2005: 494) concludes: 'Institutional racism describes the collective effect of acts, policies, unwitting prejudice and the invocation of stereotypes that sustain an atmosphere which is hostile to the full participation and success of racial minorities.' Dani students' comments provide evidence of 'unwitting prejudice and the invocation of stereotypes' (Foster 2005: 494) by lecturers and other staff. Women and men both experience racism, though it seems that racial logics more often invoke symbols of 'primitive' masculinity (like the penis gourd) or are used to confront men, and relate to accusations of violence or political resistance.

Campus Quality: Power through Procedures

Lyn Parker (2003: 226) suggests that school is a 'physical construct at the outer reaches of a long, hierarchical and extensive education bureaucracy that is also an integral part of people's lives' in Indonesia. Dani students also propose that interacting with administrators and conforming to bureaucratic procedures is an influential part of their education abroad. Although not what students are seeking and not the kind of vision of education put forward by the Indonesian government, which describes technical capacities, moral development and commitment to key values such as democracy and peace, facing down Indonesian bureaucrats, following obscure and malleable regulations, and writing letters are some of the forms of expertise that come to define the education that students gain abroad and ultimately influence their contributions to 'progress' back home.

Schooling provides in-depth experience of the idiosyncrasies of Indonesian institutions and convoluted administrative procedures. Bureaucratic procedures bring students into interactions with campus figures on a regular basis. In most of these situations, students are requesting assistance that may have a significant impact on their academic achievement. Students describe their experiences using terms such as 'stress' (*stres*), 'impossible' (*setengah mati*, literally, 'half dead') and 'dizzying' (*bikin pusing*). Some students become experts at navigating the university bureaucracy, typically after several years in school and after receiving wisdom from other Dani who are ahead of them in the process. They are kept busy at certain times in the year helping other students with administrative objectives, but look at it as an achievement, and enjoy having their skills recognized by others. It is a mark of senior status and an achievement in terms of self-development to have learned how to register, how to reenrol every semester, how to get a new student card each year or how to get accepted into the required classes. More complex achievements include helping students pass courses for which they have not successfully completed the requirements or negotiating payment at the end of the semester instead of the beginning.

Still, despite these moments of prowess, students express that they often feel out of place in their campus' head office. Their experiences encourage them to question themselves and to question why they sometimes receive rude treatment from administrative staff. As I observed at Unsrat, Dani students would run into friends in the foyer down the stairs from the administrative offices, discuss their problems and go up together. They would enter with a clear purpose in mind, but often emerge confused and with nothing accomplished. Exiting the head office, they reported that what they wanted to do required more money, or involved a requirement they did not know of, or required a letter from somewhere else on campus first, or the correct person to help them was not in the office, and they might be in any time from after lunch to next week. On occasion, there was no problem, but the reaction of the staff behind the glass-enclosed counter made students feel like they were mistaken, at which point they left to think more about what they needed to do. One senior student, Paulus, for example, came out of the Unsrat head office one day and said to me: 'I am confused. I thought I wanted to pay my registration fee, but when I asked the staff made an ugly face, like they did not understand. I do not care anymore; I will come back tomorrow and try again.'

Anton: 'They Have Dollar Signs in Their Eyes'

On the morning of 5 September 2006 a normally shy Anton came crashing out of the bathroom at his dorm in Manado, drunk, smiling, talkative and apologizing to those present, including myself, for his condition. It seemed to me that Anton and his friends had been drinking heavily, singing and playing cards for days. His friends said he was suffering from 'stress', which in Indonesia conveys that a person has been pushed beyond their coping capacity. Soon after Anton 'stressed', he and his friends packed up and disappeared to Tondano for a week.

Anton was supposed to take his final exams in May 2006, but his family was too late sending money, so he missed the examinations. Anton was then told that there were not enough students ready for final examinations from his faculty to warrant holding a final examination. At his university, as is common in Indonesia, final exams are conducted orally. Having completed coursework and thesis requirements, students meet with five to seven lecturers who each question them for 5–15 minutes. These are normally held in a group setting in a large classroom where long tables are set up in such a way that professors sit in a row on one side of the table and students queue for seats adjacent to professors. Each professor will ask the student a few questions and test them on his or her subject material. The professor then signs the student's examination paperwork. This interaction is repeated until students have enough signatures. Thus, despite having completed his requirements, he waited over four months for the university to provide him with a final examination so that he could finally graduate, seven years after starting his undergraduate programme. Each month, from June to September 2006, he was told that the examination would be held soon.

During this period of time, Anton's family in Wouma, a village on the outskirts of Wamena, was in constant contact with him through his mobile phone. They reminded him that they had spent a lot of money on his education and were eager for him to graduate and return home. Eventually, Anton announced to his friends in Manado that he was writing a letter to the administration begging for a final examination. It was held three weeks later. Anton explained to me some of his feelings about the process. He had not been able to attend the examination in May, he said, because he had no money. It is expected, he clarified, that students give an 'envelope' (*amplop*) containing 100,000–500,000 rupiah (equivalent to about US$10–50) to their professor in order to take part in the exam and get a good result. This experience was the last in a series of frustrating encounters with the university bureaucracy. As Anton described:

> When I was preparing my thesis I paid my professor some money so he would review my draft. I did not hear from him for a long time. Then I found out from other students that the university had changed the procedure. They gave my thesis to another professor so I had to start again with the 'bonuses' . . . All the students know, if you do not pay the professor or you pay very little you will get a slow response. If you want to get a good grade you must give a bonus. A good thesis or assignment will get you a 'B' or a 'C' but if you want an 'A' you need to pay.

These experiences lead Anton and others to assert that people who work on campus have *mata uang* or 'dollar signs in their eyes', because they are always thinking of how to leverage financial gain from students.

Students thus say they are expected, and sometimes directly asked, to give money to lecturers and administrators in the following situations: to receive a final result in a class or to receive an 'A' grade; following a research proposal seminar or oral examination; for their supervisor to look at, give advice on or mark a thesis in progress; to organize an examination, thesis submission, graduation, diploma or work experience placement; and, finally, to get an office worker to write a letter (and get it signed by the appropriate authorities) or to get a student identity card. Letters are particularly annoying for students. Letters, usually needing to be signed by several officials, are required to transmit information between campus departments, faculties and officials. Besides having to go through all of the 'face work' (Rawski 1999: 185) to get the letters signed by the right people, students say they also have to pay a variable amount for *administrasi*. The more they pay, the 'lighter' (*ringan*, as opposed to *berat*, heavy or cumbersome) and 'quicker' the task becomes.

Minke's Computer Lessons: Frustration and Indifference

Minke, born in the Wolo Valley, came to Sulawesi through the support of her eldest sister and her sister's husband. Her father is a preacher with the Evangelical Church of Indonesia and he runs a small church. Both of her older sisters dropped out of school and got married. Minke moved to Wamena for junior high school, living with a nurse next to the hospital, for whom she performed cleaning and housekeeping duties in exchange for room and board. She said she dropped out of high school for a while when her friends started dropping out. Her parents were angry with her, she recalled, and they threatened to marry her off in the village to a local man. At that point she asserted that: 'I do not want to hold a shovel, I want to hold a ballpoint pen.' Her older sister convinced her parents that she must go to university. As Minke remembered it, her sister said to them: 'Even if she is dumb, she should go to university.' 'So here I am!' she exclaimed.

Minke had been at Unima in Tondano for about two years. She heard that Manado was a good city from her sister's husband, who graduated from Unima, and from a group of former students in Wamena: 'They said, the courses are good and you will get away from this environment in Papua, where people are drunk and quitting school. At Unima there is much spirituality [*rohani*], there is worship every day, and discussions and organizations where you can stand up in front of people and improve your confidence. When you return you will be respected and have the authority to tell people what to do.'

Minke came home to the dorm in Tondano one day, exasperated, and said that her lecturer expected her to learn computers for his Economics class, but he only took them into the computer lab once. In order to practise on her own, she would have to pay by the hour to use the computers on campus. Even if she did pay money to practise, she was not clear what to do in the lab, since one lesson from a lecturer who himself did not use a computer on a regular basis was not enough to comprehend the concept of a computer, let alone master the use of a keyboard, mouse, and English-language software and operating system. There was a female staff member in charge of collecting money for computer usage who sometimes helped students learning to use the computer and was not terribly strict with charging them by the hour. This relationship encouraged some students to test out the computer lab, particularly those who wanted to take computer courses but were afraid to enrol and then fail. The stakes were high: some programmes required students to demonstrate computer skills in order to graduate. Minke's older cousin Etinus had managed to purchase a computer with some funding from his extended kin in Wamena. She was allowed to go to his house to practise, but the electricity supply in his shack on campus was not sufficient or stable enough to run a computer – even Etinus was reluctant to use it for his most critical assignments for fear of ruining the computer or starting a fire.

Minke marvelled at how Indonesian students all seemed to know how to use the computer, not just for typing assignments, but for other things she did not quite understand – 'They are just used to it', she would explain. Besides the main computer lab, there were other locations at Unima where students could use the internet. Many Dani students were aware of their locations, but never went there themselves. In Manado a few Dani students were known to have mastered the use of a computer and they were constantly in demand by others who wanted to learn from someone they knew. Minke said: 'I have to master [*kuasai*] this thing otherwise I will fail my class, but it is so hard. Nobody can help me do it, and we feel afraid to go into places like that when we don't know what to do, they will think we are stupid, I am embarrassed.' At the end of that semester, Minke did drop out of school – her heart was not in it and, as she said, it was all just 'impossible, and makes me just not care [*bikin malas*]'.

Becoming savvy with technology, namely computers, is promoted by the government as an important part of education and human resource development for Indonesia's young generation. The National Institute of Sciences (LIPI) articulates a primary focus on *Iptek* (*ilmu pengetahuan dan teknologi* or science and technology) – an acronym that is popular among university students who associate themselves with an emerging revolution in technology. In their speeches and formal discussion groups, Dani students identify themselves as part of the new *Iptek* generation. Indonesian views accuse Papuans of lacking technological skills, yet students confront structural conditions that make it very difficult to acquire this expertise. The effort from the instructor seems negligible, the campus housing power supply is not sufficient to support a computer, and Papuan students may feel embarrassed and uncomfortable to go to a campus computer lab and be exposed as not knowing how to use the computer in front of Indonesians precisely because they are racialized as inept. The stigma of being considered *bodoh* (dumb) by local Indonesians constrains Minke as she avoids a situation where Indonesians may see her in this light.

Laurence: No Dreadlocks Allowed

When Laurence was in semester four, he did not have any money to pay the fees, so he took a leave of absence (*cuti*). As he explained, this was the start of his administrative problems: 'If you take a leave of absence you have to pay for that time off, even if it is two or three semesters. If you are absent for that long though, they will likely not accept you back unless you pay a large bribe. If you do not pay then they cancel your program and you have to start over.' Laurence was active in student politics, frequently organizing and participating in demonstrations about social justice issues alongside other Papuans and Indonesians in Manado. He said that because of these experiences, he was not intimidated by authority figures. He said that it is common for Papuan students to feel embarrassed to confront authority figures, but that this tendency holds Papuans back from achieving their potential. As a result, he expressed that it is important to him to speak his mind to professors.

Laurence said that in a number of instances throughout his time at Unsrat, he had encountered problems with his professor and one of the assistant deans. The problem started when he challenged the professor who told him to cut his hair if he wanted to remain a student:

> When I reported to the Dean's Third Assistant that I was ordered to leave class by my professor because my hair was in dreadlocks, he did not support me. He reported back to my professor. My profes-

sor, on another occasion, demanded money from me as payment for marking my assignment. I refused and also reported this to the Dean's Third Assistant. My professor must have been told about this report because he came back to me and said that I would never graduate. He said, 'Just wait until you want to have your final exams!' After this I felt that I could not possibly succeed in my department unless I had money to smooth everything over. They would inhibit my progress. So I wanted to change to Stisipol [the Institute for Social and Political Studies located in Manado], even though some of us think that place is not really a legitimate school because too many people reportedly just pay money and get through their requirements quickly. So I felt forced to change to Stisipol even though the quality there is poor. But then in order to do that I needed to get a letter of permission and explanation from my professor and the Dean's Third Assistant to give to the new school and transfer my credits. But they do not want to give me such a letter. So, I thought, I am tired [*malas*] of dealing with these people, so I just went and had a stamp made and wrote the letter myself. It is a very common practice for teachers to ask for money, sometimes it is not too much, and we are used to it, but when they are really bad and threaten this and that and make us keep waiting and waiting for every little thing, well a person could really lose it. This has happened to other students. Look around, there are many who are not actively studying, because once you get into trouble it is hard. Other students just pay and that solves the problem but you know our parents are just farmers, we do not have money like that.

These cases highlight experiences of technocratic racism, administrative corruption and delays that inhibit students' progress, as well as bribery and discrimination. The intense campus environment throws racialized tensions and hierarchies into relief as students are confronted with the views of Indonesian students, lecturers and administrative staff. Anton's case raises the issue of bribery and the freedom that professors and administrators have to determine fees and to demand 'bonuses'. According to students, the time and effort one must put into successfully completing university can vary depending on one's ability to pay. In one of my favourite comments, a student named Etta explained: 'Everyone is treated the same . . . whoever has money can finish quickly.' It is possible, students said, to 'buy your diploma' (*beli ijazah*).[1] In general terms, this means that it is possible for some students to skim through their programme requirements because they pay to get passing grades, to skip a few courses or to avoid delays that other students deal with. One student reported that a university staff member said that he supported this practice because he was sympathetic to the extreme need for human resources in Papua.

Moreover, some lecturers perceived Papuan students to have funds available to buy a diploma precisely because of new regencies and decentralization funds in Papua. They could ask for more money, or ask for money even if they normally would not. Thus, the objective of 'filling up the positions' in local governments in Papua, coupled with racial views of Papuans as intellectually inferior, promoted discriminatory practices like asking for bribes. Undoubtedly some students take advantage of this system, but the majority of Dani students view the need for favours, friends and patronage as a huge obstacle to academic progress, and one that interferes with their ability to actually learn about their chosen subjects. Laurence felt forced to switch to a lower-quality institution because he complained about racist treatment and bribery, and was therefore threatened by his supervisor, who asserted that he would never allow him to graduate.

Crossing an authority figure is glossed as 'creating a problem (*bikin masalah*). If a student complains to a higher authority, nothing happens. Moreover, the lecturer may be informed and may retaliate. As Gigi said, 'whoever makes trouble with a lecturer will definitely slow down his/her progress'. It is typical for students to have one main lecturer who is assigned as their advisor for the entire period of their programme. As lecturers are public servants, they are hired for a guaranteed term of at least five years. Students cannot manoeuvre around disgruntled staff, and some transfer to other institutes if they want to finish their degrees.

Procedures and formalities become part of an economy of favours, friends and enemies where formal codified procedures are used in ways that reflect prevailing racial and social logics, as well as the personal objectives of staff. In this economy, perceptions, appearances and impressions mean everything. Cutting one's hair, wearing a collared shirt and trying to exude confidence (or submissiveness) are all potential strategies for shaping the way one is perceived by others. Campus figures are primarily local Indonesians who hold certain stereotypes about Papuans: not tidy enough, irresponsible with money, separatists, drunks and intellectually slow. The interesting thing about the experiences of Dani students is that it may not be the official routines of bureaucracy that most challenge them, but the 'more localized social values' (Herzfeld 1993: 4) that influence the way in which procedures are invoked by campus staff. Networks, personal friendships, heritage and appearances all have an influence on the extent to which campus figures enforce or create rules and procedures. To say that this situation reflects contingency is correct; to say that it is totally arbitrary would ignore the local racial and social logics that shape decisions and interactions. Moreover, bureaucratic and campus scenes that evoke 'primitiveness', alleged inferiority and political threat are part of an already racialized and stigma-rich social context.

The general perception campus figures have of Papuan students puts these students at a disadvantage to begin with. They are perceived as intellectually slow, undisciplined, unsophisticated (lacking in so-called neat hair and attire) and as possibly wanting to use their education against rather than for Indonesia. The stigma attached to being Papuan, and existing far outside the local network of elites and power brokers, inhibits developing relationships with campus staff and officials, so the only alternative is to use money to foster such relationships and to ease the burden of campus bureaucracy. In 2009 a new policy was introduced to combat the common problem of professors writing students' theses for them (Tombeng 2009). The new policy, rather than banning those activities, formalizes such 'collaborations' and supports the publication of theses with university funds in order to prevent behind-the-scenes transactions. Under the new policy, a professor is permitted to assist up to four students with thesis research and writing. This policy confirms statements made by Dani students that those with enough money, leverage or personal connections can access special academic support.

On campus, students find that some of their education objectives are difficult to achieve. Minke's case shows that professors promote and expect certain ideal skills without offering any way for students to achieve them. When studying is already a tangled web of formal and informal financial expectations, arrangements, deals and delays, unrealistic expectations can push students over the edge, out of university altogether or into various states of what they call *stres*.

University education appears less prestigious when viewed from the inside, where students discover an economy of friends, favours and enemies. From their descriptions, rather than gaining tangible skills and experiences that might allow them to become human resources, improve their quality or transform the Papuan highlands, they are overwhelmed by the need to navigate the education system from positions of vulnerability caused in part by racism and stigma. In terms of navigating bureaucracy, procedures, paperwork and academic authorities, they become well equipped for particular roles and activities back home, and there is no doubt that time in North Sulawesi imparts certain styles of management, administration and governance. Specific academic programmes and lessons merely form the backdrop for these more significant challenges and occasional triumphs. Dani forays into urban cosmopolitanism, multiculturalism and more Indonesian affiliations are cut short. Experiences of stigmatization and vulnerability, including fears of violence, are formative in shaping Dani preferences for the company of other Wamena people and consolidating Dani networks. Given that together Dani and Lani are the majority cultural groups in Papua province (Ananta et al. 2016: 460), shared experiences of racialization and being cut out of Indonesian networks may significantly affect ethnic relations and other social and political dynamics in West Papua.[2]

Notes

1. Lee (1999) reports that bribing professors and administrators to obtain a diploma also occurs in Maluku.
2. The 2010 census captured ethnic self-identifications, but there is still some blurring of categories that may have resulted in the inclusion or exclusion of central highlanders. For example, the 'Dani' category includes Dani/Ndani, Lani, Lani Barat and Lani Lembah (Ananta et al. 2014: 49). There is a separate Hupla code that could possibly be a reference to Hubula, a term that some Valley Dani use (see the discussion in Chapter 1).

5
Belonging, Expertise and Conflict in Highlanders' Social World Abroad

Dani students are not incorporated into Indonesian society in North Sulawesi in any clear-cut fashion, and racialization hampers efforts to build relationships that could facilitate cultural mixing and new regional or national identities. Can deterritorialization from home take place if migrants cannot develop deep connections to their new place? For students, intensified connections and identities with other central highlanders mitigate against deterritorialization. This chapter focuses on what happens instead of new connections, or while once hoped-for affiliations are still beyond reach. It documents how highlanders connect with other highlanders in the absence of deep new connections in Manadonese society, and also what divisions and tensions arise. Education abroad not only confers experiences of shame or frustration, but, against the odds, pride and confidence. The close-knit social world of central highlanders in North Sulawesi provides cultural continuities and a strong sense of identity. Dani students live together, study together, go out and about (*jalan-jalan*) together, and sometimes get married and have children together. If on-campus dynamics facilitate Dani understandings of the hierarchical and discriminatory workings of Indonesian bureaucracies, and the power of money to ameliorate discrimination from lecturers and administrators, the highlanders' world in North Sulawesi heightens and affirms important cultural sensibilities. It is not cut off from Indonesians, but responds to and partially ameliorates conditions of stigma, poverty and insecurity. Interactions with Indonesians provide Dani with a strengthened awareness of their own cultural expectations and values. Students pursue goals of personal and collective improvement in a highlanders-only context via their student organizations.

There are tensions and divisions amidst common goals and circumstances, in particular around men's alcohol consumption and leadership roles. Distinctions between 'Valley' and 'Western' Dani come back to the fore in North Sulawesi. Dani struggle to achieve and maintain their own expectations of appropriate behaviour in light of being stigmatized as 'drunken', 'primitive' and 'promiscuous' by Indonesians and, perhaps to a lesser but still important extent, coastal Papuans. Highlanders try to regulate one another's behaviour for the sake of maintaining a 'good name' – their own or someone else's – and they use a loose kinship system comprised of elder and younger siblings. This chapter reveals how students feel they change because of schooling abroad, both in terms of improvements to their abilities and because challenging conditions may also produce the opposite: a sense of deterioration, disempowerment and lost capabilities. If anything, the migration of Dani students reveals that a militarized, 'underdeveloped' and politically tense West Papua offers more of a sense of belonging than the 'developed', peaceful and stable cities of Indonesia so long as there is a Dani community to join. These experiences of connection, identification and networking are formative for highlanders, who are the most numerous, politically active and mobile Indigenous in Tanah Papua.

'Mountain People' and Coastal Papuans

Most highlanders in North Sulawesi have social lives that revolve around other self-identified highlanders, or, even more narrowly, with people from their extended family or clan alliance. Dani, Lani and Yali also refer to themselves as highlanders (*orang gunung*, meaning 'mountain people') and differentiate themselves from coastal Papuans (*orang pantai*). These differentiations are at least partially rooted in colonial declarations about the 'primitiveness' of highlanders relative to coastal Papuans (see Chauvel and Bhakti 2004; Rutherford 2012), but continue to be reworked in relation to present-day politics. Not long after moving into the Dani dorm in Tondano, I met a student from Biak, a large island off the north coast of Papua, who told me in front of the Dani man who had accompanied me that day: 'If you want to learn about culture you should ask the kids from Wamena, they are still backward.'

However, for Wamena people, being highlanders is associated with a strong communal ethic, garden labour and humility:

> Highlanders are obliged to help each other out. We cannot just take care of ourselves individually and leave our friends to their fate. That is why we say, we all go forward [*maju*] or none of us go forward. It is us kids of farmers that really want to study and work for Papua. The kids of the bosses [*bos-bos*, meaning wealthy people like landowners, entrepreneurs and higher-status politicians and civil servants] do not care because they have money. They come here to North Sulawesi as well, and we see them playing around. Many quit school and many, many go home. (Lavinia)

> We are different from other Papuans because we are farmers. Look, not one of us has soft [*halus*] hands, and wherever we go, we garden [*kerja kebun*]. Our elders say God gave you two hands and two feet, now get to work. You will not see us walking around wearing expensive things and showing off [*pasang gaya*]. (Jhon)

These self-characterizations reiterate students' roots in the highlands. They identify themselves with a strong work ethic and ability to sacrifice and suffer to get what they want. Wamena students frequently argue that they are hardworking farmers and that they accept and acknowledge obligations to share and take care of each other that they do not see amongst other Papuans. There is thus quite a bit of pride about being from Wamena that persists in spite of contexts of stigma and shame.

Relations among groups of Wamena people are close – like extended families, they move freely between residences, move about town together and express feeling obliged to assist one another. They spend the vast majority of their time together, either on or off campus. When clothes, toiletries and food may be shared, 'home' is a loosely defined place. If a female student visits her friend's residence after classes, she probably changes out of her campus wear – jeans, a clean or new-looking shirt or blouse – and borrows short trousers and an old shirt for cooking, lounging around, playing volleyball and sleeping. To bathe she will take her friend's *mandi* bucket (a plastic scoop to douse oneself while bathing), which usually contains a bar of soap, a toothbrush and perhaps shampoo, and will borrow a towel. It is equally common for male students to visit a Dani friend, or even an acquaintance, take a nap, eat, bathe and borrow a clean shirt before leaving. Besides living together, and attending classes and

Figure 5.1. Students at a soccer match featuring Persiwa, the team of Wamena, in Manado. Photo by author

extracurricular activities together, students also go shopping together, work in gardens together, wash clothes together, attend church together and keep each other informed of news from Wamena and elsewhere.

These practices show supportive, positive relations in contrast to relations with local Indonesians, or even other Papuans, that cannot be relied upon. Even students who do not know each other well are able to place each other in a network of kin and friends, and feel some obligation to help each other out. One main feature of student relations is the dominance of the 'elder sibling' (*kakak*)–'younger sibling' (*adik*) relationship. This is a hierarchical relationship of expectations and obligations that applies to all students regardless of kinship relations, and a relationship that is ultimately used to try to control and police behaviour in a stigma-rich setting. 'Elder siblings' are expected to be good examples, to take responsibility for 'younger siblings' and to assist them to be worthy of respect and status. Male and female 'younger siblings' should heed advice and do chores. While in traditional Dani gender conceptions, women are in some way or another regarded as junior to men, in North Sulawesi this is not the case because there are women who are regarded as senior due to their status and achievements.

For 'elder' and 'younger' siblings, it is difficult to meet expectations. For instance, more senior students tend not to have much money to assist or take responsibility for a junior sibling. A senior student probably has the social resources to get money together in an emergency, such as sickness or hospitalization, but the irony is that most new students arrive in North Sulawesi with money they recently acquired in Wamena, and find themselves financially assisting or supporting senior students. Taking care of 'younger siblings' is important to students' sense of adulthood, is important for maintaining a good reputation back home and is a difficult, long-term task. Senior students speak about younger siblings who make them feel ashamed when they get into trouble or do not take education seriously.

Although being a good sibling is generally important, it is more important when the people involved are actually members of the same family or clan. 'Older siblings', in particular, are expected to control the behaviour of 'younger siblings' in order to maintain a good reputation with relatives back home. For women, who are far fewer in number and largely away from the watchful presence of kin, living abroad means trying to stay focused on school in spite of attention from men. This can be partly achieved by close relationships with male kin, but then these relationships might entail another set of obligations and expectations that could take time away from their studies. Minke's refrain, 'We are all students here', was deployed by most of the women I knew on a daily basis to refute the expectation that women should do the cooking and cleaning. Minke's mother, for instance, is the younger sister of Etinus' mother. Minke looked up to Etinus as an older brother and a source of protection, advice and assistance. Etinus helped Minke with the campus bureaucracy, lent her money at times and helped her with schoolwork. Minke sometimes cooked meals for Etinus and washed his clothes. Etinus was always kind to her, as she explained: 'I have many other "older brothers" here but if they are rude and order me around too much then I do not feel like helping them out.' As she frequently retorted when some male relatives at the dorm ordered her to wash the dishes or pick vegetables: 'We are all students here. I am a student too, so we all have to do the work.' When Minke decided to quit school, she was not worried for herself, but was concerned that her family would blame Etinus for not taking proper care of her.

Besides the respectfulness that is expected as part of the 'elder sibling' and 'younger sibling' dynamic, Wamena students consider politeness and deep social interaction to be important characteristics of being highlanders. Careful interactions form the basis of socializing and echo what goes on in Wamena. When they meet in the street, students approach slowly, they take a long time looking, placing the face, the name, the relationship. They greet each other with a handshake, except if they live in the same house or are close kin whom they see often. The level of enthusiasm of the greeting tells each person about the current state of the relationship – a big hug and a yell signals good friendship, while a half-hearted handshake may signal that someone is not pleased. They ask each other where they are going or where they have been. They ask about someone they heard was sick or in trouble. They exchange information about mutual friends. They talk about an upcoming meeting or event, or about some controversy. They promise to visit soon. All of this takes place on the roadside, in a bus, spontaneous, time-consuming and important: 'If Wamena people just see their friends and wave or say hello, we feel unsatisfied' (Jally).

Thus, relations among Wamena students are close, despite differences in clan affiliation, religion and residential patterns. They are each other's primary social contacts and sources of financial and emotional support. Even though they associate with coastal Papuans and Indonesians on campus, they spend most of their time with other members of the same extended family or culture area. One of the main ways in which they do this is in student organizations.

Discipline and Prowess: Student Organizations

Every time I visited the Dani women's dorm in Manado, I found a hub of activity. More often than not, this activity revolved around student organization productions rather than examinations or assignments. Two or three women would be huddled around Ana's computer (purchased by her older brother, a public servant in Jayapura) typing and printing the programme for an upcoming event or writing out the words to Christian songs so that the group could sing well together at the next prayer session. Two others would be heading out the door to distribute invitations, either simple pieces of paper folded in three or fancier versions wrapped in cellophane and sealed with a bow. Each invitation would be addressed to a particular individual or dormitory. Fundraisers took place almost every weekend.

These commitments offer insight into students' understandings and productions of 'quality', including attributes associated with 'human resources' (SDM), 'experience' (*pengalaman*), 'results' (*hasil*) and 'confidence' (*berani*). The quality to which students aspire incorporates ceremony and propriety as well as tangible, demonstrable skills of value. Student organizations also provide an arena to view social relations and conflict. If Dani students prefer to develop and demonstrate their capabilities without Indonesians around, what exactly do they do, and does stigma disappear? What are the consequences of shame and risks of 'failure' in front of other Wamena people?

Although I focus on highlanders, it is not only highlanders or Papuans who form student organizations. Other longstanding groups in Sulawesi include local branches of the National Indonesian Students Movement (GMNI) and, mentioned below, the Union of Catholic Students of Indonesia (PMKRI). Only a small number of Dani are involved in the PMKRI, but the organization does provide residence to those students in a dormitory in Manado and creates an opportunity for Catholic students to bond with Indonesians of the same faith. These groups have elaborate costumes and flags that they wear to marches and demonstrations or just to meetings. They also have their own anthems that they sing along with the Indonesian anthem at formal gatherings. The highlands students' groups tend to be more recently formed; they are also less well funded and have smaller membership bases.

Membership in the major student organizations is based on regency (*kabupaten*) of origin in the highlands, though there are also organizations based on religion; one group is made up of members of an extended family from Wolo village, north of Wamena. The Jayawijaya student's association (Rupmawi) is the longest-standing regency-based student organization in North Sulawesi. Before the regency of Jayawijaya, centred on Wamena, was divided up and new regencies formed, it was a massive group. The Manado and Tondano branches are run somewhat separately from each other. The main activities include Easter and Christmas celebrations, the annual induction of new members, which incorporates new student orientation activities, and formal group discussions. Catholic and Protestant students are part of this group; in cultural terms the group represents a spectrum of Dani from the 'Valley' and the 'West' as well as Yali students. The organization was founded when senior students realized that they needed a way to represent their interests both locally and to the regional government back home. Each year Rupmawi leaders distribute government scholarships to later-year students if their name is on the right list in Wamena. Distribution of scholarships is one of the main sources of conflict in the regency-based organizations. It is not always clear to students which organization they should be going to for their scholarships and their perspectives may conflict with government paperwork in the highlands. Rupmawi is often in a state of conflict due to tensions between Catholic and Protestant Dani.

Student groups are also formed on the basis of religious links. The Communication Forum of University Students of the Evangelical Church of Indonesia in North Sulawesi (FKPM-GIDI) and the Big Family of Catholic University Students of the Jayapura-Timika Diocese (KBMKKJ-T) are the two main religious groupings of Dani students. FKPM-GIDI is dominated by Dani students, but fundraisers and celebrations attract other Papuan students as well. The Big Family of Catholic Students covers students from the expansive Jayapura-Timika Diocese. The group used to be dominated by Wamena students, but many students also come from the Paniai and Merauke regions of Papua.

The AMPTPI (Association of Central Highlands University Students, Papua, Indonesia) is the newest student organization, formed in order to push political issues that highlander students feel strongly about. The founders feel that they have aspirations and agendas that differ from non-highlanders and that the province-based group, IMIPA, does not adequately represent them and is not interested in supporting political activism. As it is not directly linked to any regency, the AMPTPI is also more able to criticize government practices and promote Papuan nationalism.

Student organizations promote social activities such as discussion groups and Christmas and Easter celebrations, and support new students through their induction programmes. The organizations provide formal and informal sessions of advice on being a student, on their responsibilities and on dealing with the new environment. They are also the direct link to the regency governments, and group leaders are responsible for handing out scholarships. Dani students are most active in the organizations that represent their home regency (Jayawijaya, Puncak Jaya, Yahukimo) and are less comfortable taking centre stage in the provincial-level group, which is dominated by coastal Papuans.

The organizations provide a social base as well as moral lessons and encouragement for new students. For example:

> Manado is a good place to study because here we can join organizations with other Papuans or just Wamena people. In Wamena, people do not mix too much. Here I am involved with organizations such as IMIPA, Rupmawi, AMPTPI and others. (Lex)

> We were told to go to the FKPM-GIDI induction. Maybe other new students went to other ones but we went to this one. Mainly they told

us your parents sent you here with their hard-earned money for you to study. You may not drink alcohol and get drunk, you may not mess around, you may not quit school, you must learn well and you must be successful. (Minke)

Students also assert that they are learning skills they say they lack (and require for success): organization, discipline, public speaking, leadership and developing confidence to express themselves in front of others, particularly Indonesians. Organizations provide an opportunity to socialize with others in what is seen as a productive, disciplined and religious environment. Students hold elections to choose their leaders. A committee is formed for each major event. The committee is divided into several task-based units, such as the 'consumption unit' (in charge of food preparation), the 'fundraising unit', the 'budget unit', the 'communications unit' (in charge of disseminating information about meetings and invitations) and the 'event unit' (in charge of operations on the day of the event). Events take much work to prepare. If they want to hold a major event such as a Christmas celebration, new students' induction, or commemoration of their organization or church, they organize several fundraising events first. Each fundraiser builds on the previous one; money gained is spent creating a bigger event at which they hope to attract more money. The more developed groups have put their mandates and rules to paper, creating such paperwork as 'rules of the organization', 'the importance of the organization' and other mission and vision statements.

The commemoration of the founding of the Evangelical Church of Indonesia (GIDI) in Papua was organized by Dani students, mainly from Wolo, via their student church group (FKPM-GIDI). Over the course of two fundraising events, the students raised almost two million rupiah (US$200) for the final production. About one hundred people attended the event, held at one of the buildings on Unima campus. A few coastal Papuans participated in the singing competition. A Dani minister gave the sermon. He asked us to think about all the problems in Papua and argued that the way forward is for Papuans to unite and to serve Jesus. The head of the FKPM-GIDI organization asserted: 'What students do and learn in Manado reflects what we will create later in the field. So why does it seem that smoking and drinking are on the increase instead of decreasing?' He encouraged fortitude for all those who will go home to parents who are estranged from the Lord or who need to be convinced to serve the Lord. Personal habits and morals reflect collective achievements, and what happens in Manado is directly relevant to what happens in Wamena, almost as if students are not in a separate geographical location, but amongst other Dani feel tangibly connected to home. Another senior student used the opportunity to encourage those who have been in North Sulawesi a long time to hurry up, go home and fill the jobs. This comment echoes what Indonesians tend to say

Figure 5.2. GIDI followers leading an event to mark the founding of the church. Photo by author

to Papuan students. These presentations thus reveal important extensions of regulation and racialization. After the speeches, attendees were served lunch – rice, pork and bottled water – and then left to socialize with friends.

Catholic students spent several months planning for the election of new KBMKKJ-T (Big Family of Catholic University Students of the Jayapura-Timika Diocese) leaders. Leaders were first elected to be in charge of the election committee and to organize the day-long event held at a beautiful complex on a rural property outside Manado called Wisma Lorenzo. The session that students developed for the election follows the pattern of other events: an event theme, banners, a programme, speeches and lunch, except that the session also included candidates' debates and the election. One of the activities that the KBMKKJ-T held for many years was a retreat at Wisma Lorenzo at which students gave seminar presentations around a particular theme, such as human resource development or developing a Christian identity.

Students put serious effort into their organizations and focus on getting the details right – banners, invitations, programmes, plenary sessions and committee reports, rules of order, packed lunches, sometimes bus transport or security guards, and not just one but perhaps several fundraisers. Beyond planning the events, students take centre stage on the day, getting dressed up in their church clothes, leading prayers, singing and making speeches (planned or impromptu).

Group meetings and discussions also follow this pattern: highlanders showing, teaching and practising discipline, order and participation amongst, for the most part, other highlanders. Rupmawi comprises students from different dormitories (who are mainly friends and some who are also kin). Each group of students forms a unit expected, on a rotating basis, to prepare materials for discussion and host discussion groups at their dorms. On a more spontaneous basis, a few students may decide to hold a meeting to discuss political issues. A notice announcing the meeting is usually posted in a dorm for residents and visitors. If possible, the students hosting the meeting will prepare invitations and deliver them to other members at their dorms. Rupmawi meetings are very formal, especially considering everyone knows one another quite well. Generally, whoever is hosting the meeting leads an opening prayer, introduces the topic, the presenter, the moderator and the discussant, and describes the format of the discussion. The presenter, moderator and discussant sit at a table while the rest sit on the floor in front of them.

One such meeting I attended on 28 November 2005 was a discussion of 'Recent Developments in Papua', according to the announcement posted in Yepmum dorm on Unima campus. The meeting opened with prayer and introductory speeches as outlined above. Then, the presenter spoke for about 20 minutes in formal Indonesian on the topic of Papuan political history, specifically concerning the history of Indonesian occupation since the 1960s. He asserted that many students still did not know the story of how Papua came to be incorporated into Indonesia. The discussant offered agreement with the main points and added some comments. The moderator organized question time. Before speaking, each student who made a comment or asked a question thanked the group for the opportunity to speak and acknowledged each of the previous speakers by name, mentioning their specific contributions to the discussion. The speaker then spent several more minutes making a point and thanked everyone again for taking up time. There was actual content to the discussion – it was clear that some students were paying a great deal of attention (some took notes). Beyond content, much more attention was paid to the formal procedures and the ceremony of holding a discussion: behaviour was extra polite, and discussion leaders took their roles and presentations very seriously. The presenter had prepared his notes on paper and the moderator similarly held paper and pen to take note of questions. Besides the attention to detailed, formal procedures, the meeting was an exercise in group discipline.

According to Lavinia: 'We learn from each other here. Like through Rupmawi we learn how to organize and have meetings, how to develop, and we pass this on to the new students.' Benyamin commented:

> It is good for us to learn, in class or outside, how to speak up . . . It depends on personality but also on our level of experience and knowledge. You cannot buy this in class on campus. You have to learn about things from the media, from television, and you have to learn how to talk about things. For me, I always want to participate and dialogue. If we do not, it is our loss.

Discussions, like other group events, are organized entirely by students for students, because they feel they are learning important skills in these settings. The meeting example described here shows us what students mean when they say they want to learn to debate and to be 'brave' (*berani*) and speak up in front of others. Students are displaying skills, confidence and capabilities. The forms of expertise they demonstrate in their organizations and meetings are important and can be used to help highlanders 'go forward'. Courage in public speaking, organizational and procedural skills, and discipline are sought-after capabilities that are culturally relevant and respond to technocratic racism that defines Papuans as poor quality human resources.

It is evidence of the potency of technocratic racism that Dani feel they lack skills in leadership (governance, in a sense), organizing and group communications, considering that these are some of the hallmark cultural skills of highlands societies. Organizing large-scale social gatherings reflects expertise that is traditionally valued in highlands cultures (Ploeg 1996: 212). Giving advice, speaking at ceremonies, leading discussions and solving problems are some activities undertaken by Dani leaders. Large-scale events are the hallmark of highlands social life, and the ability to orchestrate collective activities is a mark of male influence and power. Even acknowledging that in the past not everyone (and certainly not women) had the same opportunities for leadership, given that celebrations, public speaking and social leadership styles are prominent cultural traditions, it is troubling to find that young Dani today think they lack this expertise and need to learn it from Indonesians. At the same time, perhaps this is an area in which students are trying to translate between Dani and Indonesian understandings and practices of governance by incorporating new styles. As younger people, they also might not have had the opportunity to take leadership roles in Dani settings, even if they are aware of what traditional leaders do and how they operate. Traditional social structures are still relevant in the highlands, but less so in urban areas like Wamena, and older Dani argue that their powers and practices are greatly diminished compared to even a few decades ago. Dani students have mainly seen Indonesian forms of leadership and governance, and associate governance with the state rather than big men. The explanation by Laurence, below, a Valley Dani student, gives some sense of what students might be thinking as they observe male leaders who are grappling with new conditions, even as they continue to embody traditional knowledge and customs:

> The *ap kain* is what we call the tribal chief in our [Dani] language. He is a good fighter, brave in battle, kills many enemies and steals women. Nowadays we do not do that anymore so there are fewer and fewer *ap kain*. Maybe he becomes a 'bos' instead, works in the government. He is also an expert at organizing events, solving disputes, and he tells people what to do, how to help themselves with their issues. When he talks, people listen, because they believe in him. He knows customs [*adat*] and everything about our history. He monitors everything. He is always in motion, visiting people, discussing matters, organizing the community.

Although Dani leadership is a male domain, in North Sulawesi, women as well as men take on roles in leadership and organizing events. However, women are less prominent as student leaders and are much fewer than men in number. At some events, women are concentrated in predictable gendered activities like cooking, but gender segregation is much less rigid than it would be back in the highlands, where men would be very unlikely to take part in cooking activities, for example. Women are sometimes requested to manage event finances because of the perceived risk that men might steal funds or succumb to pressure to give money to other men.

Student organizations and activities provide a venue in which students can cultivate attributes they desire without concern for how Indonesians (or sometimes other Papuans) may perceive them. Atmospheres are highly supportive. No one is ridiculed during discussions, and respect for the group leaders and for each other is of the utmost importance. Beyond creating venues for expressing prowess and for self-development, they are also a stepping point for political activism. In the organizations they say they want to improve on shyness and being embarrassed to speak in front of others. Indeed, in these settings, with other highlanders, they do not appear to lack confidence or avoid attention. In demonstrating their expertise in these forms of organizing and performance, students challenge the stereotype that presents them as primitive and uncouth. At the same time, if we fast-forward to imagining these students as graduates taking up jobs in the public service back in Papua, we can see that student organizations provide an important cultural and gendered context for the formation of styles of management, roles, and performances of expertise and governing.

Conflict amongst Highlanders

Despite the relatively secure and familiar settings students create for themselves by affiliating primarily with other central highlanders, the organizations and the broader community of *orang Wamena* are also often embroiled in conflict. Valley Dani students clash with Walak Dani or Western Dani over supposed poor conduct – drinking, fighting – that disrupts events and give them a bad image. Historically, Valley Dani and Walak engaged in tribal warfare. Today, relationships amongst highlanders are also affected by the rapid creation of new regencies and districts, which may amplify divisions, especially if decentralization funds assist students from new regencies while students from older regencies like Jayawijaya struggle to survive. The supportive atmosphere of discussion groups and events disappears, and the effects of being saturated with racial hierarchies and barriers become visible. Even though relationships are often based on kindness, sympathy and camaraderie, students are quick to judge and sometimes exclude those who are accused of bad habits. The experiences of those students are important for understanding the moral and cultural distinctions that strain and reshape what otherwise looks like an intensified experience of highlander identity and connection in North Sulawesi. Distinctions and exclusions reveal a more intimate manifestation of racialization amongst highlanders that picks up on older cultural divisions and emerging power dynamics. Valley Dani are stereotyped as 'rough' (*kabal*) and may be excluded from the activities of the majority. Valley Dani students reveal narratives of waning influence, morals and numbers in North Sulawesi, wondering whether in future there will continue to be Valley Dani studying in North Sulawesi.

Walan, a Valley Dani student, looked older than his twenty-eight years. He came to North Sulawesi in 2000 when his best friend Petrus came to study at Unsrat. He could not imagine life without his friends, he said, so he hopped on the ship as well, although he did not really intend to study. Walan always looked drunk, even though his friends said that sometimes he was not drunk, he just looked that way. He wore his hair in long braids and was the life of every social event, mostly due to his drunken antics, but also because of his generosity. Even though he lived off his friends' money most of the time, if he ever had any money of his own, he spent it all on the biggest pork feast he could afford, which sometimes extended into several days of drinking and eating. He explained his academic activities: 'I used to study, I used to be smart, I used to be good at sports and helped out with the organizations, but for the last few years I just don't care anymore', he laughed, and went back to playing a neverending game of shuffleboard with one of the other students at the Catholic men's dorm in Manado where he lived periodically. When he was drunk, Walan liked to discuss politics, ranting and raving about injustices in Papua, and he liked to sing Dani and Papuan tunes on a guitar that he 'borrowed' from a friend. When he stayed at the dorm, he usually left unexpectedly wearing a set of someone else's clothes, someone else's sandals – that's just Walan, the other students would say. Walan's adventures frequently involved his friend Jon. The last time that Jon and Walan got together, their good friend (and Jon's cousin) Daniel ended up in hospital lucky to be alive after losing two litres of blood in the courtyard of the dorm – Daniel got on Jon's nerves and Jon pushed his head through a glass window at two o'clock in the morning.

Walan, Jon and Daniel are part of a group of several Catholic Valley Dani students who were excluded from student group activities by other Wamena students, who said they do not want 'drunks' at their events. Other Dani Catholics used Walan, Jon and Daniel as an example of their purported diminishing image and reputation in North Sulawesi.

In September 2006, Rupmawi held its annual new member orientation and induction. The governance of Rupmawi, dominated by Western Dani Protestants, did not extend invitations to the Catholic Valley Dani on the grounds that some of them had a pattern of attending such events in a state of drunkenness. As a result of not being invited, the few new Catholic students also missed out on being inducted as new members into Rupmawi and missed meeting other new students from Wamena. The 2006 event was organized by Walak students, a clan-based group of Dani Protestants from the Wolo Valley who desperately wanted to put on a high-quality event. The organizers even went to the trouble of hiring a Papuan security guard to patrol the forested event site to ensure that no uninvited guests gained entry.

The AMPTPI produced a graduation celebration in Tondano with a similar programme of events, although it was less well-funded and well-prepared, relying mainly on graduates spending their own money on preparations for the *bakar batu*. They invited a local government official to give a speech, and a group of students led the prayer service. Local government men and their families sat on dining chairs inside the dorm and were served steamed pork and potatoes on plates while students ate with their hands out of communal pails outside. Even though the AMPTPI represents Catholic and Protestant students, the event was held at the Protestant-dominated Yepmum dorm at Unima and Catholic students were surprised to find out that AMPTPI banners were displayed at the ceremony, to which they had not been invited. They held their own, smaller party at their off-campus dorm.

Besides the reason of alleged alcohol consumption, the students in charge of invitations also cited the fact that several of the Catholic Dani live in a dorm with Indonesian Catholics, and therefore it was not on their typical path for visiting friends around town. To invite them would require a special trip there. In response to not being included in the event, senior Catholic students refused to be of assistance in organizational matters and discouraged new arrivals from getting involved in Rupmawi. As an event got under way elsewhere, Catholic Dani at one dorm held a meeting and expressed frustration at the situation. According to Anton: 'We used to run Rupmawi. Our seniors [*kakak-kakak*] developed the whole organization, modelled after the KBMKKJ-T. They prepared the organizational materials. And now they give someone else the role of presenting the history of the organization to the new students.' Some did get drunk, which was said to be the 'normal' response to a distressing situation. Walan asserted: 'It's fine, it's better this way, the new kids are all in boarding houses anyways, they live with locals, with Catholics. The dorms are in chaos anyways, it is better if they are alone.'

These comments evoke a sense of desperation about the waning influence and presence of Valley Dani in North Sulawesi, and show tensions and divisions that exist beneath the surface of highlander identity, affiliation and mutual support. Anton remembers a time when their prowess was unquestioned. The loss that Walan finds most disturbing is that of the role of the 'elder sibling' or senior student who shares knowledge and wisdom with new students. Valley Dani students themselves assert that current conditions in their villages and in Wamena are affecting young people before they arrive in North Sulawesi. Laurence, whose older cousin used to be President of Rupmawi, described feelings of regret and disappointment at the chaotic state of their student organization, which holds events that are often disorganized and marred by alcohol:

> When I arrived here, our older siblings took charge of us constantly. If we went drinking or got together with a girl and they found out, they would toss us in the water tank. They forbid everything. Even if they were sometimes drunk, as younger siblings we were not allowed to do it. But now, if we try to control the young guys, it is really difficult. They are stubborn [*kepala batu*] and they do not listen. In Papua, they are accustomed to drinking and fist fights so they come here and just keep on doing it.

Etinus commented more broadly on some of the conditions and challenges in North Sulawesi that make drinking alcohol an enjoyable pastime:

> Sometimes students feel like they are finally here, they have achieved something, but then they have no money for fees. Their families think they are adults and they can fend for themselves. They do not know what it is like here – we have no gardens to sell produce, no pigs to raise. Are we going to get a job in Megamall, or driving a bus? If you fall behind with your fees then you are in a really bad situation – your friends go on ahead without you and you have nothing to do all day. This feels really bad. Sometimes men have troubles with women, and

this makes them want to drink, but mostly it is just stress. Nobody wants to quit. Then sometimes you get a group of friends, they are all out of school, and then they can entertain each other with drinking. Drinking becomes normal.

From the beginning of their time abroad, students are warned (especially by other highlanders) about the dangers of alcohol. Sometimes they spoke of students who were believed to have passed away because they became ill after months or years of heavy drinking. Alcohol consumption has clearly emerged as a critical challenge for collective activities and identities (see also Munro 2019; Munro and Wetipo 2013). Alcohol is readily available in North Sulawesi and is much more available than it is in Papua. Alcohol in the Papuan highlands has been banned since the Dutch colonial era (1954) and the provincial government has recently enacted a province-wide ban on the sale, production and consumption of alcohol. In Wamena, alcohol is either smuggled in through the airport or is produced locally using yeast, water, sugar and sometimes fruit juice. Students state that locals in North Sulawesi introduce them to the local homebrew, *cap tikus*, early on. Alcohol consumption is mostly linked to celebratory activities, and most students will only buy it when they have received a large sum of money from home. Consumption is a primarily male social activity. Like Etinus, Dani in Wamena also say that drinking has become normal, is a new activity associated with Indonesian colonialism and the loss of Dani control over territory, people and the flow of goods into the highlands, and contributes to violence (Munro 2019; Munro and Wetipo 2013). In North Sulawesi and in West Papua, Papuans, especially central highlanders, are racialized as drunken and violent. There is evidence that alcohol shapes contact with Indonesians and especially police in North Sulawesi, as mentioned in Chapter 3, and this is an important and emerging area in which to examine racialized relations between Indonesians and Papuans.

Tensions, Alcohol and Colonialism

In conditions of vulnerability and stigma, students ultimately spend most of their time abroad not with Indonesians or other Papuans, but with other central highlanders. Their activities, norms and conflicts affirm the relevance and importance of highlands cultural identity and of returning home to the highlands to enjoy feelings of security and belonging. For highlands students living outside of Papua, it is not just that they experience a heightened awareness of cultural difference or closeness to other highlanders because of the dominant presence of others, as is commonly described in contexts of migration, but there is a political edge to identity formation in contexts of stigmatization.

Positive, if in some cases essentializing, views of highlanders demonstrate ways in which young educated highlanders may be 'reversing the gaze' (Gillespie 2006; Rudolph et al. 2002) by pushing back against dominant views that want to position them as primitive and unintelligent.

Dani capacities to sustain themselves through gardening and social networks have helped students to survive away from home and have aided migration and settlement in new communities around Papua. In recent years I was surprised at the views of coastal Papuans about the growing Dani presence in their areas, notably Manokwari (see Sari (2016) on highlanders around Jayapura), where locals told me, for example: 'Us and the Indonesians have a new common enemy now: Wamena people.' For these commentators, 'Wamena people' were associated with tight-knit residential groups, violence and alcohol, babies out of wedlock and political activism that ended up attracting reprisals from the state. Coastal versus highlands identities are not new rivalries: Danilyn Rutherford (2003: xviii) describes a joke told by coastal informants about highlanders who figure that in an independent West Papua, Biak people would be the new 'foreigners' (*amber*, a Biak word, also used to refer to Indonesians), while highlanders would be Biak people. These views exist among coastal Papuans in North Sulawesi too. Yet the extent to which these divisions are moving beyond the space of politics writ large into everyday life is disconcerting. One way to consider such growing tensions asks questions about inequality and the imbrication of blame and violence in everyday social relations. In North Sulawesi, the atmosphere of stigma and scrutiny amplifies divisions between coastal and highland Papuans, between Valley Dani and Western Dani, and between Catholic and Protestant Dani, even as it also requires them to work together and defend one another.

In the absence of new affiliations and social connections with Indonesians, education abroad advances, rather than reduces, feelings of inadequacy, vulnerability and insecurity. If anything, Papuan highlanders become more aware of the impossibility of them being accepted as fellow Indonesians, which may generate further questioning of the nation-state and national values. Living, working, studying and organizing together provides highlanders with a modicum of control over these circumstances, but the aspiration to succeed as a group in which students take care of each other, monitor one another's behaviour and go forward (or fail) together may also amplify internal divisions and tensions. School mobility for highlanders is less conducive to broadening horizons, experiencing other cultures or making cosmopolitan connections than it is to displaying skills in front of other highlanders and coming up with ways to show their achievements back home that others will recognize as 'modern' as well as 'traditional'.

Unlike what students hope for, North Sulawesi does not offer much in the way of a new sense of Christian belonging or new ties by virtue of being educated. Ethnic tensions arise even in peaceful, stable and 'developed' places because racialization defies geographical boundaries. The pressure on youth to succeed against the odds in this disabling environment continues as in West Papua. While being away provides them with new shared experiences and support networks, it also generates new stigmas, conflicts and feelings of exclusion that will have social and political reverberations back home.

6

'Study First'
Sexuality, Pregnancy and Survival in the 'City of Free Sex'

Living in the *rantau* (space of migration) means that for better or for worse, students make their own decisions and are more or less left to their own devices. The fate of 'migrant youth' (*anak-anak merantau*), as students sometimes refer to themselves, is to make mistakes and to be vulnerable to the influences of the local environment, which includes novel configurations of freedom. When students are involved in sexual relationships during their studies, they are disobeying instructions from their parents, preachers and other authority figures in Wamena and in North Sulawesi. Yet many are also clearly questioning this regulation of sexuality and marriage, and the need to postpone family formation until after they graduate for the sake of becoming good human resources.

Indonesian youth are increasingly delaying marriage for the sake of education and career development (Kim 2010; Nilan 2008; Smith-Hefner 2005, 2006; Utomo 2012). These apparent choices are shaped by significant social pressures, including national discourses of progress and improvement. Self-control, being disease-free and piety are all promoted by the Indonesian state as characteristics of 'good' human resources. The nationwide call for young people to develop themselves into good-quality human resources stands out as a form of moral regulation that promotes education and technical skills packaged with values of piety, patriotism, health and abstinence. Even though they define what 'modern' Indonesian youth should do for the sake of personal and national development, contemporary expectations are shaped by what Pam Nilan (2008: 66) calls 're-traditionalisation' – 'a hegemonic discourse about the importance of moral and social order' that relies on Islamic cultural views of faith and family. Premarital relationships are highly stigmatized, being viewed as a violation of national cultural and religious norms, and may be punished by ostracism and shaming (Bennett 2005; Davies 2015). Sex education is limited and unmarried men and women are not allowed to access contraceptives (Bennett 2007), so advanced educational achievement increasingly relies on the regulation of youth sex and sexuality. Youth are expected to become tech-savvy experts for the national workforce by successfully managing sexual desire, romance and public impressions, not by using modern technologies like birth control.

Indonesian discourses tend to racialize Papuan sexualities as promiscuous, drawing on wider conceptualizations of Papuan cultures as 'stone age', especially in the highlands (Slama and Munro 2015). These depictions draw on caricatures of 'naked' men whose traditional dress was a penis gourd, as well as polygyny (Butt et al. 2002), and stories of 'tribal leaders [*kepala suku*] who have the right to do as they please to any woman and spread their biological desires to any woman in their tribe' (Bramantyo 2014). These alleged practices are contrasted with the myth of Indonesian 'moral sex': monogamous, regulated by birth control and contributing to national development (Butt 2005a). Modern Papuan sexualities are also criticized for supposedly not being constrained by cultural controls (e.g. Umasugi 2010; Zeth et al. 2010); thus, in Indonesian dominant views, there is no Papuan sexuality that is permissible. In North Sulawesi, if Papuan students do not forgo sex and reproduction for study they can be accused of sabotaging their own human resource potential, while allegations of promiscuity become part of technocratic racism that questions their skills and capabilities for development. But Dani students also challenge racialization in relation to sexuality, pregnancy and marriage. Unlike Sonia and Margaretta, the young women in Wamena who were stigmatized as promiscuous and ostracized because they were not in school (see Chapter 1), university students are more likely to question dominant perspectives on sex, education and marriage. Questioning is increasingly possible because highlanders become more aware of how their own values differ amidst Indonesians in North Sulawesi.

In North Sulawesi, young people are instructed to 'study first' (*kuliah dulu*) or 'finish first' (*selesai dulu*) – in other words, complete their education before sex, marriage and family life begins. Students are also warned by people in Wamena not to have sex or get (anyone) pregnant. They warn each other of the dangers of ruining their education because of romantic or sexual feelings and behaviour. Students assert the importance of finishing their studies first, but they still get involved in romantic and sexual relationships. Some are said to be married. They also say that producing the next generation of Dani is a crucial political pursuit to allay the devastating population effects of Indonesian colonialism, captured in Indigenous discussions of 'saving Papuans' (Munro 2019). They argue that educational and reproductive achievements are both essential for securing the future of Dani and other Papuans, including preventing extinction. Sexuality is also a 'normal' part of adulthood, a view that challenges dominant perspectives. At the same time, pregnancy before marriage is frowned upon by Dani cultural norms, Christian teachings and Indonesian expectations.

This study probably reflects men's experiences more than women's. There are certainly many more Dani men in North Sulawesi than Dani women. Yet, some of my closest informants were women, and I had significant opportunities to hear about their experiences and views. When I visited Dani women, happy chatter often turned to who was seen with whom or who was receiving a steady stream of text messages at all hours of the night (such as, 'HP bunyi terus!', meaning '[Your] phone is always making noise!'). Some of the women I got to know in North Sulawesi got married while they were students, and others went home pregnant. Some stayed in North Sulawesi to raise their children and pursue an education at the same time. It is somewhat stereotypical that I am discussing women's experiences most strongly in relation to themes of sexuality and pregnancy, but it should be clear that these domains are crucial to racialization and resistance, and have cultural and political resonance. It is women whose bodies bear the signs of sexuality for Indonesians to see and judge, and it is women who ultimately had to choose whether to seek an unsafe abortion, have a baby out of wedlock or return home in the hope of acceptance from kin and a quick marriage.

Highlanders engage in a tight-knit social world, and marriage and pregnancy are important ways in which they are connected to one another. When I say marriage, I do not mean formal, legal marriage or necessarily traditional Dani marriage arranged by kin and recognized through the payment of bridewealth. Students use the term 'married' (*kawin* or *sudah kawin*) fairly loosely and know that they are not formally married. It can refer to having had sexual intercourse (i.e. no longer a virgin) or to being in a relationship regardless of whether it is short-term or long-standing, but most commonly it connotes being in a serious, committed, monogamous, live-in relationship. Anyone who has children together is considered married, whether they stay together or not. The term 'boyfriend/girlfriend' (*pacar*) is also used, usually to convey less serious and not necessarily sexual relationships. Almost every female student I met was involved in some sort of relationship with a male, although some of these relationships are long-distance with students in other cities and involve flirtatious telephone calls and text messages. Sometimes these relationships are just for fun, though students are careful not to let their various boyfriends find out about each other. These relationships may also be considered more serious or may develop into something serious, as happened with Minke and Kodar, who are discussed later in this chapter. In one example, I was repeatedly told by different students that a student named Albert had a Dani wife studying in Java. Albert's wife would telephone Albert or a mutual acquaintance to request that he send her photographs of himself and some phone credit (*pulsa*) for her mobile phone. I was surprised to find out later that Albert and this woman whom everyone referred to as his 'wife' (*istri*) had never met in person.

Looking at students' intimate relationships also adds another dimension to our understanding of their lives abroad. They are not just 'siblings', fundraisers, gardeners or protestors; Dani in North Sulawesi are connected through marriage, love, sex and babies. Who was 'dating' or sleeping with whom, even who was sending or receiving text messages from whom, was always a hot topic of conversation, a daily negotiation and an important part of social life. Early on I noticed Dani children running about on campus and living in dormitories. Their visibility elicited condemnation from some Indonesians, who saw this as an affirmation of 'promiscuity' and a reason to ban women and men from sharing a dormitory. Of course, they did not realize that the women and men who shared dormitories were usually not having sex or making babies with one another. Not only were many students in the dorms related to one another in some way, they would find having sex with a housemate too close for comfort. Sex happened with people in other dorms, as far away from home as was logistically practical. Students in a marital relationship would most likely move out of the dorm into their own residence. This is what other students would expect of them, as having a married couple in the room next door would be embarrassing for other students. Nevertheless, local Indonesians were not aware of these nuances in social organization. In spite of the stigma of 'free sex', Dani and other highlands students celebrated these children and they were displayed in all kinds of social spaces, including those that were dominated by Indonesians. This is not to say that all pregnancies were wanted or that having children was not a disruption, particularly for female students. Without access to birth control, and with very different and reduced kinds of surveillance from kin, pregnancy was a fraught but not uncommon part of living and studying abroad.

'Promiscuity' and Racialized Sexuality

University lecturers, government workers and Christian leaders described the correct moral and educational path for young people in terms of a need to 'finish first' (*selesai dulu*) or 'study first' (*kuliah dulu*). Students were instructed to avoid sexual or marital relations until schooling was completed. Father Wetenge, a Minahasan minister who lived above his church on campus, explained the idea of 'study first' and its significance for Papuan students as follows:

> We tell them to study first because this is part of the formula for success. This is particularly important for our brothers and sisters from Papua, because their region is very poor and people are depending on them to have success and to help the people at home. Also from

what the Papuan students tell me promiscuity is a very big problem in Papua and leads to destruction of the young generation. Some of their parents are still in the dark about this. We encourage students to take the message home with them . . . many students around here live in dorms, especially the Papuans, or in boarding houses where they may easily fall into sin.

Dr Sisi, a Javanese obstetrician, said: 'I treat many Papuans at my hospital. They have careless sexual relationships [*kawin sembarang*], get pregnant and then no one takes any responsibility.' Indonesians expect to facilitate Papuans' technical improvements as well as moral and Christian lessons. Sexuality is intimately connected to the production of good human resources and thus accusations of promiscuity feed into racism that denies Papuan skills and capacities. The accusation of alleged promiscuity or unrestrained sexuality was a significant source of tension for Dani students because as William, a law student in Manado, stated: 'Actually this is the city of promiscuous sex. My parents told me to be careful of sex here, because this is where the prostitutes work openly in the market at night and a source of sex workers for Papua too.' Thus, Dani students question local moral claims and proscriptions.

In West Papua, as in other parts of Indonesia, young people are instructed to avoid sex altogether in order to keep themselves safe from the threat of HIV. Images of schoolchildren asserting that they will 'take care of themselves and avoid HIV/AIDS' are displayed around Jayapura. Perspectives from Dani students also suggest that HIV is a threat to human resources and that the main way to keep safe is to stay away from sexual relationships (Munro 2004). While it was not obvious at the time, some students did return home HIV positive. I am aware of several who have since passed away and others who are getting by on anti-retroviral therapy.

It is not only state agencies or religious authorities that assert that sex ruins a young person's future. Students said that their parents warn them not to have sex while they are studying. Besides important warnings about avoiding sexually transmitted infections, parents argue against marriage, according to students, because marrying without permission, guidance and bridewealth is seen as causing trouble for other family members. Young people's bodies and reproductive capacities are not their own to do with as they please; rather, their parents and the wider clan may still claim authority and decision-making power over these domains. According to traditional Dani norms, marriage should be arranged to suit the clan's political interests, expanding and consolidating exchange relations (Alua 2006). Marriage practices and values were highly concerned with wider relationships and producing clear lineages, so on these grounds, extramarital and premarital sex would be punished. The mother's chastity appeared less significant than whether or not the child would have a clear father and thus an affiliation in the patrilineal clan system (Butt and Munro 2007; O'Brien 1969). Today, men have less control over the marriage system, bridewealth is not always paid and young people may establish their own relationships even if the family disapproves. There is evidence of the continuing practice of intrafamily adoption of infants born to unwed mothers, but the pressure to live up to Indonesian standards of sexual and moral order has a potent influence on decision-making around unplanned pregnancy (Butt 2007; Butt and Munro 2007).

Sin and Survival

The 'finish first' ideology pervades students' considerations of pregnancy abroad. Being a university student (*mahasiswa*) is about more than attending classes or completing assignments, which could conceivably fit into married life. Being *mahasiswa*, students articulate, is about morality, discipline and self-control, wisdom and devoting time to community, religious and student affairs. Rika, whose relatives had recently had babies in North Sulawesi, supported abstinence, saying: 'Our parents send us to study, not to have sex.' As Rika and other students explained, relatives might ostracize and stop supporting a daughter who became pregnant or allegedly had sex. Some women and men said that parents did not follow through on threats of ostracism or that they were not that supportive at any rate, so the threat was not much of a deterrent. In fact, women might also gain material support from sexual relationships with other students. Nonetheless, Rika elaborated: 'We have to finish first, because we came to study not to get married. As Christians, we know that sex outside marriage is a sin. That is why people are ashamed if they have sex outside marriage. In Wamena if people have sex outside marriage they must pay compensation or they must get married.' Similarly, Stina said: 'Anyone who says that it is okay for us to get pregnant is wrong, very wrong. Our parents would be furious, and we would be very ashamed.' Edward agreed: 'They say "finish first" because our objective is to study, not to mess around with women or get into trouble.' He added: 'My relatives here don't allow me to get close to women, they watch [*jaga*] me.' Yet many other students argued that sexuality was an inevitable part of growing up and living independently, regardless of education ambitions:

> It is normal to have a girlfriend or boyfriend; it is just part of life. Whoever says he or she has never had a boyfriend is lying. We do not really announce it to everyone. Even though Siska and Martha are my cousins, I do not know what they are doing, but if we lived together, ate together, yes then I would know. But sometimes we see, where

is so-and-so, and if her mobile phone is inactive we say ohhh she is probably with her man. And it is probably true, because she turns up a day or two later and no one has seen her until then. Yes, we will ask where have you been and she says oh, with so-and-so, her 'elder sibling' [kakak] or some other woman but we know the truth. (Minke)

Minke continued on to explain how the environment of North Sulawesi enables men to express and act on sexual desire openly:

It is difficult here, men have too much desire, they just look at us from afar and they want to have sex already. They call us on the phone, send us mobile phone credit, and sometimes invite us out to eat. They would never do this so openly in Wamena. Sometimes we want things they give, and it is difficult to say no to men if they are determined to have sex. I do not want to be known as a tease or as a person who has *seks bebas* [free sex].

Daniel said that the local sexual culture of Manado promoted promiscuity, commenting: 'Around here it is the locals who are having promiscuous sex, just go down to the boardwalk and they are there every night.' Students were sceptical of the 'study first' imperative, questioning the feasibility of being abstinent adults, as well as the idea that sex was necessarily destructive to educational goals or broader family relationships.

The need to 'finish first' was particularly questioned by students who argue that reproduction is a political and cultural matter that links to Indigenous continuity and sovereignty in the face of Indonesian colonialism. As previously mentioned, students expressed that Indonesia wants to eliminate Papuans, and Papuans need to struggle 'through whatever means'. Black stated:

Indonesia does not want us to have more children so that is why they give birth control and they send prostitutes with AIDS. The men sleep with them and bring AIDS home to their wives. This ruins their womb. They want our black skin to be finished; they want to eliminate our race. So we think it is important for our race to keep the blood line going by having children.

It was male students who more often spoke of reproduction in racialized and politicized ways. In the highlands, the politics of reproduction is traditionally men's business (see Butt (2001), for example). Indonesian fertility control policies have been criticized by Dani men and women who see birth control as supporting the state's genocidal intention of eventually eliminating Indigenous people, and because it interferes with the cultural ideal of producing as many healthy descendants as possible (Butt 2001). Male students are also much less exposed to the actual consequences of premarital pregnancy than women, though the consequences for them really depend on whether the woman has a family who pushes them towards marriage and insists that the father to take responsibility and pay bridewealth. These assessments of reproduction emphasize the political and cultural contributions of childbearing in the context of a perceived diminishing Indigenous population rather than the possible ways that pregnancy and sexuality threaten educational achievements or lead young people into sin.

Marriage, 'Mutual Desire' and Pregnancy

Students argued that pregnancies were not, as Indonesians thought, mistakes resulting from unrestrained desire and casual sex. Rather, pregnancy was usually part of relationships that were not casual. Sex could not be particularly casual because of the difficulty of keeping a sexual relationship secret amongst Dani friends and fellow students, the shame associated with 'free sex' and women's concern over ruining their 'good name'. Students said that 'free sex' most often arose if women and men drank alcohol together. This did not happen very often, and when it did, a woman often had her female friends around to prevent her from having sex that would mark her as promiscuous. If pregnancy did result from a drunken act or a one-time encounter, a woman might seek an illegal abortion. If she could not access an abortion, then she would most likely give the baby to her parents or older sibling to raise. A baby is only legitimate, and its mother's reputation intact, if there is a relationship that surrounds it – this relationship might be legal or customary marriage, or it might be publicly acknowledged through the financial contributions of the father or his kin. Most pregnancies took place in the context of a relationship that was described as 'marriage'; the infant was proof of the seriousness of the relationship. Minke explained:

> Sometimes we use the term 'cari anak' [literally, looking for a child] when people have sex, because we understand that sex causes pregnancy. So the man might ask us, 'do you want to 'cari anak?' when he means have sex. If someone has sex, the woman might become pregnant, but if people are 'married' [sudah kawin] then they will most likely make a child. They know this and can't deny it.

Pregnancy was also described as resulting from mutual desire, using the expression 'mau dengan mau', literally, 'want with want', implying that the man and the woman equally know and accept the consequences of sex.

With low numbers of female students, women were able to choose boyfriends or husbands according to their standards, desires and needs, and they often expected financial support. Some relatives, upon hearing that their younger brother had a 'wife' or girlfriend, let alone a baby, would be more likely to send money to help support the young family because the baby belongs to the wider clan and they would not want to be accused of not taking responsibility. The lack of women also limited the number of marital relationships, testing Indonesian views that Papuan students were vigorously engaged in family formation. Yusuf commented: 'Look around, all these women, they are all married [*sudah kawin*], you cannot bother them or their husband [*paitua*, a colloquial term meaning 'old man'] will come after you.' Gigi explained: 'Even if you are married you can still leave your husband and marry someone else, but once you have children, it is very difficult to leave or remarry.' 'Marriage' thus referred to a monogamous, adult relationship established over time and through sex and pregnancy. Students also acknowledged the challenges of marriage abroad:

> You really cannot get married here anyway because you cannot have a celebration/event [*acara*]; you have no family, no parents. We say that so and so is married [*sudah kawin*] or has a wife [*maitua*] but they have not held the event. It can become a big problem. Even if you wait until you are going to finish, like Etinus and Ina, well they are still in big trouble back in the village. Because if you go home like that, about to give birth, you cannot get married in church and you have to go to the village and talk with everyone, all the elders and the family, it's really difficult. They have to decide whether Etinus is good enough, has he ever hit Ina. (Jhon)

According to this description, marriage for highlanders abroad is practically impossible. Getting married in the Papuan highlands traditionally requires the involvement of the couple's family members in arranging the match in the first place and would take place in a large, important celebration (see Butt 1998; Heider 1970: 150–52). Even if the couple were to marry in church, bridewealth would still need to be negotiated between the families, and relatives would be called on to donate pigs for the bride price and/or the celebration. Weddings often take place in natal villages far from town so that elders in the extended family can acknowledge the new marriage. As Jhon noted, it would not be possible to bring the wedding, the pigs, the elders or the village to North Sulawesi. It would be possible for the couple to make a trip home to get married, but in the midst of their studies, very few do. Students said that such a trip would require money they do not have and would necessitate dropping out of school for what could turn into a long absence, depending on the length of time needed to arrange the marriage and the wedding. But there seem to be other explanations for why students do not immediately seek to return home when their relationship turns serious – one of which Etinus points to below. Going home with a diploma is a good way to smooth over relations with relatives and others who are likely to be unhappy they have had no input into the marriage. Indeed, students conveyed that it was laughable that they find their own partners and simply take them home to Wamena for their parents' approval, expecting that they will just arrange a marriage. Parents and other kin tend to have a vested interest in the choice of partner and the extended family relations that result from a marriage. But a pregnancy or a baby might force parents to be more receptive to the marriage and more willing to expedite a wedding.

Marriage might create problems for students or it might solicit additional financial support from relatives, but it could also be a way out of university for unhappy students. In her second year of studying economics at Unima, Minke became increasingly dissatisfied with her situation. She said she might want to study literature, but her sister's husband graduated with a degree in economics and he was paying the bills – she would have to take economics as well, even though she was hopeless at mathematics and only got by because she copied her friends' assignments. Bubbly, sociable and fun, Minke received lots of attention from male students. There were rumours that she already had a baby back in Wamena – she always denied it, but they were enough to put her reputation into question and thereby encourage males to flirt with her, according to her older cousin Dana. Minke said she had two previous sex partners (referred to as 'boyfriend', *pacar*) since she started university. When I knew her, she was busy avoiding attention of one of her ex-boyfriends, refusing the advances of a fellow dorm member and spending quite a bit of time on the phone flirting with two other Papuan students – one who was living in Makassar, South Sulawesi, the other a recent graduate who had returned to Papua. Minke described herself as someone who is:

> [T]oo free with people. It is difficult. I am hot-blooded. I already had these two boyfriends, if anything else happens ... people will think badly of me and I won't have a good name. I did not even do anything with these men, but they want me and that is enough to cause trouble. If they talk about me to others...

Partly because of her weariness with economics and partly to escape her growing reputation for having boyfriends and possibly even being promiscuous, Minke decided to abandon her studies and her friends, disappoint her financial supporters, and risk hostility and punishment from her family to marry a recent Unima graduate, a Yali man of whom she was certain her parents would disapprove. She returned to Wamena. The marriage was the talk of the Dani community, as Minke arranged it all covertly by telephone with Kodar, who was then in Wamena. Their courtship consisted of agreeing to meet up at the April graduation ceremony at Yepmum dorm after two months of text messaging. They developed their communication after a photo of them was taken by Kodar's younger relative, Nina, who was a friend of Minke's in Tondano. The photo made its way to Kodar's relatives in Yahukimo regency, who asserted that Minke and Kodar were a good-looking match. Then Kodar contacted Minke by phone through Nina. After the initial introductions, Minke hid her developing relationship from Nina because, she said, Nina could spoil it by telling Kodar things about her. After they met up at the Yepmum dorm for the graduation ceremony, Kodar flew back to the highlands to put in his application for employment in the public service before the deadline. Minke packed up her room on a Sunday morning while the rest of the dorm residents were at church, loaded her belongings into a van and moved to the residence of two of Kodar's younger relatives in Manado. She never went back to Yepmum dorm, fearing her male relatives would detain her there. We said goodbye at the port a few weeks later as she boarded a ship for Papua. When we caught up a few months later, she told me of how, when the new couple reunited in Wamena, some of Minke's relatives beat up Kodar. Only her father was interested in arranging her marriage because she told him she might be pregnant. The other family members would have nothing to do with her.

In the dorm where Minke lived in Tondano, she was surrounded by kin, though not all dorm inhabitants were her relatives. Still, Dani and other central highlands men were able to overtly seek relationships with her and she could initiate relationships in ways that would be far more difficult to do in Wamena, where every interaction between nonrelatives of the opposite sex would be noted by someone who could report to others or intervene. For Minke, who she married and his prospects could become part of her own improvement, including a restored sexual reputation. Perhaps Minke's 'elder sibling' (*kakak*) Etinus, her ostensible protector, was busy with his own relationship drama, which became clearer when he graduated and returned home with his pregnant girlfriend. Amidst forms of diminishment that encouraged her to question herself and be ashamed of sexuality, Minke demonstrated a sense of being in charge of her own fate and future. She analysed her situation and prospects, and took a necessary risk: her family would be angry and disappointed, but, she surmised, they would be more disappointed if she acquired a bad reputation or got pregnant by someone who was not a good marriage prospect. However tenacious she was in arranging her own marriage and going against the wishes of her family, she faced an uncertain future dependent on her husband and his family (so long as her family remained estranged).

Dani men and women value childbearing and education because Indonesian colonialism threatens the existence of Indigenous Papuans in ethnic and cultural terms. Both educational attainment and the perpetuation of Dani cultural and ethnic lines constitute forms of resistance to diminishing numbers and power. Dani students also try to manage their sexual reputations by forging relationships that are known and accepted by other highlanders, even

Figure 6.1. Three generations at a Unima graduation ceremony. Photo by author

if most Indonesians do not know these nuances. Their views diverge from the dominant perspective that pushes young adults to choose education over marriage and childbearing for the sake of becoming good human resources, and is mainly concerned with curbing population growth and constraining sexuality to marriage. Divergent understandings are complicated by Christian values,

Indonesian racialization of Papuan sexuality as promiscuous, and the expectations and hopes of Dani kin back home. Women's experiences of premarital pregnancy while studying shed light on these dynamics. Premarital pregnancy can occasion shame for some Dani women, but other women reject the dominant view of premarital pregnancy.

Premarital Pregnancies

Students said that pregnancy was never accidental. Pregnancy was a logical outcome, and a necessary risk, of couples having sex. Pregnancy was most likely to become a problem if other students thought the mother was promiscuous or if the father refused to take responsibility for the child. Regarding a baby born in North Sulawesi who was taken to Wamena to live with relatives, a number of students said things like 'That child has many fathers' (*Anak itu punya bapak banyak*) or 'That child belongs to many people' (*Anak itu banyak orang punya*), meaning that the child's mother was perceived to have had sex with different men before the baby was born, so the identity and thus affiliation of the baby was unclear.

Pregnancy among students was a regular occurrence. Sixteen of the twenty-six Dani women I knew pretty well in North Sulawesi described themselves as 'married'. Some women undoubtedly chose not to reveal relationships or were not currently in a relationship but had been in previous relationships. Of these sixteen women who described themselves as married, nine had children and a further three were pregnant in 2006. Of course, it is likely that pregnant women would describe themselves as 'married' to protect their reputation.

Betty: Avoiding Shame

Betty, a Lani student, was a busy young woman. While pursuing a bachelor's degree in management, the 21-year-old acted as housewife in her Lani boyfriend's dorm and cared for two children aged seven and ten left with her by a relative. She was also dedicated to an evangelical church on campus. In February 2006, her boyfriend Julianus left for Wamena for a few months, or possibly longer, to carry out the fieldwork requirement of his degree. Soon after, Betty telephoned home in search of funds so that she could return to Wamena as well, ostensibly to conduct her own research. But it was clear to me and her female friends that she was eager to return home as soon as possible because she was pregnant. She hoped to marry Julianus. Betty explained that she would feel too ashamed in her intimate neighbourhood, home to university students of various ethnic backgrounds as well as professors and church ministers. Her evangelical orientation strongly emphasized the sinfulness of sex. But she was most acutely aware that people around her would not know that Julianus was the father and that their relationship would not look like marriage: 'I knew I could not just wait and get big. What would people think? I do not want to be like Nelly, like Sela, just walking around when the father is not clear.'

Betty's father sent her some money and she left for Wamena before many people knew of her pregnancy. Betty said she planned to get married and then return to finish her studies, but at the completion of my fieldwork, she still had not returned to North Sulawesi, and her friends had no news from her. This affirmed a sense among her fellow female students that: 'Once you go home and get married you cannot escape' (Minke). Betty was one of the young women who I was not able to locate in Wamena when I visited there in 2009.

Betty's deep entanglement in housework and childcare was not particularly common among women students in North Sulawesi; she was almost already treated like a married woman and her relationship with Julianus eventuated from there. There are interesting structural conditions that shaped her circumstances, related to land re-divisions and funding changes occurring in the highlands. Betty had been living with other women in the Yepmum dorm, sponsored (loosely speaking, since they did not receive much support) by the Jayawijaya regency government. But then her home regency of Puncak Jaya leased a dormitory on Unima campus and officials encouraged the Puncak Jaya students to leave Yepmum and move into this new dormitory. Betty was the only woman in the dorm. It was not long before she and Julianus started a relationship. Betty described fear, shame and guilt resulting from premarital pregnancy. As she had only recently started her degree programme, she could not claim that she had achieved her study goals. She had only been with Julianus a short time, so most of the Lani, Dani and other highlanders in Tondano and Manado did not know of their situation. Julianus was known as a drinker and students assumed that he had sex with different women. Betty was deeply engaged in a tight-knit Christian evangelical community, which made it difficult for her to reject the association of pregnancy with sin. She was able to leave Tondano and presumably avoid shame, but it would seem that she had to leave her studies for good and faced an uncertain future back home in the highlands.

Linda: Questioning Stigma

Linda completed her bachelor's degree in economics at Unima in 2006. She was seen taking graduation photographs around campus with her one-year-old daughter Mei and her parents, who had travelled from Wamena. Her husband, also a highlander, graduated in 2005, left a pregnant Linda in Tondano and started working as a teacher in Wamena. Linda lived in a crowded two-storey house on a large plot of land with excellent views of rice paddy fields around Tata Aran. Her sister and other students who lived with her had helped look after Mei so that Linda could finish her studies and would soon go home to join her husband. Her husband, although he did not earn much money, had been able to periodically send money that Linda used to support other students in her household.

To other students, Linda's situation was acceptable, especially since her husband sent money and acknowledged Mei. To outsiders, it looked like Linda was just another unmarried mother living in a crowded Papuan house. Linda reflected on these dynamics. She expressed feeling close to the members of her church, many of whom were Indonesian, and explained that they were kind to her and the other students:

> Actually, we feel that we do not have a problem with our minister, or our friends at church. They love to play with the babies. They always shake our hands and they are happy to see us. They have met our husbands, so maybe they think we are married.

But she felt uncomfortable with people who did not know her circumstances:

> I usually feel there is no problem, but also you know we do not go out that much, we stick around here. The people who do not know us can be a bit arrogant [*sombong*], I am not sure if it is because they are looking at the babies or not. Sometimes they stare, or they whisper to each other. We know that they think we have free sex [*seks bebas*] but actually that is not the case. So what can we do? We just let it be, just ignore it. Soon we will all be back in Wamena, and over there everyone knows the child's identity.

Linda laughed at the idea that her parents might be disappointed: 'What do they have to worry about? My husband is a teacher, I have just graduated, and the baby and I are going home soon!'

Linda shows that the stigmatizing effects of premarital sexuality can be mitigated by other achievements, especially graduation and her marriage to a highlands man with urban employment. Feelings of discomfort existed, but were not overwhelming because she had support from Dani students and, against the odds, some Indonesians in her neighbourhood. She felt racialized as promiscuous, but because she had some Indonesian friends and she knew her parents would be proud of her accomplishments, judgements did not produce shame. She emphasized that back in Wamena, her status as an educated wife and mother would not be in question and Wamena is the context that matters. Students' experiences of racialization, being treated as outsiders or looked down on, are heterogeneous, and one way that they may differ depends on the extent to which students have achieved important social and educational goals. Linda confirms that education and reproduction are highly, even equally valued. This may be especially true for women because regardless of their educational or career achievements, they will be judged inadequate by Dani standards if they do not marry and have children. This is not to say that men (or their relatives who might contribute to bridewealth) see no value in an educated wife (see Munro 2017), but traditionally young brides were sought-after and producing children is a persistent expectation and desire of most couples. Women who are perceived to be 'old' (i.e. over about twenty-five years of age) because they have delayed marriage for the sake of education might face difficulty in attracting a husband.

Betty and Linda's pregnancy experiences are shaped by the racialization of Papuan sexuality in North Sulawesi by Indonesian church ministers, doctors and professors as well as strangers and, potentially, other Dani. Betty found stigma and the likelihood of shame to be overwhelming. Linda, like some other women I knew, described feeling scrutinized by Indonesians, but expressed that judgemental views may be challenged.

Dealing with potential shame requires careful and gendered negotiations. Students having babies out of wedlock is in some ways a Dani parent's worst nightmare, or is certainly foreshadowed as such by the way that women are described as needing protection or monitoring. Not only are marital decisions and reproductive capacities being taken, to a certain extent, out of the purview of male relatives, but if pregnancy does bring about an end to studies, then some parents say that years of investment have been lost. Feelings other than shame are possible because these women have achieved a degree of independence and status due to their education (cf. Butt and Munro 2007). Indonesians might not recognize these achievements, but for some women, their relatives and other Dani do. If it is timed right, and gains legitimacy through eventual bridewealth, women may also be strategically managing their marriageability, which is perceived to decline sharply in their twenties.

Contests over the proper alignment of educational aspirations versus sexuality are, for Dani students, also contests over racial stigma and Indigenous continuity in the face of what looks and feels like elimination (Munro, forthcoming). Marital relationships and cultural understandings of reproductive legitimacy challenge the racialization of Papuans as promiscuous and thus unable to 'study first'. These constructions of sexuality racialize Papuan men as violent, irrational and dangerous, a threat to Indonesians, women and the nation-state. Women are racialized as passive victims of forced sex and male control. In North Sulawesi this is captured by Indonesian impressions that Papuan men get Papuan women pregnant and take no responsibility. In West Papua, the racialization of women as victims contributes to the rape and other sexual violence that Indonesian soldiers perpetrate (Komnas Perempuan 2010). In West Papua, violence shapes sexualities, and Indigenous sexualities continue to be pathologized. When some students argue that sex is normal, even productive and justifiable, they are also reclaiming Indigenous sexualities from Indonesian colonialism.

'Study first' is an example of the convergence of technocratic racism with 're-traditionalisation' in Indonesia (Nilan 2008: 79):

> [O]perating at a national security and stability level, the hegemonic discourse of ensuring moral and social order encourages the re-sacralisation of faith and family as a means of heading off the kind of social disorder that can lead to social anarchy and personal misfortune.

What young people do in terms of sexuality and family becomes subject to national judgement and surveillance. Young Indonesian human resources should be single, abstinent and childfree in addition to having technical skills and managerial knowhow. Retraditionalization enables the belittling of critical populations, such as educated Papuan youth who question the link between chastity and development, who surmise that marital legitimacy might have more to do with practice than legal documents or ceremonies, or who see through claims that proper Indonesian youth are postponing sex for the sake of education.

This chapter, more than the others so far, has thrown into relief the effect that the temporality of migration has on students' experiences and understandings. They are highly attuned to the fact that their time in North Sulawesi is limited and so are clearly considering how they might be received back home, and how things like premarital pregnancy might be understood differently in Wamena. Conceptions of success might even include going home with an educated spouse or as a newly graduated mother who can demonstrate her intellectual and reproductive capabilities. It is in relation to decisions about family formation that Dani most fervently reject Indonesian views and defend their cultural understandings and political strategies. The opportunity for marriage and childbearing abroad for potentially thousands of young Dani contributes to changing marital dynamics in the highlands, where bridewealth is becoming less common and more marriages are going unrecognized by the state, churches or traditional means. Where control over fertility and the future was integral to men's political and social standing and occurred via alliances and exchanges of wealth, today's Dani are taking control of their fertility (and, they feel, diminishing numbers) in relation to other kinds of politics. Dani sexual relations reveal Indigenous nationalism and cultural pride vis-à-vis Indonesian racialization.

7
Doing Good Things in a Dani Modernity

As students finish their educational journey with fanfare and celebration, they focus more clearly on what will become of them back home and what results they will produce. Dani graduates use their education to do good things for others in the relative absence of individual opportunities. There are limited opportunities for them to contribute to development in the ways they had imagined, and the public service is not necessarily brimming with paid jobs. Besides working for nongovernment organizations that focus on Indigenous-led development, graduates are helping other highlanders with Indonesian bureaucracies and state institutions using skills they developed abroad. In doing so, they are helping others to avoid humiliating experiences and, in a sense, are using their education to interrupt diminishment. Experiences of racialization, humiliation and discrimination influence Dani graduates to imagine a modernity characterized by segregation, protection and high levels of control over how, when, where and why highlanders encounter Indonesians and their institutions.

Graduation Stories

It seemed that *Kakak* Etinus had been inside the Unima auditorium since dawn. His female relatives had come to the Yepmum dorm after helping him iron his clothes early in the morning. While all around us students were queuing for the bathroom, males in various states of undress racing by in towels, radios left blaring pop music, Minke, Ina, Mama Gina and I got dressed in grubby shorts and collected garden tools. The men would take care of the pig and the firewood, but we had to dig, peel and wash enough cassava for the crowd of about a hundred people who would join Etinus and other graduates in celebrating their success later in the day. The money was flowing in from Wamena. Several times already this week, Minke and I had been handed a wad of cash and told to go shopping for pork and accompaniments at the market. But now we would cook a pork feast under hot rocks (*bakar batu*) for our own Etinus using produce from the garden plots of Mama Gina and Mama Yenny on Block D, Unima campus. The yard behind the dorm was coming alive with activity as we piled our tubers into giant laundry pails for scrubbing. There was a dead pig in one corner, lying on its back on some carefully arranged banana palm leaves. Two students were cutting it open and organizing the internal parts. In the middle of the yard there was a smouldering pile of wood, where some other men were starting to use giant wooden tongs to heat rocks for our pig feast. An hour or two later, our fingers raw from peeling cassava, it was time to get ready to meet Etinus at the auditorium. After bathing, Minke, Ina and I left the older women and the young children to walk up the hill to campus.

The sun was high in the sky and it was hot and bright in the large crowd of people outside the auditorium, and there was nothing to do but sit and wait. We were hungry, but imagined how hungry Etinus must be and did not complain. Every few minutes, a rumour would spread through the crowd that the ceremony going on inside was just about over. 'Is it finished?' and then the disappointing answer 'Not yet'. People looked at each other. They took photos of themselves. Some ate peanuts and oranges. From inside the auditorium, it was obvious to graduates what was taking so long – an endless series of congratulatory speeches from government and campus officials – but from outside, it seemed like graduates must be going through something arduous and important, the final step in their training. After years of hard work and setbacks, the daily grind of assignments and lectures, was the hard work still not finished? Then, about six hours after Etinus and others had taken their places in the auditorium, the doors started opening. Impatient relatives rushed in. Some graduates were rushing out. I was afraid for Ina, five months' pregnant, but she was determined. We spotted Minke's boyfriend Kodar first; standing next to him was Etinus. Minke, Ina and other relatives rushed over to him. There was shrieking, crying and hugging. Wobbly photographs were taken by me, crashing into others while trying to clear a space to capture the moment. It was the only time I saw Dani students expressing themselves freely without regard for the formal, public occasion or the crowd of people, or, as I wrote in my field notes that day (26 April 2006), 'going nuts in public'. The graduates looked so happy, proud and relieved. I thought we would be heading back to the dorm to open up the feast of steamed pork and cassava, but after two hours of photography (everyone wanted a picture in front of the wooden 'National University of Manado' sign), we arrived at the dorm in time for the start of another ceremony, this one organized by students themselves to mark the occasion. Another series of prayers, speeches and songs began, and we did not eat until dark. No matter how punishing, such great accomplishments had to be marked with the right amount of ceremony, discipline and propriety.

The ceremony held at Yepmum dorm was repeated at Dani dorms around Manado and Tondano. Typical social divisions were maintained. The Catholic

Figure 7.1. A graduation moment, Unima, 2006. Photo by author

Dani held their own coinciding ceremony in Tata Aran II, as did the Baptist Lani students.

The event at Yepmum was led and organized by Dani students who were not graduating yet. Banners announced the theme: 'Success inside the Embrace of God' (*Sukses dalam Perlindungan Tuhan*). The graduates were treated as guests of honour. They remained in their gowns and took positions near the front of the crowd of about 150 people. They were not expected to stand in front for the entire ceremony, but they were called to the front on several occasions so that other students could sing to them, lead prayers for them and talk about them fondly. Individual graduates (there were five that day from the Dani/Yali Protestant community at Unima) were asked to lead prayers of their own and give speeches to the students. Graduates made tearful and provocative statements that perfectly capture highlander identities and aspirations. Siko said: 'I am just a village boy born in the garden but I wanted to learn and now I have. I am going home to help the community.' Kodar expressed:

> I feel so blessed, and I give thanks to God for my success. I would not have been able to accomplish this without Him and without the support of friends and family. Except my family did not really support

Figure 7.2. Unima graduation. Photo by author

me, I did this on my own. I hope I will become Regent some day and bring modernity to Yahukimo.

A Lani preacher gave the sermon. He criticized the theme that students had chosen to mark the occasion, saying he would change it to 'the beginning of success' because in his view they did not really have 'success' yet. Rather than a hero's welcome, he asserted that they would probably encounter insults and suspicion back in the highlands, particularly if they had not learned their material well. Student speeches generally expressed the need to develop Papua and the important role for graduates. Etinus, for instance, posed the following question: 'If we do not do it, who will?' Some seven years later, I encountered a slightly revised version of the statement 'If not us, who? If not now, when?' in Papua on a daily basis during the election campaign of Lukas Enembe, a Lani man who became the first highlander governor and who also graduated from Unsrat in 1995. The ceremony effectively conveyed that graduates had reached goals of improvement and experience, and were rightfully acknowledged and respected by their peers, but questions were continually raised about translating their newfound confidence into results in Wamena. According to Kodar: 'Development means making Papuans prosperous, safe and healthy. It means turning on the electricity and teaching old people to read. This is what we want to do.' Jhon said: 'I want to go home and teach the children, my little brothers and sister to read and write, and to speak English.'

This sort of confidence at being graduates derives in part from the many years of being belittled for not yet being finished – the quizzing by virtual strangers and professors, as well as their own kin back home, about how long they have been at it and when they will be done. Indonesian professors racialize Papuan students as slow learners who lack the discipline and commitment to finish their degrees efficiently, and who therefore must take short cuts by paying for services and achievements. Because of structural constraints not limited to poverty and lack of tuition money, discrimination, violence and insecurity, being unable to finish university, or taking a long time to finish, is not that uncommon. Students may return home in search of more funds, a bit of belonging and reconnection, or to do their research component, and never get back on the ship to Manado. Being finished is a triumphant and powerful experience, and likely reflects overcoming significant challenges, navigating precarity and dodging near-misses.

Still, they face the prevalent theme that whatever they have achieved does not matter until they have achieved something in the Baliem Valley, in Yahukimo or in Manda, in Wouma or in Wolo:

> There is so much support in Wamena if the kids will just take the money and work hard, finish quickly. The kids have to learn well here, because over there it is all in the field. If you do not know what to do it will be obvious. The people will think there is no use in supporting students. (Yos)

Many students want to take up this challenge. Their time abroad has taught them that there is little to be gained by engaging with non-highlanders. Forays into 'learning about others' has affirmed the feeling that the highlands is the only world that feels comfortable, welcoming and right for them, and that success abroad means little if it cannot be demonstrated back home.

Homecomings (c. 2009)

> When I got home my father killed a big pig that he had been saving for me and we had a huge party. Everyone in my family was there, and even the neighbours came. I had not been home to Wamena since 2000 or 2001. I met my brother's two children who were born while I was away, and I cried. Several of my old grandparents died while I was away and I cried for them too. My family cried because they had not seen me for a long time and they were happy I was home. Everything

is back to normal now. I live in a *honai* [traditional round thatched hut, Dani language] with some men, I eat *hipere* [sweet potato, Dani language], I shit in the woods. In Manado I got fat and white, here I am skinny and dark again. (David)

We got home just in time to get to our village and organize a proper marriage before Viktor was born. Ina was enormous and we could hardly get there, as we had to walk part of the way. Our families agreed that we could get married. As soon as Viktor was born, we returned to Wamena. I started work right away as a teacher with no salary. I experienced so much stress I thought I might explode, but things are better now. I am still a teacher but I have a salary and I like teaching. I might test for another type of position next year. Everything is good. Viktor even has a younger sister now. I had some hard times in Tondano but everyone supported me. It was a long time to be away but my friends and family were there to entertain me, lift my spirits and cook *bakar batu* with me. That is one great thing about Manado; we sure ate a lot of pig! (Etinus)

My informant Anton from the Catholic dorm in Manado returned home without his diploma after all, as he spent the required funds elsewhere. This seemed to be a surprising move, considering how important it was to Anton and his family, particularly his older sister who was supporting him financially, that he finish his final examinations and return home. Yet after all the effort he made to get his final examination held, he returned home a graduate with no diploma to prove it, and thus he was unable to apply for employment for about two years. He was reluctant to join the public service anyway and worked for a legal aid NGO. He then landed a job on the local electoral commission, where his task was to keep the votes safe from tampering. In 2009, he was hiding out somewhere in Papua with the votes from Jayawijaya regency and reportedly received huge amounts of money for this responsibility, lest he take bribes to 'misplace' the votes of rival political parties. Although he was more involved in the logistics of elections rather than party politics, this is an example of how politics is a new domain of opportunity opening up for some Dani and other Papuans (especially those in areas where there are new districts requiring political representation), in the relative absence of opportunities in the private sector. These avenues depend on alliances and networks with more powerful or connected men, and suggest a reinvigorated space of masculinity where competition, social skills and strategic networks that were a hallmark of highlands society flourish once again. Alliances with Indonesians might be sought after, but given the racializing experiences of most educated Dani, their chances of success are greater if they collaborate with other highlanders.

Minke lived in Wamena with her son in a small house in Wamena for a while where she grew vegetables and helped her in-laws. She then moved to Yahukimo regency with her husband Kodar when he got work in the public service. Kodar paid bridewealth in instalments: one large pig worth 10 million rupiah and 200,000 rupiah a month for six months, according to Minke. They spent some time in Yahukimo together with Kodar's relatives who adore Minke and are proud of the bride that Kodar 'stole' from the Walak Dani. Minke described her time in North Sulawesi as boring, difficult and frustrating. She was initially proud and excited about being a student, and still argues that she acquired new skills and potential even though she did not finish her degree. But after her female relatives transferred from Unima to Unsrat, she felt lonely and miserable. When I met Minke again in June 2009, she was in high spirits, on her way to the airport to send vegetables from her relatives in Wolo to her husband in Yahukimo regency. Back in the highlands, educated men outnumber educated women, and women feel pressure to marry, produce children and, to a lesser extent, be housewives. These are not the only options available to them, but these, not formal employment, continue to be the minimum standards for successful womanhood. Today, formal employment can also be combined with traditional gender expectations, and some husbands and fathers do prioritize egalitarian relations with and treatment of wives and daughters (Munro 2017).[1] Minke, as far as I know, did not pursue further study or take up formal employment.

Returned students and graduates express that the camaraderie they achieved in the intensive environment abroad dissipates once they are home, possibly related to competition for employment and success. The organizations they have built are no longer relevant, and alumni from the same university or student organization do not necessarily support each other back in Wamena. Returned students do not hold their own *acara* (events) to mark Easter, Christmas or personal milestones, though they may take up leadership roles in the community events produced in their villages. Still, this does not mean that the intensified experience of highlander identity or the networks they built have no lasting effects. There are a good number of graduates who continue to know each other well and keep in touch with one another. However, perhaps back in Wamena, among family, and where everyone knows one another and (with exceptions) is constantly connecting and strategizing, graduates feel there is less support and protection because it is not needed in the same way as it was in North Sulawesi.

At the same time, fears of being identified as fakes or failures who did not really learn appear largely unfounded. In Wouma village, for example, people complained about two graduates who were considered unimpressive, but both were criticized for failing to live up to Dani norms, not because they had failed to study properly, bring about electricity or otherwise transform the community. The first was semi-employed at the Wamena branch of a student organization (AMPTPI), but was a disappointment to his family because he was in a relationship with a woman who was, according to the moiety system, his relative. He refused to end the relationship and they lived together as a married couple. His mother Helena stated:

> We have no one to help us develop our family. Joseph should be the leader of our family since his father is deceased but he does nothing for us because he is busy with this woman, bringing shame and sickness to us all. We supported his education for nothing.

The other poorly regarded graduate had recently completed a graduate degree at Unsrat, returned home with a large amount of mysteriously obtained money, bought a four-wheel drive Toyota Kijang (a type of sport utility vehicle) and held wild parties at his home on the outskirts of Wamena. He was accused of never helping out any of his younger relatives, even those who were studying at Unsrat. One scorned informant said that the man had promised to help him pay his final examination fees, but when he telephoned to ask for assistance, he was berated and treated harshly.

Despite what students propose while they are in North Sulawesi, it does not seem to be the case that Dani are waiting with great anticipation for young educated sons and daughters to return and unleash the region's potential for modernity. Helena said: 'My son will be coming home soon I think. He has been there for ages. I supported his education because I want him to have an easier life than I do. Working in the garden is hard work and we never have any money. It's nice to just relax, smoke a cigarette, take a nap.' Anton said: 'I think our parents just want us to be able to take care of ourselves, so they do not have to take care of us.' Rather, relatives left behind might simply hope that their graduates will be able to provide for themselves, not cause problems or be a burden on them, and may be able to share a little of their earnings someday. Thus, it seems the high expectations students anticipated from their sponsors had, in some cases, more to do with what they expected of themselves, related to the heroic identity of 'university graduate' or 'educated person'. At the same time, it is equally probable that the dreams of parents, sponsors and community members are also diminished; ultimately, they expect very little from Indonesian modernity.

Modern Poverty: Dani in the Public Service

In 2009, a handful of North Sulawesi graduates made it into the public service, mostly as teachers. Even with the supposed emphasis on hiring Papuans, and in contrast to accusations that Papuans are hired without any qualifications, it normally takes several attempts, a family connection or a great deal of luck to get into even the lowest-paid positions in the public service. Twice a year, regency-level governments recruit new employees. Candidates must submit the appropriate application documents and undertake an examination specific to the job they wish to hold. Positions are limited, and passing the examination is not sufficient to gain employment. According to Dani informants, actually getting a job depends on having family members already employed by the government who can 'push' one candidate's application ahead of another's. It is no longer true to say that all government positions and positions of power are held by Indonesians, but it is still true that Indigenous employment is highly concentrated in the public sector. Even in the public service, Dani and other highlanders are in the minority.

In June 2009, several local governments announced the successful job applicants by listing their names and positions in the *Cenderawasih Post*, Papua's major daily newspaper. Working with several Dani assistants, I analysed the family names of the new employees accepted into the Jayawijaya regency government to classify them as 'Indigenous Wamena' and 'non-Indigenous Wamena'. 'Indigenous Wamena' refers to employees whose family name identifies them as belonging to one of the main Indigenous groups of the central highlands: Dani, Yali, or Lani. 'Non-Indigenous Wamena' refers to all other employees, both other Papuans and Indonesians. We identified 41 per cent or 112 of the 275 new recruits in the June 2009 selection to be 'Indigenous Wamena' people, while 59 per cent of the new employees were from outside the central highlands. The only field of employment in which Indigenous Wamena recruits outnumbered non-Wamena recruits was in the 'nurse-in-training' field of employment, which requires the least amount of education. No Indigenous people gained employment as doctors, pharmacists or laboratory technicians. Most of the Indigenous Wamena candidates (58 out of 112) were accepted as teachers in elementary and secondary schools, but even in this field they were outnumbered by non-Wamena recruits. There were 99 non-Wamena candidates accepted into teaching positions in the June 2009 selection round.

Informants said that Indigenous Wamena candidates should have an advantage over migrants, especially since this was eight years after the introduction of the Special Autonomy Law that is supposed to favour Indigenous candidates. From the list of names, it appeared that many of the non-Wamena recruits were not Papuan, but rather Indonesian migrants, particularly in the specialist occupations such as doctors and laboratory technicians. I also looked at the list of new employees accepted into the provincial government in Jayapura. I would not expect to find that many highlanders gained employment in the provincial capital as these positions tend to go to local people from Jayapura regency, but it is still somewhat surprising that three out of a total of 173 new recruits accepted into the provincial government in Jayapura originate from the central highlands (*Cenderawasih Post,* 22 June 2009). Similarly, in Mamberambo Raya, a newly established regency that covers territory immediately to the north of Jayawijaya regency, just three out of 264 new recruits are from the central highlands, despite the fact that the regency capital is not far from Wamena (*Cenderawasih Post,* 22 June 2009). David and Mama Mateus in Wamena say that they were encouraged to apply for positions in the new regency because it would be accepting a large number of new employees. Mama Mateus did sit the examination for Mamberambo Raya regency, but she was not accepted into the service. It is significant that Indigenous Wamena people were still a minority in government jobs because the public service continues to be the main source of employment; they are outnumbered even more in the private, commercial, financial and service sectors.

Those who did get a government job sometimes expressed disappointment with this form of 'success'. Government jobs did not present an opportunity to transform anything or earn much money. Former students I met up with in June 2009 who had been accepted as teachers expected to receive a salary of about 3,500 rupiah (about US$0.35) per hour. In June 2009, 3,500 rupiah would buy 140 grams of rice, 175 grams of sugar or a short ride in a pedicab (*becak*) in Wamena:

> When I got here I was a bit confused about what to do. This year I applied for a job in the public service. My friend helped me so that I could take two tests, one for a teaching job and one for a better job in the legal section. I was accepted as a teacher. I still probably will not have any money because teachers only get 3,000 rupiah an hour. But I cannot complain too much because other people who took the test did not get accepted at all. (David)

When I was in Wamena in June 2009, David was staying with Mama Mateus, a home I often visited. He had a habit of disappearing whenever it seemed like food was about to be served. Mama Mateus explained: 'He is just like that. He is embarrassed that he has no money and he refuses to eat our food because we have two children and grandma to look after and my husband's wage is not enough for us either.' While education had not yet translated into increased wealth, David's opinion was valued by others and he was invited to Dani community discussions about social problems or other issues. He was perceived to have knowledge and experience that is of use to other Dani, which translated into social status, if not money. Getting into the public service was an ambivalent achievement for David and other graduates.

Good Hearts, Good Hands

Although the results educated Dani achieve are much smaller in scale than they spoke of during their education in North Sulawesi, the vision of 'making good things happen for others' (Zimmer-Tamakoshi 1997: 110) prevails. A desire to do good for others is part of demonstrating that one has a 'good heart', which is necessary to gain prestige and influence in the community. Alua (2006: 154) writes: 'A leader who has a good heart can make decisions for the greater good. He will prioritise the needs and interests of the people over his personal needs and the interests of his family.' In June 2009, I visited graduates involved in local nongovernment organizations. Working for such an organization is an opportunity to build one's network of contacts and reputation, and the work offers a sense of purpose and achievement. Graduates working at these organizations did not generally receive a salary, but if the organization had obtained funding for its activities, volunteers might receive 'taxi fare' (*uang taksi*) for a day's efforts. If they were experienced enough to help lead field activities in the community, they would receive several hundred thousand rupiah (approximately US$30–50) for a day's work. Still, even 'taxi fare' of 15,000 or 20,000 rupiah helps to secure a graduate's position as a breadwinner in someone's household. The ability to make small contributions is enough to differentiate them from graduates who do not work and from people with limited education who do not earn money.

One such former student, Markus, was spending his days working for an NGO. Markus lived with the family of Mama Mateus. She described what a delight it was to have Markus around, perhaps in comparison to other relatives who turned up for meals or to help with cooking, but were not able or willing to lessen the financial burden Mama Mateus felt over trying to provide for all the extra dinner guests. She said: 'Markus has not been staying with us long, but he often provides for us, not the other way around. If he has a few thousand rupiah, he will spend it on onions or a few packets of instant coffee. I am sure he will help a lot of people in the future.'

I ran into Ana (a Lani woman who graduated from Unsrat in 2007) in the airport in Jayapura. She was on her way back to Wamena after a training exercise with an NGO working on women's issues. She explained that she was just training and was not on the staff yet, but that the NGO and her older brother had paid her way to Jayapura and she was enjoying the work. She was heading off to Mulia, in Puncak Jaya regency, she said, to inform people there of the NGO and its activities. Even though she has a degree in management, she expressed excitement about her role as an advocate for women's empowerment:

> I just talk to people and listen to their problems, sometimes I help them solve problems or look for ways to improve their situation. In the inte-

rior people do not really know about empowerment. The NGO has limited resources so I am just volunteering because I think it is important.

After working for NGOs, Ana eventually began working in a bank and married a Papuan from the coast. She still lives in Wamena.

Besides as a means to qualify for government employment, the major way in which educated Dani men and women utilize literacy and formal education is by dealing with what Tania Li (2003: 387) calls 'power-saturated encounters' with the government bureaucracy and mostly Indonesian professionals, teachers and civil servants, on behalf of other Indigenous people. Among my informants, it was typical practice that if a visit to a government office, school or hospital was unavoidable, rural or less-educated individuals would be accompanied by an educated relative or friend to avoid the confusion, discomfort and embarrassment that resulted from being treated badly by staff. In some cases, the efforts of educated individuals did translate into assistance to others. On the day that school students received their report cards, mothers and fathers from Wouma village gathered at the home of Mama Mateus to discuss who would have to go and collect the reports. Parents, mostly without formal education, said they were afraid they would be asked to sign their names, something they did not know how to do. Children were crying about the problem. Some university students were enlisted to visit three different elementary and junior secondary schools to collect reports on behalf of five children. One of the university students, Laurence, explained that:

> Someone has told them they will have to sign their names, which is probably not true, but the fear of being embarrassed is too great . . . at school, in offices, in front of others, they would appear strange. We cannot let them go through this, so we do it for them . . . We do not feel so embarrassed because we have to do it, and we have more experience.

University students and graduates may be able to use literacy skills and experience with Indonesians to help others avoid humiliation or discrimination. In such cases, educated men and women may experience some sense of achievement in cultural terms because they are able to do good things for others. Yet the 'go to' person who accompanies a neighbour on a visit to the doctor or types a letter does not achieve much prowess, prestige, influence or social standing in the absence of tangible results and material benefits. Educated people often remain at the mercy of impoverished relatives for daily sustenance and lodging, until and unless they manage to acquire low-paying government jobs, often years after graduating. Thus, returning home from university, graduates like David expressed that 'everything is the same again'. From the perspective of Indigenous parents with no formal education, a little bit of literacy could help alleviate shameful encounters such as those they feared would take place at school on report card day. But for educated individuals, small acts of mediation do not produce the hoped-for benefits, whether tangible or intangible, that should or might result from many years at school or university. At the same time, Dani understandings of human resources were never limited to technical skills and public performances, always included values of helping others, and financial success was never mentioned.

What is noteworthy in Laurence's explanation of how educated people may help uneducated relatives and friends is the lack of self-promotion or sense of high status. He is merely resigned to the fact that: 'We have to do it . . . We have more experience.' In another place, perhaps such as McKeown (2006) describes in highlands Papua New Guinea, educated youth might be advertising their literacy skills around town, emphasizing their accomplishments and how important they are in terms of helping community members. In Wamena, literacy sometimes just means more opportunities to encounter Indonesians and the government system in ways that produce disappointment, if not feelings of inadequacy, as a result of one's inability to make good things happen. As of yet, there is very little indifference to the arbitrariness of bureaucratic outcomes. This could be because bureaucratic outcomes are not arbitrary, but quite consistently discriminatory, and Dani know this. It may also be because controlling institutions and flows of people and goods in Dani territory is still very sensitive and contested.

Via technocratic racism, Papuans are accused of being low-quality human resources and may be excluded from jobs (and development more broadly) on the basis that they lack knowledge, experience and skills (among other things). But when they acquire these capabilities via an Indonesian education, there is no flood of opportunities. It is not surprising that education does not fundamentally change racial hierarchies or that it reaffirms existing inequalities, but it is crucial for understanding West Papua today that young Indigenous men in particular experience economic exclusion amidst what seems like an abundance of work opportunities for others, especially Indonesians (Munro 2019). In this era of empowerment for Indigenous Papuans, why are there more Indonesians in West Papua than ever before? This study has shown that arguments that Papua needs Indonesians (and other external experts) because Papuans lack skills, particular technical abilities, disciplinary commitments or do not subscribe to Indonesian values are the new prevailing racial logics that promote discrimination and exclusion.

Belonging and Danger: Modernities of Protection and Control

When I met Ana in June 2009, I asked her if she missed Manado. 'Not really', she replied. She continued:

> All of my friends have left there and are now mostly in Wamena. I probably would not know anyone there if I went back. I am glad I went there, because the education here in Papua is of lower quality, but I also went there because my brother paid for me to go there. He chose the place. Living in Wamena is so much harder, like the weather is cold and everything is too expensive, but I could never stay away permanently. I will always come back to Wamena. Orang Wamena are not suited to living in other places for too long.

When Ana points out that she does not know anyone in Manado besides her highlander friends, who have all left, she indicates that she did not form any lasting relationships with non-highlanders. Other students were more critical of the people they met in North Sulawesi. When I met up with Lex, who had acquired a teaching position in Wamena, I asked him to reflect on his experiences in Tondano. He asserted that:

> The people there are more arrogant towards us than the Indonesians here in Wamena. Here people are afraid of us. I think people here are actually more polite, because this area is dangerous. We still have land issues here. I mean, this is our place, we are many, and they are bringing us trouble.

The social world Lex described suggests that in Wamena, Dani and Indonesians are separated by conditions of fear and potential danger. According to Lex, Indonesians keep their feelings hidden to avoid causing trouble that may lead to violence and because they know that it is not their land. Perhaps young, strong, educated men like Lex inspire some politeness or fear in Indonesians, but for most Dani, this is not the case. Others, such as the Dani women I met at the public health clinic who felt belittled and confused, or village elders visiting a government office, had different experiences.

For graduates like Lex, it is possible to argue that the feeling of being looked down on is more penetrating in North Sulawesi because, at least initially, students want to enter into the social worlds of Indonesians. Conditions in Wamena may largely mitigate against such desires and possibilities in the first place. In line with Lex's gathering view of himself and other Dani as rightful landowners with territory to control and defend, some students become politically active in North Sulawesi and remain so back home. A student I call Sam was arrested and imprisoned in 2011 for participating in the Third Papuan Congress, a peaceful political gathering in Jayapura. He was jailed for three years. Political work, in the sense of activism that draws attention to human rights abuses, critiques Indonesian rule and/or promotes Papuan independence, is a primarily male domain in West Papua. This relates to the very real possibility of violence and arrest or physical harm by Indonesian authorities. The prevalence of risk, confrontation, violence and stigmatization marks nationalist politics as a primarily masculine space. Being on the frontline of politics tends to eclipse the possibility of formal employment, so it furthers poverty and isolation for some men. In other cases, students who did not seem to be involved in politics in North Sulawesi later apparently became quite active after returning home. I was surprised to hear that a student I knew well in Manado, whom I refer to as Herbert, was shot and killed by Densus 88 (short for Detasemen Khusus 88 or Special Detachment 88), an Australian-trained and supported special forces unit in the Indonesian police, in Wamena in 2012. At the time, Indonesian news reported that he was a leader of a militant section of the now-banned West Papua National Committee (*Komite Nasional Papua Barat*). When I knew him, he spoke cogently of discriminatory dynamics and injustice experienced by students in Manado, but he was not, to my knowledge, politically active. Herbert and Sam are not the only students who may have become more critical, politicized or even radicalized by their experiences of racialization, surveillance and diminishment in North Sulawesi. Politicization and exclusion converge with intensified cultural identity and territorial commitments.

For example, Ana's statement that 'Wamena people are not suited living in other places' and 'will always come back' reminded me of my first trip to West Papua three years earlier. My arrival in Papua began in the provincial capital, where I descended from a passenger ship on a very hot night, pressed through a crowd of people, cartons and containers, manoeuvred ungracefully into an overstuffed minibus and rode until we reached a steep path into (eventually) a Dani housing complex. In areas of Jayapura such as Dok Dua, where I stayed, Dani people live together and make a living through formal employment as well as gardening (see Farhadian 2005). Women sell produce at particular spots in the city with other Dani. They mostly marry other Dani. Their homes become transit hubs for Dani coming down from the highlands and going back home again. They are fully involved in all communal rituals, particularly funerals. I spent a few days with the family of a student in Jayapura in June 2006. Patrick was busy working odd jobs while I was there, so I spent quite a bit of time with his mother-in-law, who told me about her childhood in Wamena. Mama Mantu and her daughter claimed to despise living in Wamena because it is 'cold, backward, and dirty'. They had settled down in Jayapura despite the fact that: '*Orang Wamena* take risks by living in Jayapura.' There was almost always a Dani funeral ritual going on in Mama Mantu's neighbourhood. She argued that this was because Jayapura was a bad environment for Wamena people. Not understanding, I asked her why they did not go somewhere else on the coast where the weather is also warm, thinking she meant that Jayapura was too urban or Indonesian. In her raspy voice she barked: 'I do not have any people in Sorong [a city on the coast]! If I went to Sorong, who would help me?' She explained that Dani are only safe in the highlands because that is their place, their land, and that is where they have 'people', both living and deceased. Ancestors who are satisfied with the funeral rites in their name protect the living, while secret ancestral knowledge perpetuates the continuance of clans. Her other comments suggested that it was difficult to be with Dani all the time, but it was the only way to live:

> We get into fights all the time. I fight with all of my relatives and hardly speak to half of them. But I do not have anyone else. Yesterday, I screamed at my daughter's husband's sister. Tomorrow, someone will send vegetables from Wamena and I will have to share them with her. This is how we are.

In other words, Dani must engage, exchange, fulfil obligations and reciprocate in order to continue being Dani and in order to survive. In light of the experiences of Dani students described in this book, it is likely that Dani in Jayapura also find it difficult to create relationships of reciprocity and trust with non-Dani. A fuller examination of the experiences and perceptions of the 'homeland' among Dani in Jayapura is beyond the scope of this book, but it is significant that for Dani in Jayapura, North Sulawesi and Wamena, being amongst other highlanders is seen as the best and perhaps only safe place. This does not mean, however, that Dani cannot create new communities in other places.

Highlanders in North Sulawesi committed to education abroad at a time of unprecedented violence between Indigenous people and Indonesian migrants in the highlands, when new freedoms were swiftly crushed by Indonesian forces. In spite of efforts to mount their own acts of reform after the fall of Suharto's authoritarian regime in 1998, Papuans were largely forced to watch from the sidelines as Indonesians took advantage of an atmosphere of political openness to demonstrate in the streets and critique state power in ways that were previously impossible without violent retribution. It quickly became clear that political tolerance was not extended to Papuan concerns or critiques (see Mote and Rutherford 2001). The more that Dani students learn about subjects like economics, law or governance, the more obvious it becomes that such norms and principles do not apply in Papua. Moreover, many in North Sulawesi watched as friends and family, mostly fellow students, were treated as enemies of the state in Papua for criticizing duplicitous government practices or for no apparent reason at all. Sometimes students also got caught up in violence in Papua. In March–April 2009, there was an atmosphere of fear and tension related to numerous killings, violent incidents, and increased police and military operations leading up to and during the 2009 national legislative elections. On 9 April, according to national news services, a crowd of Papuans attacked the local police station next to the Cenderawasih University campus in the middle of the night. The Vice Chancellor's building was also set on fire. Police opened fire and then went hunting for Papuan students in the vicinity. Papuan reports suggest that the 'attack', like other incidents surrounding the election period, was orchestrated by others and that the police may have seen the crowd and attacked first (as has frequently happened in West Papua). Police spoke proudly of having killed the 'attackers'. A student who arrived in Manado in 2006 and lived in the same Catholic dorm as I did was shot as he fled from police in Jayapura. His name was Erik Logo and he was shy, polite and helpful to others. He was a good 'younger sibling'.

Dani students in North Sulawesi have thus far escaped physical violence at the hands of Indonesian police, but their experiences of stigma and being looked down on (*gengsi*, literally, superiority or arrogance) reveal practices of emotional violence, or Indonesian attempts at diminishment. Students' experiences encourage resistance, protectionism and avoidance of Indonesians and even, potentially, coastal Papuans. Dreams of recognition and relationships are severely circumscribed and dramatically reoriented in the process. In this modernity, Wamena people assist, compete with and try to impress one another. They try to create exclusive spaces of security and authority. These are not the effects commonly associated with education, urban mobility and migration. The modernity that Dani graduates express hopes for is one that shelters Wamena people, that ensures their survival and that allows them to determine how, when and for what purposes Dani interact with Indonesians. The racializing experience of education abroad engenders these sentiments and fosters cultural momentum. Dani elders may talk more of political power writ large (independence or Indigenous reclamation), but young Dani also want to reveal and change the everyday inequalities that may produce experiences of diminishment.

Note

1. This publication looks at the experiences and views of Dani men who actively consider and try to pursue modern gender ideals, but whose efforts may be thwarted, go awry or result in unpredictable outcomes. I conclude that innovative gender ideas are not always translated into practice, and practising equality in gender relations may be challenged by broader conditions that make unequal relations the path of least resistance.

Conclusion
Koteka Questions

> The old people used to wear *koteka* and did not feel ashamed,
> but now, we know the feeling of shame. (Benyamin)

One morning (19 April 2006) at the Yepmum dorm, Benyamin, Minke, Lepis and I were watching television. A domestic Indonesian travel programme advertised that on the next show, the Javanese presenter would be 'on location' in the interior of Papua. Some footage of highlands men wearing penis gourds followed. As always, students were excited that something about the highlands was on national television. However, there were shouts of 'Oh no!' and, 'Oh my God!' when the pictures of the men in penis gourds appeared. Lepis, a Yali student, said: 'Oh no, everyone will see our parents wearing penis gourds. This is really embarrassing. But it is our culture and we cannot escape it.' Benyamin laughed: 'The government tried to give them pants but they refused to wear them!'

The penis gourd (*koteka*) features strongly for students as an emblem of alleged primitiveness unique to their region. Although students are well aware of the dominant perception of the penis gourd (some report being teased about penis gourds in North Sulawesi), they still speak respectfully of those who wear it. These men tend to be older, and students argue that that those who wear the penis gourd find it to be comfortable, appropriate and are making a statement about their cultural identity. In spite of his comment about people refusing to wear trousers from the government, Benyamin went on to say: 'Clothes are from the government and the missionaries. Some of our people were happy about clothes. We like wearing clothes. But some people prefer the penis gourd, no matter what others think or say.'

Many male students claim to have worn a penis gourd for annual battle re-enactments (*perang-perangan*) put on for tourists during the Baliem Valley festival, for dance competitions in Jakarta or even at political demonstrations. It is said to be exciting to wear because it takes great courage to overcome the shame of being almost entirely nude and to expose oneself to others in this way. Thus, while students understand the primitive connotations associated with not wearing clothes or still wearing penis gourds, this is not the whole story for them. Wearing the penis gourd can be a preference. Wearing it also demonstrates, for students and others, courage, tenacity and commitment. It is the opposite of shameful. What I take from this is that when highlanders are allowed to see themselves according to their own perspectives and standards, they are tenacious and courageous. What worries them is having to see themselves through the gaze of others.

Figure 8.1. Indonesian tourists at the Baliem Valley Festival battle re-enactment. Photo by author

Contact between Dani and Indonesians sometimes, but not always, elicits a confrontation of perspectives. Indonesians typically see Dani as black, poor, slow, politicized and anti-Indonesia, immoral, promiscuous and possibly seeking a fast, superficial route to a public service job. Dani students criticize and challenge much of this racialization, and thus threaten to upset the 'natural' order of things – Papuans may be educated, intelligent, sophisticated, have money (at times) and ask pointed questions about belonging and equality in the Indonesian nation. As a result, Dani students are encouraged to be shy, embarrassed and even ashamed (captured in the term *malu*). This is the subjectivity most commonly made available to them, even when they have increased their skills, education, urban experience and an open and humble attitude. Dani students avoid Indonesians because they are anticipating embarrassment and because in their experiences, Indonesians think poorly of them. Students reject the grounds on which they are excluded, but the feeling of not belonging, or of being out of place, is harder to dispel. Discomfort, awkwardness and the feeling of being scrutinized are perhaps the more insidious effects of stigma, because they place limits on students' ability to assert themselves and take prominent positions.

The racial logics evoked and tested in Dani–Indonesian encounters are gendered – on some level 'primitiveness' is associated with masculinity (with penis gourd as shorthand) and Dani men are seen to butt heads with, or sometimes be dominated by, Indonesian men. Being seen as a good labourer invokes men's physical features, but women are also stigmatized as a bit 'wild' or at least unrefined – they go along with the men, after all, hiking up into the jungle to cook with hot rocks, sitting in the dirt and scrubbing clothes in a stream. Being good for labour is the flipside of alleged intellectual inferiority or slowness, and men therefore seem to experience this more than women. When it comes to sexuality, however, the stigma of promiscuity is directed at men and women equally, but women feel more of the shame of this because female sexuality is, in Dani, Indonesian, and Christian practices, judged more harshly than male sexuality. Male students, many of whom are pursuing Dani women, hardly seem concerned about being seen as promiscuous.

On the whole, educational journeys abroad are in many ways more fraught for women, who are outnumbered by men, are forced to be more concerned about their reputations and whose education represents contemporary questions about appropriate roles for men and women. For women, is education and a career really a more viable, or desirable, option than marriage and children? Certainly Dani women – and, to a lesser extent, men – are grappling with questions of how much education and career potential can be achieved before marital and reproductive prospects are diminished. Some remaining questions are: what level of education and achievement are Dani men willing to embrace in their wives? How much education will women want to achieve if they get stigmatized for not having children? Women are supporters of independence from Indonesia and do not escape surveillance and intimidation in North Sulawesi or West Papua, but men bear the brunt of this reputation and are more public about their political aspirations. It is men who are seen as a threat to the local Indonesian community – indeed, the nation – and thus they are in more danger of reprisals and repression from the authorities.

Public and scholarly attention has been directed at state violence and human rights abuses in Papua, but the circumstances I have described also point to more subtle forms of violence through which inner processes are reshaped. These forms are not unlike what Papuans refer to as Indonesia's 'refined politics', or covert strategies of control and genocide. The national narrative of education, in West Papua and elsewhere, invites young people to believe in the possibilities of transformation and equality, but is silent about structural and political violence: the realities of in-migration, poor-quality schooling, prejudicial hiring practices and racialization that goes unacknowledged by broader society. In fact, these inequalities are hidden behind technocratic racism, or claims that Papuans lack skills, expertise and human resource qualities for effective participation in development and governance. In spite of the critical assessments of highlanders who have experienced the silent, everyday violence of Indonesian modernity, the inflated possibilities of transformation set Indigenous men and women up to fail. Rachel Shah (2016: 244) proposes that nowadays Papuan highlanders know that conditions will constrain what they can achieve, are aware of different kinds of educational 'success' and pursue formal education anyway. I agree that perhaps nowadays there is more widespread awareness of the limitations of education precisely because of highlanders' experiences trying to translate education, especially university degrees, into tangible results over the past decade. But, in addition, this study shows that highlanders' awareness of political, racialized and other constraints on achievements sits in tension with the very palpable, confronting and ongoing ways that they are diminished and blamed for failures of development, expertise and governance.

A keen sense of the political implications of knowledge, literacy and employment, including the possibility of transforming existing inequalities, has also emerged out of Dani experiences of colonialism and Indonesian 'progress'. Stigma forms parts of a broader context of diminishment that informs and hampers personal and political dreams. Highlanders' educational journeys have shown that diminishment operates at different scales and in multidimensional ways. As a crucial mechanism of Indonesian colonialism, diminishment is not just about discourses or confrontation with foreign agents and authoritative judgements. Diminishment can be experienced, and contested, through the body, population numbers, self-understandings, and relationships, networks and alliances. It can be profoundly local, as well as embedded in national procedures and institutions.

Humiliation does not convince Dani students that they are inadequate or consolidate desires to be like 'modern' Indonesians. In fact, it intensifies their commitments to home and other highlanders. Shame promotes avoidance and resistance rather than assimilation or identification with national social norms. It promotes an affiliation with 'our' social norms, a hardening of group identities, and, sometimes, new forms of antagonism within the community as individuals try to live up to expectations borne out of stigma and scrutiny. Thus, stigma causes dreams of transformation to be limited, refashioned and politicized. Dani dreams of development, broadening horizons, cultural improvement, prosperity and power are translated, reshaped and perhaps narrowed towards political dreams of independence and sovereignty as a precursor to any other meaningful change. So when we try to analyse what is happening in West Papua today with the appearance of new ways of ostensibly promoting Papuan interests and empowering Papuans, we need to look at interactions, at contact and at how power operates in relationships, whether these are amongst couples, entrepreneurs, public servants or government officials. We need to consider racialization, scrutiny and intimidation, and ask how these conditions might affect the decisions that Papuans make and how they treat others. Racialization limits relationships with Indonesians, constrains aspirations and prevents national identification, but it also creates and intensifies other relationships, aspirations and identities.

Formal education emerges as an experience characterized by exclusion and division. It encourages little in the way of Indonesian nationalism, urban cosmopolitanism, cultural blending, broadening of horizons or learning from others. The education of West Papuans in Indonesia fosters critical consciousness, cultural resistance and decolonization. It is therefore important to keep asking, in other Melanesian and Indonesian contexts, how and under what circumstances schooling fosters unexpected aspirations for the future and consolidates local cultural identities.

In the 1980s, Douglas Hayward (1983: 3) characterized Dani as 'living on the fringes of Indonesian society'. It still appears to be true that even if highlanders take up Indonesian education, follow Indonesian understandings of modernity and develop skills regarded as important by Indonesians, they cannot become part of Indonesian communities in North Sulawesi, Wamena or anywhere else. After education abroad, the world of Indonesians is something that highlanders may question, looking instead for opportunities, connections and success via other highlanders. The 'price of admission to the national community' (Rosaldo 2003: i) is too high. Unless highlanders wish to put aside self-esteem, cultural pride and longstanding criticisms of the nation, they will never be part of those communities. For now, it is a struggle to engage on their terms. Using the metaphor of the *koteka*, it is a struggle to continue to see courage and tenacity where others only want to see nudity and primitiveness.

There Are No Small Acts

I began this book with a conversation I heard in Wouma, a village on the outskirts of Wamena, in which a ten-year-old named Andy was jokingly threatened with marriage if he did not hurry up and get ready for school. Andy's reluctance to go to school also reflected broader questions his family was considering about tradition (staying home, gardening, early marriage to a Dani woman) versus education (going away, a degree of independence, an urban career). These questions arose because Andy's eldest brother Darius died suddenly away from home in October 2006 in Jayapura, where he was a university student with a young family. After he died, Andy's father lamented that if only he and other relatives had been with Darius when he fell ill after a fishing trip, they might have been able to apologize to the ancestors and spirits and save his son. Going even further back, they suggested that if Darius had not gone away to university, which also opened the door for him to become a husband and father, he would not have needed to take up dangerous activities to earn money. Were he at home in the village, garden produce and market earnings would have taken care of his basic needs and those of his wife and two daughters.

Andy's relatives, including his father, had quiet conversations about his education. As the last son of a big man, should he stay close to the farm to learn the family *adat* (customs) and history, and traditional ways of achieving prosperity? What if they focused on Andy's formal education and something went wrong and he did not make it to university or, even if he did get to university, would a university education make up for the sort of clan chaos that would inevitably ensue if none of the young men knew the family traditions? Their conversations reminded me of the many things that did happen to students I knew or knew of who were studying away from home. Drawing on the stories of the students I knew, I would like to end with an imaginative reflection on the variety of forms that could be taken by Andy's future life, considering extremes of good and bad outcomes.

Andy could die. He could get sick and die, far from home, and his father would have a hard time doing anything about it. His friends would do their best to put on a funeral service, probably lasting several days, and would try to raise money for his family. His family would try to pay to have his body flown back to the highlands at a cost of 5–10 million rupiah. (If unable to do so, he would have to be buried abroad, a fate that upsets students just talking about it.) He might also struggle with alcohol, which caused the death of a prominent student in 2005, a son of another Wouma 'big man' who was among a select few to hold a special scholarship to study at STPDN (*Sekolah Tinggi Pemerintahan Dalam Negeri,* a higher education institute training future government leaders) in Bandung, Java.

Far from home, he might fall in love with the wrong girl, like Walan and Yan did. She might work magic on Andy, take over his life, humiliate him and then break up with him, leaving him to lose his way, to be depressed, to quit school and to drink too much alcohol. He might fall in love with a local Indonesian or non-Wamena woman and never return to life in the highlands. He might fall in love with a Dani woman and get her pregnant. Of course, his father would have little influence over the match and no immediate way to make it official and proper through a traditional wedding. If he were lucky, Andy would have someone raising his pigs, or raising pigs on his behalf, necessary for bridewealth in a traditional wedding. A pregnancy abroad would also likely delay Andy's graduation, and his family might have to worry about sending him more money to take responsibility for his wife and child.

If Andy's father and other kin did not continuously get money together to pay his school fees and living expenses abroad, Andy might end up dropping in and out of university, making his four-year degree turn into a six- or eight-year degree. During periods in which he was not actively studying, there is a good chance he would drink too much alcohol and experience a considerable amount of stress.

Andy might get involved in student organizations, work hard to be an honest treasurer, get caught between factions warring over stolen funds, resign his position and, in frustration and disappointment as a result of conflict and dishonesty among fellow students from Wamena, be less than enthusiastic about university life. He might get involved in student organizations abroad, steal funds from the organization and get assaulted by angry students, as happened to one of the Rupmawi leaders. He might quit university, fleeing to another city, as one student leader did when rumours surfaced about his misuse of scholarship money. Tired of being stuck in the third semester due to a lack of funds to bribe the lecturer for a final mark, he might lash out and be expelled, or implode, spending the rest of his days drinking and getting into fights. He might get into a protracted conflict with his professor over money, attire, the length and style of his hair, or assignments, and be forced to transfer to another university if he ever wants to graduate. Someone in or out of Wamena might be jealous (*iri*) and enact some kind of sorcery that people said made him sick or blind. He might bring all of his irreplaceable university documents (proof of fee payments, report cards) on a trip home to Wamena to apply for scholarships and lose them on board the ship, causing him to quit university rather than begin again.

Andy might receive money from home, purchase an economy-class boat ticket to somewhere in Indonesia and disappear for an extended period. He could become a born again Christian under the guidance of local Pentecostal families and enjoy his new life abroad so much that he would rather not return home to Wamena.

There is a good chance that some of Andy's professors and other public servants at university would ask him for money under the table, making him dread the idea of one day becoming a public servant himself, and causing him to drag his feet to graduation and spend more time partying. Upon returning home to Wamena without his diploma, he would rather wait for an opportunity to work for an NGO than join the government. On the other hand, he might become quite experienced in networking with public servants, gain employment in Wamena and become a prominent politician. He might become very rich, expertly embezzling vast amounts of public money. However, if he finally ran out of money or was fired from his job, he might end up depressed, paranoid, prone to psychotic episodes and isolated from the family, like Andy's uncle, who was once a member of parliament in Wamena.

Andy could eventually finish his university degree, make his way home and find himself unemployed, penniless and with considerable unpaid debts to his extended family. Out of shame, disappointment and boredom, he would probably drink too much and spend his time wandering about, visiting friends and not helping his father out on the farm.

Ideally, Andy would dedicate himself to schooling with conviction and energy. As a ten-year-old, he would be confident and energetic in class, despite being hungry, and despite his embarrassment over his torn, stained and ill-fitting school uniform. His mother and father would keep paying his school fees. Throughout his teenage years in Wamena, he would resist dropping out of school with his cohort to dig sand and rocks out of the We River to sell to construction projects. He would avoid alcoholism of young and older men, and avoid the glue-sniffing of even younger males (and females). He would stay clear of young women unless they were his relatives. It would be important that Andy would avoid getting into trouble with Wamena's heavy police and military presence, but also that running, hiding or submitting to them would not make him feel like less of a man. While helping on the farm and with customary activities, he would still graduate from high school and do well on the national university entrance exam. His father, mother or uncle would sell some pigs, he would take that money and leave, getting his first aerial view of Wamena's Grand Valley and majestic mountains on his first plane ride, and then he would get on a ship. The ship would make its way from Jayapura west for days along Papua's long green coastline. Depending on how much money he carried, and where his friends have gone or are going, he would likely disembark in Manado-Bitung, Makassar or Jakarta.

Andy would spend his money on school fees, practical clothes, meals and Sunday donations at church. He would not fill his new backpack with desirable and seemingly inexpensive goods: a leather jacket, a fancy mobile phone, a volleyball or a bottle of whiskey. He would try to take care of any junior relatives from Wamena studying in the same place, and senior relatives would guide him, keep him in line, helping him sort out new challenges and confusing circumstances.

Andy would never quit, go on holiday or take a leave of absence, and he would finish in four years. His professors, the Dean, the Dean's five assistants, the Vice-Chancellor's four assistants, the staff at the registrar's office and the department clerks would not demand extra money from him to mark his assignments, process his exams and complete his graduation paperwork. His neighbours, with whom he thought he had made friends, would support him in times of need. Government officials would not make him feel too humiliated for speaking his mind and standing up for his friends. He would develop the confidence he would seek, and need, to avoid feeling inferior to the Indonesians around him, who sometimes make him feel awkward and uncertain. His friends and kin would not ask him for too much money, and he himself would not incur large debts with them. His friends would prefer to help him celebrate important milestones with a pig roast or a prayer service than with a month of binge drinking. He would not have sexual relationships with women or would choose the perfect one and carefully manage the relationship so that they would return to Wamena together after graduation.

Andy would have a close relative working in the local government in Wamena so his application to join the civil service would go forward, and he would gain employment quickly. He would engage minimally in dishonest practices, and his department would be productive and free of corruption. He would find his work satisfying; he would feel that his education made a difference and that he would be helping other Indigenous people in Wamena and making a positive contribution to development. The wants and needs of his social network, his father's people, his mother's people, his father's other children, people of the same clan and distant in-laws would be negotiated with minimal trouble. He would live on the farm, as his father might hope, but he would probably build a wooden house for himself and his wife and children on the edge of the property, like the medical assistant and the schoolteacher have done. Alternatively, he might be able to afford a simple, raggedy house in town, like his uncle, a public servant who works at the district library. The local government would be responsible with its budget and pay the salaries of lower-level government employees so that he could continue to meet his financial obligations.

Andy would never become disillusioned or despondent, despite seeing some of his fellow graduates give up on employment, his friends shot or imprisoned, and seeing some of his elders and other community members feeling embarrassed to face Indonesians. He would not be harassed, intimidated or assaulted by military personnel, and security forces would not shoot him while he was part of a demonstration or an angry crowd. He would continue to show the utmost respect for traditional customs and take his obligations as the last son of a big man in Wouma very seriously. If he were as good at solving conflicts as his father, Andy himself would become a big man. He would take care of the farm, the family and the ancestors. There would always be pig-raising and potato-growing, and the huts would be full of men, women and children. There would be another Andy who improved himself, doing a perfect job of negotiating colonialism, fear, shame, stigma, arrogance, anger, corruption, racism, love, sex, jealousy, violence, alcohol and bureaucracy. Or, unless Andy were extraordinary, he would be like most of the students, young and old, in various states of study, drunk and sober, in love and out of love, penniless and well-funded, mostly making an effort to improve themselves in North Sulawesi, from whom I learned what might happen to Andy.

Bibliography

Al-Faham, H., and R. Ernst. 2016. 'Between Society and the State: Gendered Racialization and Muslim Americans', in A. Sarat (ed.), *Studies in Law, Politics, and Society*. Bingley: Emerald Group Publishing, pp. 125–47.
Alua, A.A. 2006. 'Ap Kaintek Model Kepemimpinan Masyarakat Hubula di Lembah Balim, Papua', in A. Alua (ed.), *Nilai-nilai Hidup Masyarakat Hubula di Lembah Balim Papua*. Jayapura: STFT Fajar Timur, pp. 139–66.
Amir, S. 2013. *The Technological State in Indonesia: The Co-constitution of High Technology and Authoritarian Politics*. Abingdon: Routledge.
Amit, V., and H. Wulff (eds). 1995. *Youth Cultures: A Cross-cultural Perspective*. New York: Routledge.
Ananta, A., E.N. Arifin and L. Suryadinata. 2004. *Indonesian Electoral Behaviour: A Statistical Perspective*. Singapore: ISEAS.
Ananta, A., E.N Arifin, M.S Hasbullah, N.B Handayani and A Pramono. 2014. *A New Classification of Indonesia's Ethnic Groups*. ISEAS Working Paper #1. Singapore: Institute of Southeast Asian Studies.
Ananta, A., D.R.W.W. Utami and N.B. Handayani. 2016. 'Statistics on Ethnic Diversity in the Land of Papua, Indonesia', *Asia and the Pacific Policy Studies* 3(3): 458–74.
Anthias, F., and N. Yuval-Davis. 1992. *Racialized Boundaries: Race, Nation, Gender, Colour and Class and the Anti-racist Struggle*. London: Routledge.
Aragon, L.V. 2000. *Fields of the Lord: Animism, Christian Minorities, and State Development in Indonesia*. Honolulu: University of Hawai'i Press.
Aspinall, E. 1993. *Student Dissent in Indonesia in the 1980s*. Melbourne: Monash Asia Institute.
———. 1999. 'The Indonesian Student Uprising of 1998', in A. Budiman, B. Hatley and D. Kingsbury (eds), *Reformasi: Crisis and Change in Indonesia*. Melbourne: Monash Asia Institute, pp. 212–29.
Aspinall, E., M. Mietzner and D. Tomsa. 2015. *The Yudhoyono Presidency: Indonesia's Decade of Stability and Stagnation*. Singapore: ISEAS.
Badan Pusat Statistik (Central Statistics Agency). 2010. *The 2010 Indonesia Population Census*. Jakarta: BPS.
Badan Pusat Statistik Provinsi Papua (Central Statistics Agency Papua Province). 2013. *Indicator Pendidikan Provinsi Papua 2013*. Jayapura: BPSPP.
Ballard, C. 2002. 'West Papua', *The Contemporary Pacific* 14: 467–76.
———. 2008. '"Oceanic Negroes": British Anthropology of Papuans, 1820–1869', in B. Douglas and C. Ballard (eds), *Foreign Bodies: Oceania and the Science of Race 1750–1940*. Canberra: Australian National University Press, pp. 157–201.
Ballard, C., S. Vink and A. Ploeg (eds). 2001. *Race to the Snow: Photography and the Exploration of Dutch New Guinea, 1907–1936*. Amsterdam: Royal Tropical Institute.
Bandiyono, S. 1996. *Penyesuaian Diri Migran di Daerah Perkotaan Irian Jaya*. Jakarta: Puslitbank Kemasyarakatan dan Kebudayaan Lembaga Ilmu Pengetahuan Indonesia (PMB-LIPI).

Bennett, L.R. 2005. 'Patterns of Resistance and Transgression in Eastern Indonesia: Single Women's Practices of Clandestine Courtship and Cohabitation', *Culture, Health & Sexuality* 7(2): 101–12.

———. 2007. 'Zina and the Enigma of Sex Education for Indonesian Muslim Youth', *Sex Education* 7(4): 371–86.

Berita Satu. 2016. 'Gubernur Papua: Perda Pelarangan Minuman Beralkohol untuk Lindungi Rakyat Papua' ['Governor of Papua: Local Law Bans Alcohol to Protect the People of Papua'], 1 April 2016. Retrieved 31 December 2017 from http://www.beritasatu.com/nasional/357819-gubernur-papua-perda-pelarangan-minuman-beralkohol-untuk-lindungi-rakyat-papua.html.

Bertrand, J. 2004. *Nationalism and Ethnic Conflict in Indonesia*. Cambridge: Cambridge University Press.

Berita Kawanua. 2014. 'Keributan di Tataaran, Satu Mahasiswa asal Papua Tewas', 19 October. Retrieved 27 December 2017 from http://beritakawanua.com/berita/minahasa/keributan-di-tataaran-satu-mahasiswa-papua-tewas#sthash.HxgjnXKm.siLIJBf0.dpbs.

Bjork, C. 2005. *Indonesian Education: Teachers, Schools, and Central Bureaucracy*. New York: Routledge.

Boellstorff, T. 2004. 'The Emergence of Political Homophobia in Indonesia: Masculinity and National Belonging', *Ethnos* 69(4): 465–86.

Braithwaite, J., V. Braithwaite, M. Cookson and L. Dunn. 2010. *Anomie and Violence: Non-truth and Reconciliation in Indonesian Peacebuilding*. Canberra: Australian National University Press.

Bramantyo. 2014. 'Seks Bebas di Papua Sangat Mengerikan' ['Free Sex in Papua is Appalling'], 8 January. Retrieved 20 December 2017 from https://daerah.sindonews.com/read/824670/26/seks-bebas-di-papua-sangat-mengerikan-1389166898.

Bridges, K. 2011. *Reproducing Race: An Ethnography of Pregnancy as a Site of Racialization*. Berkeley: University of California Press.

Broekhuijse, J.T. 1967. *De Wiligiman-Dani: Een Cultureel-anthropologische Over Religie en Oorlogsvoering in de Baliem-vallei*. Utrecht: Gianotten.

Bromley, M. 1962. 'Some Reflections on Priorities for Economic Development', in L.J. Pospisil (ed.), *Working Papers in Dani Ethnology No. 1*. United Nations Temporary Executive Authority in West New Guinea – West Irian, Bureau of Native Affairs, pp. 64–6.

———. 1972. 'The Grammar of Lower Grand Valley Dani in Discourse Perspective', Ph.D. dissertation. New Haven: Yale University.

Brundige, E., W. King, P. Vahali, S. Vladeck and X. Yuan. 2004. 'Indonesian Human Rights Abuses in West Papua: Application of the Law of Genocide to the History of Indonesian Control', Allard K. Lowenstein International Human Rights Clinic, Yale Law School. Retrieved 31 July 2017 from http://www.g-a-l.info/Yale%20Report%20on%20West%20Papuah%20rights.pdf.

Buchholt, H., and M. Ulrich (eds). 1994. *Continuity, Change and Aspirations: Social and Cultural Life in Minahasa, Indonesia*. Singapore: Institute of Southeast Asian Studies.

Budiardjo, C., and L.S. Liong. 1988. *West Papua: The Obliteration of a People*. Thornton Heath: Tapol.

Butt, L. 1998. 'The Social and Political Life of Infants among the Baliem Valley Dani, Irian Jaya', Ph.D. dissertation. Montréal: McGill University.

———. 2001. '"KB Kills": Political Violence, Birth Control, and the Baliem Valley Dani', *Asia Pacific Journal of Anthropology* 2(1): 63–86.
———. 2005a. 'Sexuality, the State, and the Runaway Wives of Highlands Papua, Indonesia', in V. Adams and S. L. Pigg (eds), *Sex in Development: Science, Sexuality, and Morality in Global Perspective*. Durham, NC: Duke University Press, pp. 163–86.
———. 2005b. '"Lipstick Girls" and "Fallen Women": AIDS and Conspiratorial Thinking in Papua, Indonesia', *Cultural Anthropology* 20(3): 412–42.
———. 2007. 'Secret Sex: Youth, Agency, and Changing Sexual Boundaries among the Dani of Papua, Indonesia', *Ethnology* 46(2): 113–32.
———. 2008. 'Silence Speaks Volumes: Elite Responses to AIDS in Highlands Papua', in L. Butt and R. Eves (eds), *Making Sense of AIDS: Culture, Power and Sexuality in Melanesia*. Honolulu: University of Hawai'i Press, pp. 116–32.
———. 2012. 'Young Female Sex Workers' Experiences of HIV/AIDS Testing and Treatment in Conditions of Political Violence in Highlands Papua, Indonesia', *Western Humanities Review* 66(3): 35–54.
———. 2015. '"Living in HIV-Land": Mobility and Seropositivity among Highlands Papuan Men', in M. Slama and J. Munro (eds), *From 'Stone-Age' to 'Real-Time': Exploring Papuan Temporalities, Mobilities and Religiosities*. Canberra: Australian National University Press, pp. 221–42.
Butt, L., and J. Munro. 2007. 'Rebel Girls? Unplanned Pregnancy and Colonialism in Highlands Papua, Indonesia', *Culture, Health and Sexuality* 9(6): 585–98.
Butt, L., J. Munro and G. Numbery. 2017. 'Adding Insult to Injury: Experiences of Mobile HIV-Positive Women Who Return Home for Treatment in Tanah Papua, Indonesia', in J. Taylor and H. Lee (eds), *Mobilities of Return: Pacific Perspectives*. Canberra: Australian National University Press, pp. 147–70.
Butt, L., G. Numbery and J. Morin. 2002. 'The Smokescreen of Culture: AIDS and the Indigenous in Papua, Indonesia', *Pacific Health Dialog* 9(2): 283–89.
Chauvel, R. 2005. 'Constructing Papuan Nationalism: History, Ethnicity, and Adaptation', *Policy Studies, No 14*. Washington DC: East-West Center.
———. 2007. 'Refuge, Displacement and Dispossession: Responses to Indonesian Rule and Conflict in Papua', in E.E. Hedman (ed.), *Dynamics of Conflict and Displacement in Papua, Indonesia*. Oxford: Refugee Studies Centre Working Paper 42, pp. 32–51.
———. 2011. 'Policy Failure and Political Impasse: Papua and Jakarta a Decade after the "Papuan Spring"', in P.J. King, J. Elmslie, and C. Webb-Gannon (eds), *Comprehending West Papua*. Sydney: Centre for Peace and Conflict Studies, University of Sydney, pp. 105–15.
Chauvel, R., and I.N. Bhakti. 2004. 'The Papua Conflict: Jakarta's Perceptions and Policies', *Policy Studies, No. 5*. Washington DC: East-West Center.
Clark, J. 2000. *Steel to Stone: A Chronicle of Colonialism in the Southern Highlands of Papua New Guinea*. Oxford: Oxford University Press.
Collins, E., and E. Bahar. 2000. 'To Know Shame: Malu and its Uses in Malay Society', *Crossroads: An Interdisciplinary Journal of Southeast Asian Studies* 14(1): 35–69.
Cookson, M.B. 2008. 'Batik Irian: Imprints of Indonesian Papua', Ph.D. dissertation. Canberra: Australian National University.
Danim, S. 1995. *Transformasi Sumber Daya Manusia: Analisis Fungsi Pendidikan, Dinamika Prilaku dan Kesejahteraan Manusia Indonesia Masa Depan [Human Resource Trans-*

formation: Analysis of the Function of Education, Behavioural Dynamics and the Future Welfare of Indonesians]. Jakarta: Bumi Aksara.

Davies, S.G. 2015. 'Surveilling Sexuality in Indonesia', in L.R. Bennett and S.G. Davies (eds), *Sex and Sexualities in Contemporary Indonesia: Sexual Politics, Health, Diversity and Representations*. Abingdon: Routledge, pp. 29–50.

Denis, J. S. 2015. 'Contact Theory in a Small-Town Settler-Colonial Context: The Reproduction of Laissez-Faire Racism in Indigenous-White Canadian Relations', *American Sociological Review* 80(1): 218–42.

Douglas, B. 2013. 'Foreign Bodies in Oceania', in B. Douglas and C. Ballard (eds), *Foreign Bodies: Oceania and the Science of Race 1750–1940*. Canberra: Australian National University Press, pp. 3–30.

Douglas, S.A. 1970. *Political Socialization and Student Activism in Indonesia*. Chicago: University of Illinois Press.

Drooglever, P.J. 2009. *An Act of Free Choice: Decolonisation and the Right to Self-Determination in West Papua*. London: Oneworld.

Du Bois, M. 1991. 'The Governance of the Third World: A Foucauldian Perspective on Power Relations in Development', *Alternatives* 16(1): 1–30.

Duncan, C.R. 2004. 'From Development to Empowerment: Changing Indonesian Government Policies toward Indigenous Minorities', in C.R. Duncan (ed.), *Civilizing the Margins: Southeast Asian Government Policies for the Development of Minorities*. Ithaca: Cornell University Press, pp. 86–115.

———. 2005. 'Unwelcome Guests: Relations between Internally Displaced Persons and their Hosts in North Sulawesi, Indonesia', *Journal of Refugee Studies* 18(1): 25–46.

Elmslie, J. 2003. *Irian Jaya under the Gun: Indonesian Economic Development versus West Papuan Nationalism*. Honolulu: University of Hawai'i Press.

Epstein, A. 1984. *The Experience of Shame in Melanesia: An Essay in the Anthropology of Affect*. London: Royal Anthropological Institute of Great Britain and Ireland.

Farhadian, C. 2001. 'Raising the Morning Star: A Social and Ethnographic History of Urban Dani Christians in New Order Indonesia', Ph.D. dissertation. Boston: Boston University.

———. 2003. 'Comparing Conversions among the Dani of Irian Jaya', in A. Buckser and S.D. Glazier (eds), *The Anthropology of Religious Conversion*. Lanham, MD: Rowman & Littlefield, pp. 55–68.

———. 2005. *Christianity, Islam, and Nationalism in Indonesia*. New York: Routledge.

———. (ed.). 2007. *The Testimony Project: Papua: A Collection of Personal Histories in West Papua*. Jayapura: Deiyai.

Fife, W. 1994. 'Education in Papua New Guinea: The Hidden Curriculum of a New Moral Order', *City and Society Annual Review* 7(1): 139–62.

———. 1995. 'The Look of Rationality and the Bureaucratization of Consciousness in Papua New Guinea', *Ethnology* 34(2): 129–41.

Ford, M., and L. Parker. 2008. 'Introduction: Thinking about Indonesian Women and Work', in M. Ford and L. Parker (eds), *Women and Work in Indonesia*, vol. 5. Abingdon: Routledge, pp. 1–16.

Foster, K.M. 2005. 'Diet of Disparagement: The Racial Experiences of Black Students in a Predominantly White University', *International Journal of Qualitative Studies in Education* 18(4): 489–505.

Foster, R.J. (ed.). 1997. *Nation Making: Emergent Identities in Postcolonial Melanesia*. Ann Arbor: University of Michigan Press.

Franciscans International and Asian Human Rights Commission. 2011. *Human Rights in Papua 2010/2011*. Hong Kong: Asian Human Rights Commission.
Gardner, R. 1963. *Dead Birds*. Cambridge, MA: Harvard University, Peabody Museum.
Gardner, R., and K. Heider. 1968. *Gardens of War: Life and Death in the New Guinea Stone Age*. London: Deutsch.
Giay, B. 2000. *Menuju Papua Baru: Beberapa Pokok Pikiran sekitar Emansipasi orang Papua* [*Towards a New Papua: Some Thoughts on the Emancipation of Papuans*]. Jayapura: Deiyai.
———. 2001. 'Against Indonesia: West Papuan Strategies of Resistance against Indonesian Political and Cultural Aggression in 1980s', in I. Wessel and G. Wimhöfer (eds), *Violence in Indonesia*. Hamburg: Abera, pp. 129–38.
Giay, B., and C. Ballard. 2003. 'Becoming Papuans: Notes towards a History of Racism in Tanah Papua', *American Anthropological Association, Chicago, 19 November*.
Glasse, R.M., and M.J. Meggitt. 1969. *Pigs, Pearlshells, and Women: Marriage in the New Guinea Highlands*. Englewood Cliffs, NJ: Prentice Hall.
Glazebrook, D. 2008. *Permissive Residents: West Papuan Refugees Living in Papua New Guinea*. Canberra: Australian National University Press.
Gillespie, A. 2006. 'Tourist Photography and the Reverse Gaze', *Ethos* 34(3): 343–66.
Gietzelt, D. 1989. 'The Indonesianization of West Papua', *Oceania* 59(3): 201–21.
Goffman, E. 1963. *Behavior in Public Places: Notes on the Social Organization of Gatherings*. New York: Free Press of Glencoe.
Haluk, Markus. 2013. *Hidup atau Mati: Hilangnya Harapan Hidup dan Hak Asasi Manusia di Papua* [*Dead or Alive: The Loss of Hopes and Human Rights in West Papua*]. Jayapura: Deiyai.
Hartono, D., H. Rumdiarti and E. Djohan. 1999. *Akses terhadap Pelayanan Kesehatan Reproduksi: Studi Kasus di Kabupaten Jayawijaya* [*Access to Reproductive Health Services: A Case Study of Jayawijaya Regency*]. Jakarta: PPT-LIPI.
Hayward, D. 1983. 'From Tribal Economics to a Market-Oriented Society', *Irian: Bulletin of Irian Jaya Development* 11(2–3): 1–29.
Heider, K. 1970. *The Dugum Dani: a Papuan Culture in the Highlands of West New Guinea*. Chicago: Aldine.
———. 1979. *Grand Valley Dani: Peaceful Warriors*. New York: Holt, Rinehart and Winston.
Henley, D. 1989. *The Idea of Celebes in History*. Clayton: Monash University, Centre of Southeast Asian Studies.
———. 1996. *Nationalism and Regionalism in a Colonial Context: Minahasa in the Dutch East Indies*. Leiden: KITLV.
Hernawan, B. 2015. 'Torture as a Mode of Governance: Reflections on the Phenomenon of Torture in Papua, Indonesia', in M. Slama and J. Munro (eds), *From 'Stone-Age' to 'Real-Time': Exploring Papuan Temporalities, Mobilities and Religiosities*. Canberra: Australian National University Press, pp. 195–220.
Heryanto, A. and N. Lutz. 1988. 'The Development of "Development"', *Indonesia* 46: 1–24.
Herzfeld, M. 1993. *The Social Production of Indifference: Exploring the Symbolic Roots of Western Bureaucracy*. Chicago: University of Chicago Press.
Hull, T., E. Sulisyaningsih and G. Jones. 1999. *Prostitution in Indonesia: Its History and Evolution*. Jakarta: Pustaka Sinar Harapan.
Human Rights Watch. 2001. 'Violence and Political Impasse in Papua'. Retrieved 31 December 2017 from https://www.hrw.org/reports/2001/papua/PAPUA0701.pdf.

———. 2007. 'Out of Sight: Endemic Abuse and Impunity in Papua's Central Highlands'. Retrieved 28 December 2017 from http://www.unhcr.org/refworld/docid/46a7610f2.html.
———. 2014. 'Indonesia: Security Forces Kill Five in Papua', 10 December. Retrieved 28 December 2017 from https://www.hrw.org/news/2014/12/10/indonesia-security-forces-kill-five-papua.
———. 2017. 'Indonesia: Events of 2016'. Retrieved 28 December 2017 from https://www.hrw.org/world-report/2017/country-chapters/indonesia.
International Crisis Group. 2006. 'Papua: The Dangers of Shutting Down Dialogue'. *Asia Briefing No. 47.*
International Coalition for Papua. 2013. *Human Rights in Papua*. Wuppertal: International Coalition for Papua and Geneva: Franciscans International.
Jaarsma, S. 1991. 'An Ethnographer's Tale: Ethnographic Research in Netherlands (West) New Guinea (1950–1962)', *Oceania* 62(2): 128–46.
Jacobsen, M. 2002. 'On the Question of Contemporary Identity in Minahasa, North Sulawesi Province, Indonesia', *Asian Anthropology* 1: 31–59.
Jeffrey, C., R. Jeffery and P. Jeffery. 2004. 'Degrees without Freedom: The Impact of Formal Education on Dalit Young Men in North India', *Development and Change* 35: 963–86.
Jeffrey, C., P. Jeffery, and R. Jeffery. 2005. 'Reproducing Difference? Schooling, Jobs, and Empowerment in Uttar Pradesh, India', *World Development* 33(12): 2085–101.
Jones, G. 1977. *The Population of North Sulawesi*. Yogyakarta: Gadjah Mada University Press.
Jourdan, C. 1997. 'Stepping Stones to National Consciousness: The Solomon Islands Case', in R.J. Foster (ed.), *Nation Making: Emergent Identities in Postcolonial Melanesia*. Ann Arbor: University of Michigan Press, pp. 127–50.
Karp, I. 2002. 'Development and Personhood: Tracing the Contours of a Moral Discourse', in B.M. Knauft (ed.), *Critically Modern: Alternatives, Alterities, Anthropologies*. Bloomington: Indiana University Press, pp. 82–104
Kartasasmita, G. 1994. *Pembangunan Sumber Daya Manusia Iptek dan Peranannya dalam Pembangunan Nasional* [*The Development of IT Human Resources and their Role in National Development*]. Bandung: ITB.
Komnas Perempuan, Pokja Perempuan Majelis Rakyat Papua and International Center for Transitional Justice Indonesia. 2010. *Stop Sudah! Kesaksian Perempuan Papua Korban Kekerasan dan Pelanggaran HAM 1963-2009* [*Enough is Enough! Testimonies of Papuan Women Victims of Violence and Human Rights Abuses 1963-2009*].
Keeler, W. 1983. 'Shame and Stage Fright in Java', *Ethos* 11(3): 152–65.
Kim, J. 2010. 'Women's Education and Fertility: An Analysis of the Relationship between Education and Birth Spacing in Indonesia', *Economic Development and Cultural Change* 58(4): 739–74.
King, P., Elmslie, J. and Webb-Gannon, C. (eds). 2011. *Comprehending West Papua*. Sydney: Centre of Peace and Conflict Studies, University of Sydney. Retrieved 31 July 2017 from http://sydney.edu.au/arts/peace_conflict/practice/Comprehending%20West%20Papua.pdf.
Kirksey, S.E. 2002. 'From Cannibal to Terrorist: State Violence, Indigenous Resistance and Representation in West Papua', M.Phil. thesis. Oxford: University of Oxford.
———. 2012. *Freedom in Entangled Worlds: West Papua and the Architecture of Global Power*. Durham, NC: Duke University Press.

Kirsch, S. 2002. 'Rumour and Other Narratives of Political Violence in West Papua', *Critique of Anthropology* 22: 53–79.
———. 2007. 'Representations of Violence, Conflict, and Displacement in West Papua', in E.L. Hedman (ed.), *Dynamics of Conflict and Displacement in Papua, Indonesia*. Oxford: Refugee Studies Centre Working Paper 42: 52–68.
Knauft, B.M. 2005. *The Gebusi: Lives Transformed in a Rainforest World*. Boston: McGraw-Hill.
Koentjaraningrat, R.M. 1994. *Irian Jaya: Membangun Masyarakat Majemuk* [*Irian Jaya: Developing a Diverse Population*]. Jakarta: Djambatan.
Koentjaraningrat, R.M., and D.C. Ajamiseba. 1994. 'Reaksi Penduduk Asli Terhadap Pembangunan dan Perubahan' ['The Reaction of the Indigenous Population to Development and Change'], in R.M. Koentjaraningrat (ed.), *Irian Jaya: Membangun Masyarakat Majemuk* [*Irian Jaya: Developing a Diverse People*]. Jakarta: Djambatan, pp. 433–52.
Kompasiana. 2014. 'Lagi, Alasan Mabuk Satu Orang Papua Tewas Usai Bentrok dengan Warga Manado' ['Again, A Drunk Papuan is Killed in a Fight with Manadonese'], 20 October. Retrieved 27 December 2017 from http://www.kompasiana.com/arki.papua/lagi-alasan-mabuk-satu-orang-papua-tewas-usai-bentrok-dengan-warga-manado_54f418567455137a2b6c86ce.
Kwok, N. 2012. 'Shame and the Embodiment of Boundaries', *Oceania* 82(1): 28–41.
Lake, L.M. 1989. 'Cultural Adaptation in Vernacular Literacy Programs of Irian Jaya, Indonesia', Ph.D. dissertation. Philadelphia: University of Pennsylvania.
Larson, G.F. 1987. 'The Structure and Demography of the Cycle of Warfare among the Ilaga Dani of Irian Jaya'. Ph.D. dissertation. Ann Arbor: University of Michigan.
Lattas, A. 1998. *Cultures of Secrecy: Reinventing Race in Bush Kaliai Cargo Cults*. Madison: University of Wisconsin Press.
Lawson, S. 2016. 'West Papua, Indonesia and the Melanesian Spearhead Group: Competing Logics in Regional and International Politics', *Australian Journal of International Affairs* 70(5): 506–24.
Lederman, R. 1986. *What Gifts Engender: Social Relations and Politics in Mendi, Highland Papua New Guinea*. Cambridge: Cambridge University Press.
Lee, J. 1999. 'Out of Order: The Politics of Modernity in Indonesia', Ph.D. dissertation. Charlottesville: University of Virginia.
Leith, D. 2003. *The Politics of Power: Freeport in Suharto's Indonesia*. Honolulu: University of Hawai'i Press.
Lenhart, L. 1997. 'Orang Suku Laut Ethnicity and Acculturation', *Bijdragen tot de Taal-, Land-en Volkenkunde* 153(4): 577–604.
Lewis, A. 2003. 'Everyday Race-making: Navigating Racial Boundaries in Schools', *American Behavioral Scientist* 47(3): 283–305.
Li, T.M. 1999. 'Marginality, Power and Production: Analysing Upland Transformations', in T.M. Li (ed.), *Transforming the Indonesian Uplands: Marginality, Power and Production*. Amsterdam: Harwood, pp. 1–44.
———. 2003. 'Masyarakat Adat, Difference, and the Limits of Recognition in Indonesia's Forest Zone', in D.S. Moore, J. Kosek, and A. Pandian (eds), *Race, Nature, and the Politics of Difference*. Durham, NC: Duke University Press, pp. 380–406.
———. 2007. *The Will to Improve: Governmentality, Development, and the Practice of Politics*. Durham, NC: Duke University Press.
LiPuma, E. 2000. *Encompassing Others: The Magic of Modernity in Melanesia*. Ann Arbor: University of Michigan Press.

Lijphart, A. 1966. *The Trauma of Decolonisation: The Dutch and West New Guinea*. New Haven: Yale University Press.
Lindquist, J. 2004. 'Veils and Ecstasy: Negotiating Shame in the Indonesian Borderlands', *Ethnos* 69(4): 487–508.
Mains, D. 2012. *Hope is Cut: Youth, Unemployment, and the Future in Urban Ethiopia*. Philadelphia: Temple University Press.
———. 2007. 'Neoliberal Times: Progress, Boredom, and Shame among Young Men in Urban Ethiopia', *American Ethnologist* 34(4): 659–73.
Marx, C. 2011. 'Hendrik Verwoerd's Long March to Apartheid: Nationalism and Racism in South Africa', in B. Manfred and W. Simon (eds), *Racism in the Modern World: Historical Perspectives on Cultural Transfer and Adaptation*. New York: Berghahn Books, pp. 281–302.
Matthiessen, P. 1962. *Under the Mountain Wall: A Chronicle of Two Seasons in the Stone Age*. New York: Viking Press
McCallum, C. 2005. 'Racialized Bodies, Naturalized Classes: Moving through the City of Salvador da Bahia', *American Ethnologist* 32(1): 100–17.
McGibbon, R. 2004. 'Plural Society in Peril: Migration, Economic Change, and the Papua Conflict', *Policy Studies, No. 13*. Washington DC: East-West Center.
McKeown, E. 2006. 'Modernity, Prestige, and Self-Promotion: Literacy in a Papua New Guinea Community', *Anthropology and Education Quarterly* 37(4): 366–80.
McKenna, K. 2015. *Corporate Social Responsibility and Natural Resource Conflict*. Abingdon: Routledge.
Means, G. 1985. 'The Rural Sector and Human Resource Development in Indonesia', University of Toronto-York University Joint Centre on Modern East Asia's Southeast Asia/ASEAN Project.
Mellor, D. 2003. 'Contemporary Racism in Australia: The Experiences of Aborigines', *Personality and Social Psychology Bulletin* 29(4): 474–86.
Mietzner, M. 2007. 'Local Elections and Autonomy in Papua and Aceh: Mitigating or Fueling Secessionism?', *Indonesia* (84): 1–39.
Mote, O., and D. Rutherford. 2001. 'From Irian Jaya to Papua: The Limits of Primordialism in Indonesia's Troubled East', *Indonesia* 72: 115–40.
Munro, J. 2004. 'Taking on Development: Papuan Youth, HIV/AIDS and State Discourse in Eastern Indonesia', M.A. thesis. Victoria: University of Victoria, Canada.
———. 2012. '"A Diploma and a Descendant!" Premarital Sexuality, Education, and Politics among Dani University Students in North Sulawesi, Indonesia', *Journal of Youth Studies* 15 (8): 1011–27.
———. 2013. 'The Violence of Inflated Possibilities: Education, Transformation and Diminishment in Wamena, Papua', *Indonesia* 95: 25–46.
———. 2014a. 'Presidential Elections in Papua: a Battle between "New" and "Old"?', *SSGM in Brief* 2014/19. Canberra: State, Society and Governance in Melanesia Program, Australian National University.
———. 2014b. 'Home-Brew Alcohol, Gender and Violence in the Papuan Highlands', *SSGM in-Brief* 2014/14. Canberra: State, Society and Governance in Melanesia Program, Australian National University.
———. 2015a. 'Jokowi in Papua: Powerless or Duplicitous?', *SSGM in Brief* 2015/29. Canberra: State, Society and Governance in Melanesia Program, Australian National University.

———. 2015b. '"Now We Know Shame": *Malu* and Stigma among Highlanders in the Papuan Diaspora', in M. Slama and J. Munro (eds), *From 'Stone-Age' to 'Real-Time': Exploring Papuan Temporalities, Mobilities and Religiosities*. Canberra: Australian National University Press, pp. 171–96.

———. 2017. 'Gender Struggles of Educated Men in the Papuan Highlands', in C. Spark and M. Macintyre, *Transformations of Gender in Melanesia*. Canberra: Australian National University Press, pp. 45–67.

———. 2019. 'Indigenous Masculinities and the "Refined Politics" of Alcohol and Racialization in West Papua', *The Contemporary Pacific*.

Munro, J., and L. Butt. 2012. 'Compelling Evidence: Research Methods, HIV/AIDS, and Politics in Papua, Indonesia', *Asia Pacific Journal of Anthropology* 13(4): 334–51.

Munro, J., and L. McIntyre. 2016. '(Not) Getting Political: Indigenous Women and Preventing Mother-to-Child Transmission of HIV in West Papua', *Culture, Health and Sexuality* 18(2): 156–70.

Munro, J., and P. Wetipo. 2013. 'Prevalensi Minuman Lokal di Wamena, Papua: Laporan Hasil Diskusi dan Rekomendasi dari Masyarakat' ['The Prevalence of Home-Brew Alcohol in Wamena, Papua: Report on Discussion Results and Community Recommendations'], unpublished research report. Retrieved 28 December 2017 from https://www.academia.edu/5482245/Prevalensi_Minuman_Lokal_di_Wamena_Papua_Laporan_Awal.

Myrttinen, H. 2015. 'Under Two Flags: Encounters with Israel, Merdeka and the Promised Land in Tanah Papua', in M. Slama and J. Munro (eds), *From 'Stone-Age' to 'Real-Time': Exploring Papuan Temporalities, Mobilities and Religiosities*. Canberra: Australian National University Press, pp. 125–44.

Naylor, L.L. 1974. 'Culture Change and Development in the Balim Valley, Irian Jaya, Indonesia', Ph.D. dissertation. Carbondale: Southern Illinois University.

Nilan, P. 2008. 'Youth Transitions to Urban, Middle-Class Marriage in Indonesia: Faith, Family and Finances', *Journal of Youth Studies* 11(1): 65–82.

Nilan, P., L. Parker, L. Bennett and K. Robinson. 2011. 'Indonesian Youth Looking towards the Future', *Journal of Youth Studies* 14(6): 709–28.

O'Brien, D. 1962. 'Economic and Social Development', in L.J. Pospisil (ed.), *Working Papers in Dani Ethnology No. 1*. United Nations Temporary Executive Authority in West New Guinea – West Irian, Bureau of Native Affairs, pp. 81–82.

———. 1969. 'The Economics of Dani Marriage: An Analysis of Marriage Payments in a Highland New Guinea Society', Ph.D. dissertation. New Haven: Yale University.

Osborne, R. 1985. *Indonesia's Secret War: The Guerrilla Struggle in Irian Jaya*. Sydney: Allen & Unwin.

Parker, L. 2003. *From Subjects to Citizens: Balinese Villagers in the Indonesian Nation-State*. Copenhagen: NIAS; London: Taylor & Francis.

Penders, C. 2002. *The West New Guinea Debacle: Dutch Decolonisation and Indonesia 1945–1962*. Adelaide: Crawford House.

Persoon, G. 1998. 'Isolated Groups or Indigenous Peoples: Indonesia and the International Discourse', *Bijdragen tot de Taal-, Land-en Volkenkunde* 154(2): 281–304.

Peters, H.L. 1975. 'Some Observations of the Social Life and Religious Life of a Dani Group', *Irian: Bulletin of Irian Jaya Development* 9(2): 1–197.

Pickering, M. 2001. *Stereotyping: The Politics of Representation*. New York: Palgrave.

Ploeg, A. 1965. 'Government in Wanggulam', Ph.D. dissertation. Canberra: Australian National University.

———. 1966. 'Some Comparative Remarks about the Dani of the Baliem Valley and the Dani at Bokondini', *Bijdragen tot de Taal-, Land-en Volkenkunde* 122(2): 255–73.
———. 1995. 'First Contact, in the Highlands of Irian Jaya', *Journal of Pacific History* 30(2): 227–39.
———. 1996. 'Huge Men in the Highlands of Irian Jaya', in H. Levine and A. Ploeg (eds), *Work in Progress: Essays in New Guinea Highlands Ethnography in Honour of Paula Brown Glick*. Frankfurt: Peter Lane, pp. 213–32.
———. 2004. 'Wealth Items in the Western Highlands of West Papua', *Ethnology* 43(4): 291–313.
Pomponio, A. 1990. 'Seagulls Don't Fly into the Bush: Cultural Identity and the Negotiation of Development on Mandok Island, Papua New Guinea', in J. Linnekin and L. Poyer (eds), *Cultural Identity and Ethnicity in the Pacific*. Honolulu: University of Hawai'i Press, pp. 43–69.
Pospisil, L.J. (ed.). 1962. *Working Papers in Dani Ethnology No. 1*. United Nations Temporary Executive Authority in West New Guinea – West Irian, Bureau of Native Affairs.
Pouwer, J. 1999. 'The Colonisation, Decolonisation and Recolonisation of West New Guinea', *Journal of Pacific History* 34: 157–80.
Powell, J.P., and M. Wilson (eds). 1974. *Education and Rural Development in the Highlands of Papua New Guinea*. Port Moresby: University of Papua New Guinea.
Priest, N., Y. Paradies, B. Trenerry, M. Truong, S. Karlsen and Y. Kelly. 2013. 'A Systematic Review of Studies Examining the Relationship between Reported Racism and Health and Wellbeing for Children and Young People', *Social Science and Medicine* 95: 115–27.
Raweyai. Y.T. 2002. *Mengapa Papua Ingin Merdeka [Why Papua Wants Freedom]*. Jayapura: Presidium Dewan Papua.
Rawski, F. 1999. 'Jargon in the Jungle: Indonesian State Rhetoric at a Highland Sulawesi "Access Point"', *Review of Indonesian and Malaysian Affairs* 33(1): 157–90.
Reddy, W.M. 1997. 'Against Constructionism: The Historical Ethnography of Emotions', *Current Anthropology* 38(3): 327–51.
Rhys, L. 1947. *Jungle Pimpernel: The Story of a District Officer in Central Netherlands New Guinea*. London: Hodder & Stoughton.
Richards, S. 2015. 'Hip Hop in Manokwari: Pleasures, Contestations and the Changing Face of Papuanness', in M. Slama and J. Munro (eds), *From 'Stone-Age' to 'Real-Time': Exploring Papuan Temporalities, Mobilities and Religiosities*. Canberra: Australian National University Press, pp. 145–68.
Robbins, J. 2004. *Becoming Sinners: Christianity and Moral Torment in a Papua New Guinea Society*. Berkeley: University of California Press.
———. 2005. 'Humiliation and Transformation: Marshall Sahlins and the Study of Cultural Change in Melanesia', in J. Robbins and H. Wardlow (eds), *The Making of Global and Local Modernities in Melanesia: Humiliation, Transformation, and the Nature of Cultural Change*. Aldershot: Ashgate, pp. 3–21.
Rosaldo, R. 2003. 'The Borders of Belonging: Nation and Citizen in the Hinterlands', in R. Rosaldo (ed.), *Cultural Citizenship in Island Southeast Asia: Nation and Belonging in the Hinterlands*. Berkeley: University of California Press, pp. 1–15.
Rudolph, S.H., L.I. Rudolph and M.S. Kanota (eds). 2002. *Reversing the Gaze: Amar Singh's Diary – A Colonial Subject's Narrative of Imperial India*. Boulder: Westview Press.

Rusman, R. 1998. 'Youth, Education and Employment in Irian Jaya', in J. Miedema, C. Ode and R.A.C. Dam (eds), *Perspectives on the Bird's Head of Irian Jaya, Indonesia: Proceedings of the Conference, Leiden, 13–17 October 1997*. Amsterdam: Rodopi, pp. 364–84.

Rutherford, D. 1997. 'Raiding the Land of the Foreigners: Power, History and Difference in Biak, Irian Jaya, Indonesia', Ph.D. dissertation. New York: Cornell University.

———. 1998. 'Trekking to New Guinea: Dutch Colonial Fantasies of a Virgin Land, 1900–1942', in J. Clancy-Smith and F. Gouda (eds), *Domesticating the Empire: Race, Gender, and Family Life in French and Dutch Colonialism*. Charlottesville: University of Virginia Press, pp. 255–72.

———. 2003. *Raiding the Land of the Foreigners*. Princeton: Princeton University Press.

———. 2012. *Laughing at Leviathan: Sovereignty and Audience in West Papua*. Chicago: University of Chicago Press.

Sahlins, M. 1992. 'The Economics of Develop-Man in the Pacific', *Res* 21: 13–25.

Saltford, J. 2003. *The United Nations and the Indonesian Takeover of Papua, 1962–1989: The Anatomy of Betrayal*. London: Routledge.

Saraswati, L.A. 2010. 'Cosmopolitan Whiteness: The Effects and Affects of Skin-Whitening Advertisements in a Transnational Women's Magazine in Indonesia', *Meridians: Feminism, Race, Transnationalism* 10(2): 15–41.

Sari, Y.I. 2016. 'Papua's Time Bomb', *New Mandala*, 7 January. Retrieved 31 July 2017 from http://asiapacific.anu.edu.au/newmandala/2016/01/07/papuas-time-bomb.

Schut, T. 2016. 'Educated Young People and Un(der)employment in Rural Flores, Indonesia', Ph.D. dissertation. Perth: University of Western Australia.

Shah, R. 2016. 'Questions of Power in Schooling for Indigenous Papuans', in P. Sillitoe (ed.), *Indigenous Studies and Engaged Anthropology: The Collaborative Moment*. Abingdon: Routledge, pp. 235–66.

Sharp, N. 1977. *The Rule of the Sword: the Story of West Irian*. Malmsbury: Kibble Books and Arena.

Shiraishi, S. 1997. *Young Heroes: The Indonesian Family in Politics*. Ithaca: Cornell University Press.

Slama, M. 2010. 'The Agency of the Heart: Internet Chatting as Youth Culture in Indonesia', *Social Anthropology* 18(3): 316–30.

———. 2015. 'Papua as an Islamic Frontier: Preaching in "the Jungle" and the Multiplicity of Spatio-temporal Hierarchisations', in M. Slama and J. Munro (eds), *From 'Stone-Age' to 'Real-Time': Exploring Papuan Temporalities, Mobilities and Religiosities*. Canberra: Australian National University Press, pp. 243–70.

Slama, M., and J. Munro. 2015. 'From "Stone-Age" to "Real-Time": Exploring Papuan Temporalities, Mobilities and Religiosities: An Introduction', in M. Slama and J. Munro (eds), *From 'Stone-Age' to 'Real-Time': Exploring Papuan Temporalities, Mobilities and Religiosities*. Canberra: Australian National University Press, pp. 1–38.

Smith-Hefner, N. 2005. 'The New Muslim Romance: Changing Patterns of Courtship and Marriage among Educated Javanese Youth', *Journal of Southeast Asian Studies* 36(3): 441–59.

———. 2006. 'Reproducing Respectability: Sex and Sexuality among Muslim Javanese Youth', *Review of Indonesian and Malaysian Affairs* 40(1): 143–72.

Soepangat, S. 1986. '*Indonesian School as Modernizer: A Case Study of the Orang Lembah Baliem Enculturation*', Ph.D. dissertation. Tallahassee: Florida State University.

Sondakh, A.J. 2002. *Si Tou Timou Tumou Tou (Tou Minahasa): Refleksi atas Evolusi Nilai-Nilai Manusia*. Jakarta: Pustaka Sinar Harapan.
Spark, C. 2011. 'Gender Trouble in Town: Educated Women Eluding Male Domination, Gender Violence and Marriage in PNG', *Asia Pacific Journal of Anthropology* 12(2): 164–79.
Stasch, R. 2015. 'From Primitive Other to Papuan Self: Korowai Engagement with Ideologies of Unequal Human Worth in Encounters with Tourists, State Officials and Education', in M. Slama and J. Munro (eds), *From 'Stone-Age' to 'Real-Time': Exploring Papuan Temporalities, Mobilities and Religiosities*. Canberra: Australian National University Press, pp. 59–94.
Stoler, A.L. 2002. *Carnal Knowledge and Imperial Power: Race and the Intimate in Colonial Rule*. Berkeley: University of California Press.
Strathern, A. 1971. *The Rope of Moka: Big-Men and Ceremonial Exchange in Mount Hagen, New Guinea*. Cambridge: Cambridge University Press.
———. 1975. 'Why is Shame on the Skin?', *Ethnology* 14(4): 347–56.
Sugandi, Y. 2013. 'The Notion of Collective Dignity among Hubula in Palim Valley, Papua', Ph.D. dissertation. Münster: University of Münster.
Suparlan, P. 1997. 'Kesukubangsaan dan Primordialitas: Program Ayam di Desa Mwapi, Timika, Irian Jaya' ['Tribalism and Primordialism: A Chicken Program in Mwapi Village, Timika, Irian Jaya'], *Antropologi Indonesia* 54(21): 38–61.
———. 1998. 'Model Sosial Budaya bagi Penyelenggaraan Transmigrasi di Irian Jaya' ['A Socio-cultural Model for the Implementation of Transmigration in Irian Jaya'], *Antropologi Indonesia* 57(22): 23–47.
———. 2001. 'Orang Kamoro: Perubahan Kehidupan dan Linkungannya' ['The Kamoro: Lifestyle and Environmental Change'], *Antropologi Indonesia* 25(64): 84–90.
Suwada, A. 1984 [1971]. 'Kei Islanders', in F.A. Trenkenschuh (ed.), *An Asmat Sketchbook: A Series on the Asmat People 3 & 4*. Hastings: Asmat Museum of Culture and Progress.
Sykes, K. 1995. 'Raising Lelet: *Education, Knowledge and the Crisis of Youth in Central New Ireland, Papua New Guinea*', Ph.D. dissertation. Princeton: Princeton University.
———. 1999. 'After the Raskal Feast: Youth's Alienation in Papua New Guinea', *Critique of Anthropology* 19(2): 157–75.
Timmer, J., 2000. 'Living with Intricate Futures: Order and Confusion in Imyan Worlds, Irian Jaya, Indonesia', Ph.D. dissertation. Nijmegen: Radboud University Nijmegen.
Tjiptoherijanto, P. 1996. *Sumber Daya Manusia dalam Pembangunan Nasional* [*Human Resources in National Development*]. Jakarta: Lembaga Penerbit Fakultas Ekonomi Universitas Indonesia.
Tombeng, W. 19 June 2009. Retrieved 11 October 2009 from www.unima.ac.id.
Tomlinson, M. 2002. 'Sacred Soil in Kadavu, Fiji', *Oceania* 72(4): 237–57.
Toye, J.F. 1987. *Dilemmas of Development: Reflections on the Counter-revolution in Development Theory and Policy*. Oxford: Blackwell.
Umasugi, N. 2010. 'Sex Sebas Bukan Hal Tabu Bagi ABG Papua' ['Free Sex is Not Taboo for Young Papuans'], 14 June. Retrieved 20 December 2017 from https://news.okezone.com/read/2010/06/14/340/342548/seks-bebas-bukan-hal-tabu-bagi-abg-papua.
Unrepresented Nations and Peoples Organization (UNPO). 2004. 'West Papua: Police, Military Involved in Papua Abuses', 9 August. Retrieved 28 December 2017 from http://www.unpo.org/article/1064.

Utomo, A.J. 2012. 'Women as Secondary Earners: Gendered Preferences on Marriage and Employment of University Students in Modern Indonesia', *Asian Population Studies* 8(1): 65–85.

———. 2016. 'Gender in the Midst of Reforms: Attitudes to Work and Family Roles among University Students in Urban Indonesia', *Marriage and Family Review* 52(5): 421–41.

Van den Broek, T., and A. Szalay. 2001. 'Raising the Morning Star: Six Months in the Developing Independence Movement in West Papua', *Journal of Pacific History* 36(1): 77–92.

van Langenberg, M. 1990. 'The New Order State: Language, Ideology, Hegemony', in A. Budiman (ed.), *State and Civil Society in Indonesia*. Clayton: Monash University, Centre of Southeast Asian Studies, pp. 121–50.

Wardlow, H. 2006. *Wayward Women: Sexuality and Agency in a New Guinea Society*. Berkeley: University of California Press.

Weber, H. 1994. 'The Indonesian Concept of Development and its Impact on the Process of Social Transformation', in H. Buchholt and U. Mai (eds), *Continuity, Change, and Aspirations: Social and Cultural Life in Minahasa, Indonesia*. Singapore: Institute for Southeast Asian Studies, pp. 194–210.

Webster, D. 2001. '"Already Sovereign as a People": A Foundational Moment in West Papuan Nationalism', *Pacific Affairs* 74(4): 507–28.

Weeks, S. 1987. '*Education and Change in Pangia, Southern Highlands Province*', Educational Research Unit Report No. 56. Port Moresby: University of Papua New Guinea.

Wonda, S. 2007. *Tenggelamnya Rumpun Melanesia: Pertarungan Politik NKRI di Papua Barat* [*Sinking the Melanesian Race: Indonesian Political Wars in West Papua*]. Jayapura: Deiyai.

Wood, M., and A. Dundon. 2014. 'Great Ancestral Women: Sexuality, Gendered Mobility, and HIV among the Bamu and Gogodala of Papua New Guinea', *Oceania* 84(2): 185–201.

Yahya, A. 1997. '*Membina Sumber Daya Manusia Memasuki Abad Ke XXI*' ['Guiding the Human Resources into the 21st Century'], Kertas Karya Perorangan (TASKAP). Jakarta: Republic of Indonesia Department of Defence.

Yang, L.H., A. Kleinman, B.G. Link, J.C. Phelan, S. Lee and B. Good. 2007. 'Culture and Stigma: Adding Moral Experience to Stigma Theory', *Social Science and Medicine* 64: 1524–35.

Yoman, S.S. 2007. *Pemusnahan Etnis Melanesia: Memecah Kebisuan Sejarah Kekerasan di Papua Barat* [*The Elimination of Melanesians: Breaking the Silence on the History of Violence in West Papua*]. Yogyakarta: Galang.

Zeth, A.H.M., A.H. Asdie, A.G. Mukti and J. Mansoben. 2010. 'Perilaku dan Risiko Penyakit HIV/AIDS di Masyarakat Papua Studi Pengembangan Model Lokal Kebijakan HIV/AIDS' ['Behaviour and HIV/AIDS Risk in Papuan Society: Developing a Local HIV/AIDS Policy Model'], *Jurnal Manajemen Pelayanan Kesehatan* 13(4): 206–19.

Zimmer-Tamakoshi, L. 1997. 'The Last Big Man: Development and Men's Discontents in the Papua New Guinea Highlands', *Oceania* 68(2): 107–22.

Index

NOTE: page references with an *f* are figures; with an *m* are maps.

abortions, 148
abstinence, 157
acara (events), 164
activism, 92, 129, 171
adat (custom), 46, 180
adik ('younger sibling'), 72, 126, 127
adoption of infants, 146
advancement, 1, 80. See also progress (*kemajuan*)
AIDS, 145, 147. See also HIV/AIDS
'albinos' (*bule*), 61, 62, 63, 65
alcohol, 8, 138–40
Ale, Sobat (friend or buddy), 87
Alua, Agus, 17, 18
amber ('foreigners'), 139
Amir, Sulfikar, 23
AMPTPI (Association of Central Highlands University Students, Papua, Indonesia), 129, 136, 165
anak-anak (Papuan 'kids'), 88
anak-anak kota ('city children'), 52
anak-anak merantau ('migrant youth'), 141
Anthias, Floya, 21
'anti-social' behaviour, 27
ap kain (tribal chief), 134
Archbold Expedition, 16
asli (Indigenous), 56
asrama putri (women's dorm), 69
Association of Central Highlands Students of Papua (AMPTPI), 92
avoidance of Indonesians, 174

Badan Pusat Statistik Provinsi Papua (BPSPP), 5, 6
Bahasa Indonesia, 27
bakar batu ('stone cooking'), 18, 65, 70, 71f, 136, 158
Baliem River, 17
Baliem Valley, 15m, 68; Dani in the, 14–20; education in, 38
Ballard, Chris, 11
Bandiyono, Suko, 24
bangsa Minahasa (Minahasa nation/people), 57
baptisms, 94f
battle re-enactments (*perang-perangan*), 175, 176f
becak (bicycle-powered pedicabs), 34–35, 37
behaviour, regulation of, 123
berani ('brave'), 133
berani ('confidence'), 128
berkat (blessing), 74
Bible literacy, 38
bicycle-powered pedicabs (*becak*), 34–35, 37
Big Family of Catholic University Students of the Jayapura-Timika Diocese (KBMKKJ-T), 129, 131, 137
birth control, 144
blessing (*berkat*), 74
body, understanding of, 21
Boellstorff, Tom, 96
'boyfriend/girlfriend' (*pacar*), 143, 150
'brave' (*berani*), 133
bridewealth, 146
Buchholt, Helmut, 56
bule ('albinos'), 61, 62, 63, 65
bupati (regent), 51
bureaucratic procedures, 113–22
Butt, Leslie, 3, 22

camat (district head), 44
campus life (Dani students), 100–122, 107–10; conflict among highlanders, 135–38; 'human resources' (*sumber daya manusia*), 102–7; procedures

(on campus), 113–22; racialization on campus, 110–13; student organizations, 127–34; universities, 101–2
'caring for' (*pelihara*) hair, 111
cassava (*ubi kayu'*), 62
casual sex, 148
Catholic missionaries, 38, 40
Catholic schools, 52
Catholic Valley students, 136
celebrations, student, 71f. *See also* graduation
Cenderawasih Post, 166, 167
Cenderawasih University, 173
census (2010), Indonesia, 5
Central Sulawesi, 101
Chauvel, Richard, 12
Christian and Missionary Alliance (CMA), 17, 38
Christianity, 6, 9, 19, 25, 38, 76, 83, 154, 182; baptisms, 94f; dorm room posters, 104f; kinship, 61; Minahasan Christians, 59; missionaries, 38, 40; morality and, 49; North Sulawesi, Indonesia, 57; sex outside of marriage, 146 (*see also* sexuality); symbols of, 59, 60
churches, 40, 41, 58, 76, 83, 131, 132; Dani students, 76–77; marriage, 149. *See also* Christianity; Eben Haezer Bethel Tabernacle Church
'city children' (*anak-anak kota*), 52
Clark, Jeffrey, 20
clean living, 52
close-knit neighbourhoods (*kampung*), 86, 87
coastal Papuans (*orang pantai*), 124–27
collective suffering (*memoria passionis*), 78
colonialism, 26, 41, 58, 138–40, 147, 184
Communication Forum of University Students of the Evangelical Church of Indonesia in North Sulawesi (FKPM-GIDI), 129, 130
conditions, disappointment of, 103
'confidence' (*berani*), 100, 128
confrontation, 171
control, 170–74

cooking, 70. *See also* 'stone cooking' (*bakar batu*)
corruption, 43
cultural values (Dani), 25
custom (*adat*), 46, 180

'danger zone' (*daerah rawan*), 70
Dani: in the Baliem Valley, 14–20; contemporary perspectives on, 40–43; cultural connections, 6; cultural values, 25; disappointment of, 27; education of, 3, 4, 8, 25; first presidential visit to, 1, 2f, 3f; housing (students), 63; marginalization of, 80; modernity, 158–74; oppressive and violent conditions, 5; public service, 165–67; racialization of, 79; stigmatization, 61, 78–99; students (*see* students); traditions, 9; understanding of body, 21; university graduates, 18; in the Wolo Valley, 14–20
Dead Birds (film), 17
demographics, 24
deterritorialization from home, 123. *See also* schooling abroad
development objectives, 3, 55, 178
diminishment, 20–28, 178
discipline (Dani students), 100–122; campus life (Dani students), 107–10; conflict among highlanders, 135–38; 'human resources' (*sumber daya manusia*), 102–7; procedures (on campus), 113–22; racialization on campus, 110–13; student organizations, 127–34; universities, 101–2
discomfort (*malu*), 96, 97, 98, 177
discrimination, 111, 158, 162. *See also* racism
district head (*camat*), 44
diversity, 60
'dollar signs in their eyes' (*mata uang*), 115–16
dormitory living (Dani students), 67–70
dorm room posters, 90f, 104f
Duncan, Christopher, 13
Dutch colonialism, 26, 41, 58
Dutch explorers, 11
Dutch school, 33

Earl, George, 11
Eastern Indonesia, 7m
Eben Haezer Bethel Tabernacle Church, 76, 77, 94–96
education, 17, 20–28; absentee teachers, 37; bureaucracy, 113–22; challenge of, 103; controlling efficacy, 40–43; daily life of school, 33; of Dani, 3, 4, 8, 25; diminishment, 21; gender, 26; help to have, 169, 170; history of (in Wamena), 38–40; of Indigenous people, 105; lack of, 49; literacy, 43–45; meanings of schooling in Wamena, West Papua, 53–55; missionaries, 41; modernization of, 39; moralities and, 54; moralities of sex and school, 45–49; as political strategies, 43; postponing sex for, 157 (*see also* sexuality); postsecondary studies, 5; rates of illiteracy, 6; schooling abroad, 123–40; struggles to get ahead, 49–53; student feelings about, 113; view of, 34; Wamena, West Papua, 33–55; young girl ready for school, 37f; Yudhoyono, Susilo Bambang, 4
education-for-stupidity (*pendidikan pembodohan*), 42
efficacy, controlling, 40–43
elder sibling. *See* 'older sibling' (*kakak*)
'empowerment' (*pemberdayaan*) activities, 51
Epstein, Albert, 97
'estranged populations' (*masyarakat terasing*), 12, 13
ethnic group (*suku*), 10, 56
ethnic nation (*suku-bangsa*), 10
European explorers, 11
Evangelical Church of Indonesia (GIDI), 130, 131f
events (*acara*), 164
examination panels (Unima), 109f
'experience' (*pengalaman*), 128
extramarital relationships, 145

family (*saudara*), 58
family-run eateries (*rumah makan*), 46
Farhadian, Charles, 38

fear, 78
Fife, Wayne, 27
Fiji, 20
financial survival, 66
'finish first' (*selesai dulu*), 144, 147
'foreigners' (*amber*), 139
Foster, Kevin, 113
freedom (*merdeka*), 10
'free sex,' 144, 148
'friend' ('*nayak*'), 33
friend or buddy (*Ale, Sobat*), 87
funding: scholarships, 73; for student dormitories, 68. *See also* sponsorship (Dani students)

gardens (Dani students), 70–72, 124, 125, 164
Gardner, Robert, 17
gay men, violence against, 96
gender, education, 26
generosity, 100
Gietzelt, Dale, 13
Glazebrook, Diana, 106
Goffman, Erving, 78
'go into the field' (*turun lapangan*), 104, 105
governance, 19, 42, 134, 178
government (*pemerintah*), 41
government-appointed village head (*kepala kampung*), 43
graduation, 107, 113, 152f, 158–62, 160f, 161f
'Grand Valley,' 16

hair (racialization of), 110, 111, 118
hasil (results), 105, 106, 128
Hayward, Douglas, 179
headman (*Lurah*), 88, 89, 91
hegemony, 141
hierarchies, 11, 53, 101, 123
higher education (*kuliah*), 103
highlanders (*orang gunung*), 16, 73; characteristics of, 127; conflict among, 135–38; humility of, 127; marriage for, 149; school mobility for, 139. *See also* mountain people (*orang gunung*); students

'high-quality' families (*keluarga berkualitas*), 23
Hindom, Isaac, 79
history of education (in Wamena), 38–40
HIV/AIDS, 8, 27, 79, 145
home, returning without results, 106
homecomings, 162–65
honesty, 100
'house-mother' (*ibu kos*), 28, 68
'human resources' (*sumber daya manusia*), 23, 82, 100, 102–7, 105, 128
humiliation, 111, 158, 179

ibu kos ('house-mother'), 28, 68
illiteracy, rates of, 6
independence (*merdeka*), 10, 19, 107, 113
Indigenous (*asli*), 56
'Indigenous Papuan' (*orang asli Papua*), 14
'Indigenous Wamena,' 166
Indonesia census (2010), 5
Indonesian language, 112
Indonesian research office (*Lembaga Ilmu Penelitian*), 64
'Indonesians' (*orang Indonesia*), 11–14
Indonesian University Students Movement (GMNI), 93
'inland' (*pedalaman*) communities, 39
insecurities, 162
International Workers Day, 93
istri ('wife'), 143

Jacobsen, Michael, 57
Jakarta, Indonesia, 2
Japan, World War II, 16
Java, 2
Jayawijaya regency, 69

kakak ('older sibling'), 72, 126
kampung (close-knit neighbourhoods), 86, 87
Karp, Ivan, 25
kawin or *sudah kawin* ('married'), 143
Keeler, Ward, 97
keluarga berkualitas ('high-quality' families), 23
Kelurahan Maesa-Unima (Unima District), 64

kemajuan (progress), 1
kepala kampung (government-appointed village head), 43
'kin' (*saudara*), 96
kinship, 61, 88
Koentjaraningrat, R.M., 24
Komite Nasional Papua Barat (West Papua National Committee), 172
koteka (penis gourd), 175–84
Koteka Operation (1971), 39
kuliah (higher education), 103
kuliah dulu ('study first'), 144

land and people (*vanua*), 20
land of Papua (*Tanah Papua*), 80
languages, 27, 112
Lani, 16
leadership, 24, 100, 133
Lembaga Ilmu Penelitian (Indonesian research office), 64
Lewis, Amanda, 8
Li, Tania, 2, 169
LiPuma, Edward, 27
literacy, 43–45
local men (*orang sini*), 87
Logo, Erik, 174
Lurah (headman), 88, 89, 91

mahasiswa ('university student'), 54, 92, 146
Mai, Ulrich, 56
Malay people, 11
male: view of promiscuity, 177; view of reproduction, 147
malu (discomfort), 96, 97, 98, 177
Maluku Islands, 101
management roles, 134
marginalization of Dani, 80
marital relationships, students in, 144
markets, street, 67
marriage, 48, 148–53; challenges of abroad, 149; delay of, 141; as a problem for students, 150
'married' (*kawin* or *sudah kawin*), 143
Marx, Christoph, 23
masters of the land (*tuan tanah*), 56–61, 98

masyarakat terasing ('estranged populations'), 12, 13
mata uang ('dollar signs in their eyes'), 115–16
McCallum, Cecilia, 96
Means, Gordon, 23
Melanesian racial heritage, 14
Mellor, David, 110
memoria passionis (collective suffering), 78
merdeka (independence), 10, 19, 113
Mietzner, Marcus, 9
'migrants' (*pendatang*), 13, 19
'migrant youth' (*anak-anak merantau*), 141
migration, 79, 124
Minahasa nation/people (*bangsa Minahasa*), 57
Minahasan Christians, 59
Misi, West Papua, 36
Misi market, 36f
missionaries: Christianity, 38, 40; education, 41
mobile phones, 80
modernity, 1, 34, 59, 158–74, 178; control, 170–74; good hearts, good hands, 168–70; graduation stories, 158–62; homecomings, 162–65; protection, 170–74; public service, 165–67. See also progress (*kemajuan*)
modernization, 55
'modern' status, 28
morality: clean living, 52; and education, 54; of sex and school, 45–49; sexuality, 142
Morning Star flag, 46, 104f
Mote, Octavianus, 20
mountain people (*orang gunung*), 16, 73, 124–27
Munro, Jenny, 3
music on mobile phones, 80
Muslims, 58
mutual desire, 148–53

National Education Day, 93
National Indonesian Students Movement (GMNI), 128
National Institute of Sciences (LIPI), 118
National University of Manado (Unima), 6, 58, 62, 63, 101, 109, 111, 117, 154, 159, 160f, 161f
'*nayak* ('friend'), 33
Nerenberg, Jacob, 6
Netherlands New Guinea, 12
newcomers (*pendatang*), 56; Dani students as, 65–77; North Sulawesi, Indonesia, 61–65
New Life Minahasa Evangelical Church, 76
New Order government (1965–98), 12
Nilan, Pam, 26, 141
non-governmental organizations (NGOs), 168, 169, 182
'non-Indigenous Wamena,' 166
North Sulawesi, Indonesia, 6, 7, 7m, 8, 10, 21, 54, 57m, 112, 173; Christianity, 57; Dani students as newcomers, 65–77; Eben Haezer Bethel Tabernacle Church, 94–96; getting along with locals, 88–91; masters of the land (*tuan tanah*), 56–61; newcomers (*pendatang*), 61–65; racial stereotyping of Dani students, 81–83; relationships with Dani students, 83–86; stigmatization in, 78–99; surveillance of Dani students, 91–94; treatment of Dani students, 86–88

Office of Statistics, 44, 45f, 101
'older sibling' (*kakak*), 72, 126
oppression, 5
orang asli Papua ('Indigenous Papuan'), 14
orang barat ('westerners'), 66
orang gunung (mountain people), 16, 73, 124–27, 149
orang Indonesia ('Indonesians'), 11–14
orang lembah ('Valley people'), 16, 66
orang pantai (coastal Papuans), 124–27
orang Papua ('Papuans'), 11–14, 64, 68
orang putih (white people), 79
orang sini (local men), 87
orang Tondano (Tondano people), 66
orang Wamena ('Wamena people'), 11, 73, 95, 135, 172
Order of Saint Francis, 38

pacar ('boyfriend/girlfriend'), 143, 150
Papua, 7m, 15m
Papuan 'kids' (*anak-anak*), 88
'Papuans' (*orang Papua*), 11–14, 64, 68
Parker, Lyn, 113
'Pass valley,' 35
pedalaman ('inland') communities, 39
pelihara ('caring for) hair, 111
pemberdayaan ('empowerment') activities, 51
pemerintah (government), 41
pendatang ('migrants'), 13, 19
pendatang (newcomers), 56; Dani students as, 65–77; North Sulawesi, Indonesia, 61–65
pendidikan pembodohan (education-for-stupidity), 42
pengalaman ('experience'), 128
penis gourd (*koteka*), 175–84
Pentecostal churches, 76, 83, 94f, 182
people, 10–11
perang-perangan (battle re-enactments), 175, 176f
perempuan sundal ('prostitute'), 47
Perguruan Tinggi Pendidikan Guru (teacher-preparation college), 101
Persoon, Gerard, 12
Philippines, 59, 93
pigs, 18, 33, 70
political activism, 92, 129, 171
political agendas, 24, 54
political independence, 107
politics: Dani students, 78–81; of reproduction, 147; risk of nationalist, 171
politik halus ('refined politics'), 79
pornography, 48
postsecondary studies, 5
Pouwer, Jan, 39
poverty, 8, 162
pregnancies, 48, 146, 147, 148–53; among students, 153; premarital, 153–57
premarital relationships, stigmatization of, 141
presidential visits, 1
Priest, Naomi, 22
'primitiveness,' 175, 176, 177

primitivism, 56
procedures (on campus), 113–22
progress (*kemajuan*), 1
promiscuity, 142, 147, 148; and racialized sexuality, 144–46; stigmatization of, 177. *See also* sexuality
'promiscuous' sexual behaviour (*seks bebas*), 47
'prostitute' (*perempuan sundal*), 47
protection, 170–74
protectionism, 174
public service, 100, 104, 158, 163
Puncak, 16
putih (white), 60
putra daerah/putri daerah (sons and daughters of the place), 56

quality of human resources, 104

race, 10–11
'race-nation-people' (*suku-bangsa*), 57
racialization, 8, 10, 20–28, 123, 142, 158, 163, 178; boundaries of, 140; on campus, 110–13; diminishment, 21; promiscuity and racialized sexuality, 144–46
racial stereotyping of Dani students, 81–83
racism, 4, 22, 45, 110; technocratic, 4, 23, 25, 27, 43, 45, 78, 100, 103, 107, 119, 133, 142, 157, 170, 178
rantau (space of migration), 141
'Recent Developments in Papua' (2005), 132
'refined politics' (*politik halus*), 79
Reform era, 26
regent (*bupati*), 51
registration, 114
relationships, 88; extramarital, 145; premarital, 141; students in marital, 144
repression, 2
reproduction, politics of, 147. *See also* pregnancies; sexuality
resistance, 174
results (*hasil*), 105, 106, 128
retraditionalization, 141, 157
Richards, Sarah, 13, 79

rights, Indigenous, 107
rumah makan (family-run eateries), 46
Rutherford, Danilyn, 20, 139

sacred knowledge, 18
Sam Ratulangi University (Unsrat), 62, 63, 102, 112, 114
Sangir-Talaud Islands, 101
Saraswati, L. Ayu, 60
saudara ('kin'), 96
saudara (family), 58
scholarships, 73. See also sponsorship (Dani students)
schooling abroad, 123–40
school mobility for highlanders, 139
Schut, Thijs, 28
scrutiny, confrontation of stereotypes, 96–99
SDM. See *sumber daya manusia*
seks bebas ('promiscuous' sexual behaviour), 47
selesai dulu ('finish first'), 144, 147
sex: moralities of sex and school, 45–49; pornography, 48
sexual desire, 147
sexuality, 141–57; consequences of sex, 148; morality, 142; pregnancies, 148–53; premarital pregnancies, 153–57; promiscuity and racialized, 144–46; sexual reputations, 151; shame of, 151; sin and survival, 146–48; stigmatization of promiscuity, 177
Shah, Rachel, 178
shame, 78, 101, 141, 179; confrontation of stereotypes, 96–99; sex outside of marriage, 146; of sexuality, 151. See also discomfort (*malu*)
shopping, 67
'show one's face' (*taruh muka*), 75
shyness, 101. See also discomfort (*malu*)
Singapore, 59
skills, 106
skin colour as a racial marker, 81. See also stereotypes
Slama, Martin, 3
social myths, 83
Sondakh, A.J., 60

sons and daughters of the place (*putra daerah/putri daerah*), 56
Southwest Sulawesi, 101
space of migration (*rantau*), 141
Special Autonomy Law (2001), 9, 14
sponsorship (Dani students), 72–76
Stasch, Rupert, 17
state violence, 5, 8
stereotypes, 65, 135; confrontation of, 96–99; Dani students, 81–83
stigmatization, 4, 10, 56, 102, 107, 123, 138, 171, 178; confrontation of stereotypes, 96–99; Dani, 61; 'free sex,' 144; in North Sulawesi, Indonesia, 78–99; premarital pregnancies, 154–57; premarital relationships, 141; of promiscuity, 177
Stoler, Ann, 27
'stone cooking' (*bakar batu*), 18, 65, 70, 71f, 136, 158
Stop Sudah! Testimonies of Papuan Women Victims of Violence and Human Rights Abuses 1963–2009, 22
STPDN (*Sekolah Tinggi Pemerintahan Dalam Negeri*), 181
"straight-hairs," 37
Strathern, Andrew, 97, 98
street markets, 67
students: alcohol consumption, 138–40; campus life, 107–10; Catholic Valley, 136; celebrations, 71f; churches, 76–77; conflict among highlanders, 135–38; confrontation of stereotypes, 96–99; control, 170–74; daily life of, 72; discipline, 100–122; dormitory living, 67–70; dorm room posters, 90f; Eben Haezer Bethel Tabernacle Church, 94–96; gardens, 70–72, 164; getting along with locals, 88–91; good hearts, good hands, 168–70; graduation stories, 158–62; homecomings, 162–65; 'human resources' (*sumber daya manusia*), 102–7; humiliation (by lecturers), 111; Indonesian relationships with, 83–86; *koteka* (penis gourd), 175–84; in marital relationships, 144; marriage as a problem for, 150; migration of,

124; modernity, 158–74; as newcomers, 65–77; politics, 78–81; pregnancies among, 153; premarital pregnancies, 153–57; procedures (on campus), 113–22; protection, 170–74; public service, 165–67; racialization on campus, 110–13; racial stereotyping of Dani, 81–83; schooling abroad, 123–40; sense of purpose, 74; sexuality, 141–57; sin and survival, 146–48; social lives with other highlanders, 124–27; sponsorship, 72–76; stigmatization in North Sulawesi, Indonesia, 78–99; student organizations, 127–34; surveillance, 91–94; surveillance of Dani, 157; tensions, 138–40; treatment of, 86–88; universities, 101–2
'study first' (*kuliah dulu*), 144
submissiveness, 97
Sugandi, Yulia, 18
Suharto, Muhammad, 12, 58
suku (ethnic group or tribe), 10, 56
suku-bangsa (ethnic nation), 10
suku-bangsa ('race-nation-people'), 57
sumber daya manusia ('human resources'), 23, 82, 100, 102–7, 105, 128
surveillance of Dani students, 91–94, 157
symbols of Christianity, 59, 60

taboo knowledge, 18
Taiwan, 59
Tanah Papua (land of Papua), 80
taruh muka ('show one's face'), 75
teacher-preparation college (*Perguruan Tinggi Pendidikan Guru*), 101
tensions, students, 138–40
Tolikara, 16
Tomlinson, Matt, 20
Tondano community, 63, 67
Tondano people (*orang Tondano*), 66
trade (Wamena, West Papua), 35
traditions, 133; Dani, 9; *koteka* (penis gourd), 175–84
transformation, 178
tribal chief (*ap kain*), 134
tribal leaders (*kepala suku*), 142
tribal warfare, 135

tribes, 10–11, 56
tuan tanah (masters of the land), 56–61, 98
turun lapangan ('go into the field'), 104, 105

'*ubi kayu*' (cassava), 62
Unima (National University of Manado), 6, 59, 62, 63, 101, 109, 111, 117, 154, 159, 160f, 161f
Unima District (*Kelurahan Maesa-Unima*), 64
Union of Catholic Students of Indonesia (PMKRI), 69, 93, 128
United Nations (UN), 1, 5
universities, 101–2; bureaucratic procedures, 113–22
'university student' (*mahasiswa*), 54, 92, 146
Unsrat (Sam Ratulangi University), 62, 63, 102, 112, 114
Utomo, Ariane, 26

'Valley people' (*orang lembah*), 16, 66
vanua (land and people), 20
violence, 2, 5, 8, 19, 20, 162, 171; against gay men, 96; racism and, 22; in Wamena, West Paoua, 5
vulnerability, conditions of, 138

Wamena, West Papua, 6, 15m; access to, 35; conditions in, 37; controlling efficacy, 40–43; daily life of school, 33; education, 33–55; first presidential visit to, 1, 2f, 3f; history of education in, 38–40; literacy, 43–45; meanings of schooling in, 53–55; moralities of sex and school, 45–49; Office of Statistics, 44, 45f; struggles to get ahead, 49–53; trade, 35; view of education, 34; violence in, 5
'Wamena people' (*orang Wamena*), 11, 35, 73, 95, 135, 172
'wantokism,' 9
We Bridge, 36
Webster, David, 22
We River, 33, 49

'westerners' (*orang barat*), 66
West Papua, 7m, 10; Dutch administration of, 12; as final frontier of the Netherlands East Indies colony, 12
West Papua National Committee (*Komite Nasional Papua Barat*), 172
white (*putih*), 60
'whiteness,' 56
white people (*orang putih*), 79
Widodo, Joko, 8
'wife' (*istri*), 143
Wiru, 21
Wisma Lorenzo, 131

Wolo Valley, 136; Dani in the, 14–20
women's dorm (*asrama putri*), 69
World Bank, 23
World War II, 12, 16

Yahukimo, 16
Yahya, Achmad, 23
Yali, 16
Yang, Lawrence, 88
'younger sibling' (*adik*), 72, 126, 127
Yudhoyono, Susilo Bambang, 1, 2f, 3, 3f, 4, 8, 35
Yuval-Davis, Nira, 21–22

www.ingramcontent.com/pod-product-compliance
Lightning Source LLC
Chambersburg PA
CBHW051542020426
42333CB00016B/2065